CONTRASTS

WIKTOR OSIATYŃSKI

CONTRASTS

Soviet and American Thinkers Discuss the Future

TRANSLATED BY
Ewa Woydyłło

Macmillan Publishing Company
NEW YORK

Macmillan Publishing Company
866 Third Avenue, New York, N.Y. 10022
Collier Macmillan Canada, Inc.

Library of Congress Cataloging in Publication Data
Osiatyński, Wiktor, 1945–
Contrasts: Soviet and American thinkers discuss the future.
Translated from the Polish.
Includes index.
1. Science—Philosophy. 2. Forecasting.
3. Science and civilization. I. Title.
Q175.O77 1984 501 84–12588
ISBN 0–02–594070–8

10 9 8 7 6 5 4 3 2 1

Printed in the United States of America

CONTENTS

Introduction *vii*
Acknowledgments *xix*

Part One / On the Universe and Life

1. On Science in General *3*
    1. Linus Pauling *4*
    2. Evgenii Feinberg *11*
2. On the Macrocosm and the Microcosm *21*
    3. Iosif S. Shklovskii *21*
    4. Robert Hofstadter *31*
3. On Evolution and Mankind *40*
    5. Leonid Tatarinov *41*
    6. Paul Ehrlich *50*

Part Two / On Man and His Environment

4. On Brain and Mind *61*
    7. Konstantin Sudakov *62*
    8. Karl Pribram *68*
5. On Experimental Medicine *77*
    9. Sergei Anichkov *78*
    10. Norman Shumway *84*
6. On Language and Culture *93*
    11. Noam Chomsky *94*
    12. Guram Ramishvili *101*
7. On Human Values *109*
    13. John Kenneth Galbraith *110*
    14. Nicolai Tchavtchavadze *119*

Part Three / On the Future of Science

8. On History and the Future *131*
   15. Alvin Toffler *132*
   16. Lev Gumilov *143*

9. On Futurism and the Paradigm Shift *152*
   17. Igor Bestuzhev-Lada *153*
   18. Willis Harman *160*

10. On a New Science *169*
   19. Edgar Mitchell *170*
   20. Victor Iniushin *179*

11. On Science in Perspective *187*
   21. Sergei Semenov *188*
   22. Fritjof Capra *197*

Index 209

INTRODUCTION

For a long time I have considered writing this book because making comparisons between Americans and Russians has always been, for many reasons, a part of my thinking. For many years I have been, in a sense, a stranger in two cultures with my roots in a third. Naturally, as a Pole, I was deeply submerged in the Polish tradition, which is different from both the Russian and American cultures. Living in Poland I was, however, exposed to Soviet ideas and Russian tradition. On the other hand, for almost twenty years now, I have been studying the history of American social ideas. Six out of the eleven books I've published in Poland deal with various aspects of American life and social history—from the Founding Fathers to the history of Black Americans to the neoconservative movements in the late seventies and early eighties—and the first two were written even before my first visit to the United States in 1975.

While studying about the United States, I traveled every so often to the Soviet Union—as a tourist and tourists' guide, a scholar, and a journalist. Inevitably, I compared what I had learned about the United States with what I experienced in the Soviet Union. I read in the Soviet press many negative reports about America, and in the American Press many negative reports about Soviet Russia. The Americans I met in Poland were usually curious about the Soviet Union being at the same time frightened of its wild might. However, to my great surprise, most of the Russians I met thought highly of America. To my even greater surprise, I found that despite different histories and radically different political systems, institutions, and everyday customs, Russians and Americans had much in common. These similarities and their origin may be the subject of another, completely different book. Let me only say here that most Americans and Russians share similar beliefs and an almost identical vision of a better life, even of what ultimate happiness means—namely, material prosperity and well-being. They differ, of course, in what they perceive as the best means to reach their ideals, and these differences are, clearly enough, historically and culturally predetermined.

In time, I've come to realize that both nations seem to share the same fundamental belief as to the means by which ultimate happiness can be achieved: that through science earth can be turned into a paradise. However, the ideas about the powers of science differ slightly because of a variation in the meaning of the word *science*. In general, Americans believe that science, in the form of technology, will upgrade the level and comfort of life, but they limit the meaning of the word *science* to hard, experimental disciplines. The Russians, on the other hand, include what an American—or, for that matter, an Englishman—would call humanities or liberal arts. The Russian perspective prevails in continental Europe, where science is everything that is studied or taught in academic institutions irrespective of topic, method, or verifiability. As a result, the Russians not only share the Americans' hope that hard science will make life better and more comfortable, they also believe that the scientific method will be useful in shaping society and individuals in order to achieve the ideal social goals.

Whatever the differences in the understanding of the definition of science, neither the Russians nor the Americans doubt that science is the single most important key to the future, and the beliefs of both result in a cult of science. Every conversation, either with Russians or Americans, ends in a discussion on science's role in the shaping of things to come.

This, of course, was partly due to my personal bias, for science—at least one aspect of it—has fascinated me ever since high school: how can science help to solve some of the puzzles of the universe?

I have been looking for an answer to this and similar questions for years. I've read the entire canon of traditional liberal arts literature. It was interesting, but it didn't offer answers. There were, at best, hypotheses and speculations, based on arbitrary assumptions or sheer wishful thinking, to say nothing about contradictory opinions and conclusions. By the late sixties I was already disillusioned with philosophy, sociology, and the rest of the soft sciences. It was then that I thought for the first time about hard science. Is it more competent to answer my questions?

Placing my hopes in science, in 1972 I went to work as a writer for the weekly intellectual magazine *Kultura* (*Culture*) in Warsaw. It was—and I use the past tense deliberately, for the magazine was banned by the military government soon after the introduction of martial law in Poland in December 1981—something between the *New Yorker* and the *New York Review of Books* with, however, a much wider perspective. It covered books and theater, film and music —anything having to do with the arts and culture—as well as history and economics, social problems, and science, particularly the social sciences and humanities.

I wrote articles and essays on many of these subjects, shifting more and more to the hard sciences, particularly physics and natural life sciences. My approach was to look for the humanistic consequences of the research in these disciplines, to popularize science and the humanities. I would go to a university or research institute, talk to the scientists, witness the experiments, read some books and papers, and ask the scholar to write something for *Kultura*, or I would do it myself. In time I became more and more convinced of the advantages of one specific form of writing about science: an interview with the scientist.

An interview gives the reader an opportunity to get closer to the scientist and his personality, to know his way of thinking and reasoning and, sometimes, even to learn about his life. As compared to a piece I would write myself, the interview reduces the risk of misunderstanding or vitiating of the scientist's thoughts. Moreover, a discursive form of dialogue allows for the explanation of more difficult and controversial matters than I, alone, could write about. Scientists usually consider self-evident that which is most difficult for a layman to comprehend; popularizers, in turn, tend to avoid everything that is not understandable to them, however important it might be. An interview also provides an opportunity to link seemingly unrelated problems; for example, one can ask a physicist a question to which a biologist didn't have an answer but which a physicist would not think to ask himself.

Whatever the rationale, I soon became an expert in interviewing scientists and intellectuals in Poland, and traveling from one scholar to another was my full-time job.

In 1975 my new interests coincided with my former ones, which I had never completely abandoned—comparing my experiences in the Soviet Union with my studies of the United States. I was offered a grant to participate in the Professional Journalism Fellowship at Stanford University. For six months all resources of the university were open to me, and I began to ask leading scientists and scholars for interviews.

Within a short time I had fifteen or so candidates; only one scientist turned me down. All the others were quite cooperative and in many cases seemed very pleased at becoming known in remote Poland.

I soon had enough interviews with American scientists for a book, and I was confident that such a book would be popular in Poland, a country with a highly literate public and a profound interest in the United States. My only concern was that the book should not consist exclusively of the interviews with Stanford professors.

The three non-Stanford intellectuals—Edgar Mitchell, an astronaut who came back from the moon to found the Institute of Noetic Sciences; Willis Harman, from SRI International (formerly, Stanford Research Institute); and Linus Pauling, from the Institute of Orthomolecular Medicine—were nearby. Two other choices were self-evident: even before coming to Stanford I had translated into Polish Alvin Toffler's *Future Shock* and John Kenneth Galbraith's *Economics and the Public Purpose*, and they both agreed to be interviewed. While visiting Galbraith in Boston, I managed to talk to Noam Chomsky. Soon afterward I had to leave for Poland.

I left for home with twenty taped interviews, but two-thirds of them were still with Stanford professors. I wanted to change this balance and began to hunt for American scientists and intellectuals visiting Poland. At one point I received news that a famous physicist and Nobel Prize winner, Robert Hofstadter, was in Warsaw. We met and had a fascinating conversation that lasted several hours. Alas, when I asked him for some biographical data I learned that he, too, was from Stanford!

Soon after turning the manuscript over to my publisher I began to think about a second volume of interviews—this one to be with Soviet scientists and intellectuals. To compare opinions and views of representatives of the two scientific superpowers seemed quite natural and attractive. But I knew such a task would be very difficult to accomplish. Not only is travel in the Soviet Union restricted, but a visitor needs special permission to visit a research institute, and a scientist has to have special permission to talk to a journalist.

Yet these were problems that could be overcome. After all, *Kultura* was an official publication of fraternal Poland. *Kultura* even had a special cooperation agreement with its Soviet counterpart,

Sovietskaya Kultura magazine. My editor-in-chief invited his Soviet comrade to Warsaw and presented to him the idea of a series of interviews with Soviet scientists and intellectuals. The Soviet editor liked the idea, invited me to Moscow, and said that they would take total and perfect care of me.

It sounded frightening. I wanted to talk freely to open-minded people and I was afraid the editor would send me around to official academicians who would endlessly repeat the same trivia I knew all too well. To avoid this, I postponed my visit and started to compile my own list of scholars.

After several months I sent to *Sovietskaya Kultura* a list of seventy-five persons I was interested in meeting in the U.S.S.R. I realized that no sane person could expect to meet or even arrange for such a crowd of scientists, but I wanted the Soviet officials to make a selection from my own list.

About a year later I received a phone call from Moscow. They had arranged for over twenty meetings to take place during a two-week visit in May 1977.

I arrived in Moscow on a Thursday evening. The next morning I reported to the *Sovietskaya Kultura* office and was greeted in a manner appropriate to my young age and low rank. I was told that they had arranged one or two meetings for me in Moscow, one in Leningrad, and one or two in Tbilisi. A scientist in Tartu, in Latvia, wanted to see me, too, but they were unable to obtain my visa to Latvia. They would continue to work on this and on my schedule as well. And on my tickets, visas, passes, and permissions. They hoped I had Soviet currency, which I didn't. My editor and I considered my visit an exchange, and since we had paid the Soviet editor's expenses in Warsaw, we assumed they would pay mine. "We will see what can be done. We know you don't need an interpreter but here is your guide and protector. He will travel with you and take care of you. And now, you had better go back to your hotel and wait there, we will call you. Your guide may learn something even though it is the weekend."

One or two in Moscow, one in Leningrad, and one or two in Tbilisi. It won't make a book. I was sitting in my hotel room discouraged, helpless, and angry. I took out a copy of my list. I looked around for a telephone directory but couldn't find one. I called the reception desk.

"We have one here, come down." I went, scared that while I was there, my patron would call. I looked through the book, back and forth, but couldn't find either the scientists' names or the research institutes. I asked the receptionist for help. She smiled, "Sorry, scientists are not listed in the directory." I called information. "Sorry, they are not listed."

I went back to my room desperate and hungry. Staring at the phone, which never rang, I took out of my suitcase a bottle of Polish vodka that I had brought from Poland as a gift for the editor of *Sovietskaya Kultura*, and over an unknown number of hours I drained it to the dregs.

When the ringing phone woke me the next day about noon I didn't realize at first where I was. The Russian language brought me back to earth.

"My name is Tchavtchavadze. I am a professor of philosophy in Tbilisi. I've got a letter from *Sovietskaya Kultura* that you would like to meet me. I am now in Moscow and will be staying here for some time, so I won't be able to see you in Tbilisi. I thought we could talk here. Why don't you come to my hotel?"

I explained how I could not leave my hotel and he agreed to come visit me. A few hours later, Tchavtchavadze, a handsome man in his fifties, of old Georgian aristocracy, knocked on my hotel room door. "Let's do our job first and then go and have something to eat."

In the late evening, we were still there, sipping an excellent Georgian brandy. He sat by the phone, took out of his pocket an address book and dialed numbers. The same conversation was repeated several times.

"Hey, this is Kola speaking . . . Fine, thanks, and how are you? . . . I am staying here for some time . . . Of course, we have to see each other . . . Listen, I have here a good friend visiting from Poland . . . Yes, he's doing a series of interviews with scientists . . . He spoke to the Americans . . . Oh, yes, and has published a book . . . Yes, another volume . . . Of course, I did . . . No, you see, *Sovietskaya Kultura* invited him . . . But you know . . . Of course, he's a nice guy . . . You would . . . Great . . . No, he has to stay in his hotel, why don't you come here tomorrow . . . No, in the morning Ivan will visit him . . . Yes, he will wait for you in the afternoon . . . Thank you, see you soon."

After about an hour or so I had five meetings scheduled for the next three days, several phone numbers—in Moscow, Tbilisi, Leningrad, and elsewhere—plus information about the people he advised me to see. And, in addition, a handwritten letter of recommendation.

On Sunday the first scientists came to see me and I started my work. The scenario was almost always the same:

"I've heard from Kola about you. I know you've got some problems here. I respect Professor Tchavtchavadze very much. I would love to be in your book but you know . . ."

None of them was a dissident or underground scholar. Each did his job and tried to be honest and open-minded. For me it was an interview, for them much more. One word here or there and he might lose his job. He might not be published. Given an exit visa. And so on. But if I promised to send him the text of the interview for an authorization before publishing it, he didn't have any objections to talking.

I would promise and we would converse for hours. Eventually I was given new addresses, new phone numbers, and new letters of recommendation.

When my official guide came to see me on Tuesday, I already had five interviews taped and about fifteen other contacts. He said that *Sovietskaya Kultura* managed to arrange one additional appointment in Moscow. He gave me some money and an airline ticket. We would go to Leningrad on Thursday and from there to Tbilisi on the following day. Then, back to Moscow, since they hadn't received confirmation from Kiev. He thought that six interviews was quite a success.

Imprudently I said it wasn't enough for a book, but that he shouldn't worry; I had already interviewed a few scholars and had a few more appointments. However, he did worry. Of course, he said, they didn't mean to limit my freedom, but I should be more cautious. "You know, there are different people, and you cannot know all by yourself who is who." And I shouldn't make his task more difficult. He wished me all the best and said that he would come back to take me to the airport on Thursday.

For the next two days—as during the rest of my stay in the Soviet Union—I was taping two or three interviews a day, traveling from one suburb of this incredibly huge Soviet city to another. My greatest problem during my whole stay was meals. I didn't have the two or three hours a day it took to wait on line to get into a restaurant. At first I tried ordering a huge cold breakfast in my hotel room and saving it for dinner late in the night when I would get back from work, picking up ice cream between subway stations during the day.

Unfortunately, the maids cleaning my room took away my trays of food, and ice cream became my sole diet for most of the two weeks. Luckily, Russian ice cream is very good.

I was quite busy and happy. Once I realized that my guide's main task was to prevent me from meeting too many scientists, I simply didn't tell him what I was doing. Fortunately he was quite lazy, and he didn't accompany me to interviews. After we arrived in Leningrad he went to sleep, so I met three scholars instead of only the one arranged by *Sovietskaya Kultura*. My guide had family in Tbilisi and left me completely on my own there for two days.

On Sunday at noon I went back to the hotel; it was two hours before our scheduled departure for Kiev—which had finally been approved.

Since my guide wasn't in his room, I took my luggage and went down to the lobby to wait for him. I was then sent back to my floor to get from the floor caretaker a special pass to enable me to take my own luggage out of the hotel.

"Are you leaving?" she asked. "How come?"

"We have a plane to Kiev in less than two hours. Didn't you see my guide? I'm worried he may be late."

"Then you don't know. He came here a few hours ago and couldn't find you. So he canceled your reservations and went out with his family."

I waited for him, getting angrier and angrier with every minute. By the time he showed up, in the company of three friends or cousins, the plane had already left. I gave him hell and told him that I was going to be in Kiev by the next morning—with or without him.

There was no other plane to Kiev that day, so we flew back to Moscow—approximately twice as far from Tbilisi as Kiev—took a taxi from the airport where we landed to another—a ride of over an hour—and caught a night flight to Kiev. In Kiev we stopped at the airport hotel, the strangest I have ever stayed at—a guest was not allowed to have his suitcase to his room! Seven hours later we were back in Moscow, where I resumed my interview–ice cream routine.

The day before my departure, the deputy editor of *Sovietskaya Kultura* invited me and my guide to his office to ask how things had gone. He was amazed that I thought they had gone well. He hoped I had managed to get enough interviews. I did.

"How many?" he asked.

"Try to guess."

"Five, maybe six or seven."

"Twenty-four!" I told him.

Before he embraced me in congratulations, he looked for a second or so at my guide. This look, which I still remember, haunted me throughout the following night.

While I was waiting in the hotel lobby for a taxi to the airport, my guide suddenly appeared with his wife. He came to say good-bye. They brought me flowers, a bottle of cognac, and a very special cake. Souvenirs for friends. He really liked me very much. He gave me a lift to the airport, took my luggage, and led me to the V.I.P. entrance. He showed something to the officer and took my passport and ticket. A minute later he returned and said that all was cleared, my luggage was checked through to Warsaw, and I could go through passport control. He said good-bye and disappeared.

Astonished by the treatment I received, I relaxed and waited for my plane. As usual, it was late. I thought about my guide. Something didn't fit, but I couldn't quite identify what it was. Suddenly, the look of the deputy editor of *Sovietskaya Kultura* came to my mind. I stopped to think about it for a moment. My hands began to tremble. I remembered reading somewhere that the Russians have a magnetic chamber at Moscow's international airport. If they put my suitcase there for one second, all my efforts would have been in vain. Blank tapes. I asked a clerk if I could have access to my luggage. "No. It's all checked in. To Warsaw."

I remember neither how long we waited for the plane nor the flight itself. Later, people told me that at the airport in Warsaw I seemed insane. While waiting for my luggage, I kept looking for electric sockets and asking people if the outlets really worked. I even took a lamp from a customs officer's desk and checked a socket. When I saw my suitcase, I grabbed it, ran with it to the socket, pulled everything out onto the floor, picked up the tape recorder, and switched it on.

It worked.

In 1980 the book of interviews with Soviet scientists and intellectuals was published in Poland. It was as successful as the first one. I sensed, however, that in these two books there was a potential for something still different: a book in which Soviet and American scholars would be put together. I didn't know of anything like this, and I could hardly think that a Western journalist or writer could manage to do a book of interviews in the Soviet Union.

Usually, when Soviet and American scientists and intellectuals come together they either speak about very complicated details of their specific fields of research or discuss the most general problems of Soviet-American relations and world peace. I had something quite different in mind: Soviet and American scientists speaking freely about science itself, the relativity of scientific theories, the history and the future of the universe and mankind, and the moral responsibility of a scientist.

Once my outline was accepted by American, Bulgarian, and Czechoslovakian publishers (the Soviet Union turned it down cold) the second part of my work had to be done. I went to all of the interviewees with draft translations of their interviews. In most instances we taped new parts for the interviews, then I combined these with the old fragments, and sent the new version to the interviewees. In some cases I did a completely new interview with the same person, and I met Fritjof Capra, of whom I had no knowledge eight years ago.

When updating my book, I had one incident reminding me a little bit of my Soviet experience. In June 1983, I went to reinterview Dr. Willis Harman at SRI International in Menlo Park, California. For security reasons I was not let in, because I am a Polish citizen.

Such is the story of this book.

Years ago, when I first thought of writing a book like this, I envisioned it as a confrontation between Soviet and American science. Now I see each of them as a complement to one another. I have become convinced that there is no such thing as American science or Soviet science. There are, of course, numerous differences between scientists and intellectuals, but they have little to do with nationality. There are as many controversies among the Americans and among the Soviets as there are between the two. Perhaps there are more general national differences in the attitude toward research and science, which has to do with broader cultural differences, than with science as such. It seems, for instance, that American science in general tends to be more practically oriented, while the Soviet scientists seem to be more open to the abstract questions related to the social purpose of science and to the social values promoted by science. But also, in this respect, one can find as many narrow specialists among the Soviet scientists as one can find broad-minded, philosophically-oriented scientists among the Americans. It also seems that in both countries scientists are bound, often unconsciously, by a set of ideological assumptions, however different these assumptions may be in each country. And in both countries, there are scientists and intellectuals who question these assumptions.

Despite all the differences and controversies, all the scientists share common ideas: a respect for the truth, a sense of moral responsibility, and a belief that the study of science and humanities can lead us to becoming truly multidimensional men and women of the future.

The juxtaposition of American and Soviet scientists proves, in fact, that the aims of science are universal. It encompasses a search for an unreachable truth about the realities: the physical reality that surrounds us, the social reality we create together with other people, the images of reality continually created and re-created in our minds, and how all three of these will change in the future.

My original aim was to popularize contemporary science. However, the technical details of the sciences and humanities were not my primary concern. These are quite well known from the science sections in the daily and weekly press and from popular journals and magazines.

In this book I've tried to focus on problems that only occasionally are a matter of public discussion: namely, the general questions concerning the role of science in our culture. What is the influence of scientific achievements on our consciousness, our world outlook, and our values?

For over ten years I have been traveling around the globe, from one laboratory to another, from one scientist to another, to find out how we can use today's science to understand the world and to answer the fundamental questions of the human condition.

From my studies I know now that traditional science cannot answer these questions because, by definition, they refer to values. Science is the best of all known tools to answer practical questions, to find the best means to given ends. But traditional science has almost nothing to say about the ends themselves.

As I speak with more and more modern scientists, I am noting a subtle but profound change in the way their outlooks differ from the outlooks of their historical counterparts. They talk about both the power and the limitation of the traditional scientific method. And this realization leads them to enlarge the basic assumptions of science to incorporate human values. As one of the interviewed intellectuals put it, the new science will address not only "how to" but also "what for."

This new science is developing independently in the United States and in the Soviet Union. Because of the revolutionary potential for science itself, the trend is rejected, sometimes aggressively, by scientific establishments. But the questions the new science has already posed and the doubts it has raised are, by themselves, an important contribution to our culture and to future civilization.

Presenting this emerging new science—both in the United States and in the Soviet Union—was my main ambition for this book. It doesn't mean, of course, that the book consists exclusively of the interviews with the advocates of the new science. The proportions here reflect the proportions found in a larger scientific community where there are more traditionally oriented scientists and few others who challenge the dominant vision of science. The reader can easily tell one from the other. However, even the most traditional scientists are, at least, addressing questions of values. Most important, only very few people today consider these questions unrelated to their interests. Most agree that science should address them. Some scientists even find that the results of their own traditional research raise many doubts about what until recently seemed to be an unquestionable truth.

I hope the reader will also become more skeptical about the ultimate powers of science as well as more hopeful—in seeing that scientists, too, have met this realization by broadening the scope of their concerns to consider more actively human values. Like many of the scientists I interviewed, I believe that this new trend toward incorporating human values into the pursuit of science is necessary if we are to survive as a species.

New York City, August 1983

ACKNOWLEDGMENTS

There are many people without whose help, contribution, and encouragement this book would never have been conceived, written, or completed. I am greatly indebted to all of them. I can hardly find the way to express my gratitude to the contributors to this book, the scientists and intellectuals I interviewed. Without the time and effort they devoted to the preparation of each conversation, to the proper interviewing, and to the authorization and updating of the final form there would be nothing to publish.

There are also many people of goodwill who helped me to come to the United States, to work and stay here, and to prepare this book.

In the first place, I would never have come to the United States in 1975, when I did the original interviews, without the help of Jim Mandros, Cornellius Welsh, and other people working at the press and culture section of the U.S. embassy in Warsaw. They selected me among the scores of equally capable Polish journalists, and offered me a grant to participate in the Professional Journalism Fellowship at Stanford University in California. I was accepted as a fellow and after my arrival at Stanford was greatly helped by Lyle Nelson, Harry Press, and other members of the professional journalism staff.

I owe my return to the United States in 1982 almost exclusively to Alvin Toffler and to the president of Antioch University, William Birenbaum, who had invited me to Antioch as a Visiting Scholar. This assignment wouldn't have been possible without financial contributions by Alvin Toffler, Leo Drey, and Samuel Peabody. During my long stay in the United States I was also given financial help by Janusz Gorzynski and Barbara Piasecka Johnson. Paul Martin and Louis Henkin from the Center for the Study of Human Rights at Columbia University in New York, and Ken Smith, with the faculty of Antioch University in Los Angeles, gave me short-term assignments that permitted me to complete this book after the termination of my original contract with Antioch. I would not have been able to work on this book without the help of Richard Esterly and the staff of the Caron Foundation, who kindly agreed to defer payment for my stay at Chit Chat Farms. I owe a special debt to Gregory Wierzynski and Jim Abernathy without whom I would never have found my way to Chit Chat. Dr. Paul Krooks also took care of my health in the United States.

There are many people who hosted me, providing food and shelter at various times during my stay in the United States. At the moment of my arrival, Heidi and Alvin Toffler gave me a key to their apartment in New York. Barbara and Gregory Wierzynski shared with me their house in Washington, D.C.; so did Hillary and Lew Feldstein in Keene, New Hampshire; and Marilynn and Bob Trounson in Sierra Madre, California. I house sat for Christopher Redman in Chevy Chase, Maryland, and Joe Pipik in Washington, D.C. At different times I was a guest of Agnes and Leo Gruliow in Columbus, Ohio; Nadine and Harry Rosenthal in Silver Spring, Maryland; David Rosenthal in San Francisco; Agnieszka and Andrzej Wroblewski in Boston; Anna and Jerzy Hajduczyk in Ridgefield, Connecticut, as well as of Elzbieta Czyzewska, Jim Abernathy, Elzbieta Wyszynska, Janusz Gorzynski, and Judith and Samuel Peabody in New York City. The warmth and friendship I found in all these places eased the longing for my family in Poland.

And last but not least, there are many people who helped me in the actual preparation of this book. Harold Segel, as early as 1980, reviewed two volumes of interviews published in Polish and strongly encouraged me to prepare an English version. Barbara Wierzynski and Joe Pipik did a tremendous amount of work polishing the rough English of the book proposal and summary; the original version would have hardly been understandable to my prospective publishers. John Radziewicz helped me to reedit the proposal, and Alvin Toffler worked with me on restructuring the book. Finally, Perry Knowlton found a publisher. When my job was almost finished, Martha Carr and Penny Kiffner edited the English translation of the interviews. Lorna Dorian retyped the unreadable manuscript, and Elizabeth Kornacki helped me with the hundreds of little things needed to obtain final authorization for the interviews. When all this was completed, Melinda Corey gave the book its final shape. I want to express a deep gratitude to all these people.

I am especially indebted to two persons who provided a variety of help at every stage of this work: Heidi and Alvin Toffler, my best protectors and friends in the United States.

PART ONE

ON THE UNIVERSE AND LIFE

I

On Science in General

What is science? How do we arrive at scientific statements about reality? What is the role of imagination and intuition in scientific discovery? What is the validity of scientific statements? How is science related to everyday experiences?

These are the problems addressed by Linus Pauling and Evgenii Feinberg—two scientists who have been exploring the mysteries of physics and chemistry for more than half a century. Now they present two contrasting views on the nature of science and the usefulness of the scientific method as an instrument for understanding the world. They also discuss the relationship between science and art and the relevance of science to the analysis of mysterious psychic phenomena.

The two scientists' views differ considerably, especially where the powers and limitations of the scientific method are concerned. Linus Pauling believes that all phenomena, ethics and feelings included, can be reduced to some basic physical and chemical mechanism. In Pauling's "submolecular view of the world" there is room for neither mystery and mysticism nor religion. The world in all its manifestations is totally rational and comprehensible.

Evgenii Feinberg is much more skeptical. He points out that successes of science have produced a cult of rationality and logic to the detriment of intuition. For Feinberg, intuition is a perception of the truth that is not based on logical reasoning or experience, and the basic assumptions of science have this kind of intuitive character. From this perspective Feinberg claims that a scientific statement at its base is neither logical nor rational; logic and experiments are used by scientists to validate intuitive statements.

1. Linus Pauling

Born in 1901, Linus Pauling obtained a doctorate in 1925 from the California Institute of Technology in Pasadena, where he worked until 1964. He is now Professor Emeritus of Chemistry at Stanford University and chairman of the Board of Trustees of the Linus Pauling Institute of Science and Medicine in Palo Alto, California.

The main topic of Pauling's study is the nature of chemical compounds and the bonds between the individual atoms in molecules and compound substances. He discovered a helical structure of amino acids, forming a polypeptide chain in proteins. His further research led him to the discovery, in 1949, that there are several different kinds of human hemoglobin molecules; one that causes sickle-cell anemia as well as others that are involved in a variety of diseases. The research on the structure of proteins resulted in the theory of antibody production. In the sixties Pauling applied his earlier ideas to research on the possibility of molecular causes of mental illness and to the theoretical considerations of the evolution of proteins. Since 1937, Dr. Pauling has conducted research on the molecular theory of diseases. During the last twenty years he has been interested in the study of vitamins, especially vitamin C.

Dr. Pauling has written more than six hundred scientific works and over one hundred articles dealing with social and political issues. His most popular works include: Introduction to Quantum Mechanics *(1935),* The Nature of Chemical Bond *(1939),* General Chemistry *(1947),* The Architecture of Molecules *(1964),* Vitamin C and the Common Cold *(1970),* No More War *(1958; 1983),* Science and World Peace *(1973), and* Cancer and Vitamin C *(1979). Dr. Pauling is currently writing a book on the nature of life.*

Linus Pauling is doctor honoris causa of thirty-five universities and an honorary member of numerous academies of science. For his research on the nature of chemical compounds, he received the Nobel Prize in chemistry in 1954.

Aside from his scholarly activities, Dr. Pauling has been an active member of the international peace and détente movements. In 1961, the United States Humanist Society named him Humanist of the Year. He was awarded the Nobel Peace Prize in 1963 and has also received the Gandhi Peace Prize. In 1973, Linus Pauling received the Inter-

national Lenin Peace Prize, becoming the only person in the world to have been awarded both the Nobel and Lenin Peace prizes.

Wiktor Osiatyński: You began your scientific career in the early twenties; we all know of the incredible development of science in the course of the last fifty years. In what way has that progress been marked in the discipline you've chosen and how has it affected your work?

Linus Pauling: When I first developed an interest in chemistry, I was most curious about the relationship between the well-known chemical formulas and the structure of chemical substances. Based on the traditional categories of composition and chemical structure, you could not precisely explain many chemical properties of a substance. Some studies had been undertaken on the structure of substances, and a method of X-ray diffraction by crystals was known; distances between individual atoms could be measured, too; but there was no general theory based on these observations at that time. The nature of the force holding the atoms together in molecules was still unknown, and I considered that a fundamental problem in chemistry and all branches of science. This problem could have been solved only after 1925, when the principles of quantum mechanics were first formulated. A similar approach was applied to biological problems later on, in the thirties.

As a result, physics, chemistry, and, to a considerable extent, biology have ceased to be mysterious. Today we understand the physics of atoms and molecules quite well; immense progress has been made in the research on the structure of proteins, nucleic acids, the genetic code, and so forth. There are still questions, many of which concern life and biology, that we have not yet found answers to. But I think enormous progress has been made toward a more profound understanding of the world.

O. What kind of progress is this?

P. The world has become more comprehensible; that's progress. We've already tracked down answers to mysterious questions that have haunted man for ages. For instance, why does a child inherit some attributes of each parent? Or, what are the essential differences between two species? We have acquired quite profound knowledge on many phenomena of life; in fact, I don't think there is anything mystical about life anymore. It means that we are able now to create a rational philosophy and rational approach to the world as a whole, in all its aspects: not only physical or biological, but pertaining also to what still seems today to be supernatural and incomprehensible; in fact, a key to such phenomena can be found in quite rational principles of the functions of the human brain.

O. Do you believe that rational comprehension can really embrace all phenomena of human life? Including emotions, ethics, or spiritual "innermost life" of an individual?

P. If I were to define my philosophical stand, I'd say I am a reductionist: I believe that all phenomena can be reduced to certain basic mechanisms. As a humanist and rationalist, I think that these mechanisms can be revealed by the human mind. I reject all dogmas; I don't accept the revealed religions. I think even ethics can be based on scientific foundations.

I have published a number of articles on the scientific basis of morality; the articles were not very profound or scientific, for there is every appearance that arguments here are quite simple. Generally speaking, I don't see a necessity for mysteries and secrets. We are able to understand the world. In fact, during my over sixty-year-long career, I've noted a constant progress in the understanding of the world. That is why I hope we'll understand it entirely and fully someday—its every aspect and phenomenon.

O. I find it somewhat doubtful that such a complete understanding of the world can ever be achieved. After all, the understanding of something depends on the number and nature of the questions we ask. And every answer brings up new questions. Of course, we know more today than people did half a century ago, but over all those years, infinitely more questions have arisen.

P. I agree that today we are able to ask more significant questions than, say, fifty years ago. That is because we found answers to some of our old questions, which were originally rather general. While we've understood the fundamentals more thoroughly, we have also formulated new problems we have yet to solve. It means that today we understand the world to an extent, but there are still certain aspects we cannot understand. We have often not been able even to formulate questions until we reached a certain level of understanding of the more fundamental problems.

O. It seems to me that this process may go on forever.

P. It may be that, with the progress of science, the number of questions we are able to ask will grow. Moreover, we can hope that, sooner or later, we shall find the right answers. But I cannot tell you whether such an increase in questions will go on infinitely; we will exhaust all our questions if our understanding of these mysteries is more or less completed. Or, at least, the understanding of the fundamental scientific problems.

O. Do you mean the understanding of fundamental patterns that underlie all disciplines and fields of science?

P. Right; once we learn the general patterns, we will have to deal only with particular questions. We will have to find out how the patterns function in concrete cases. For example, in biology we may find a mechanism for the arrangement of amino acids in the polypeptide chains. It is estimated, though, that the number of possible polypeptide chains is infinitely greater than the number of atoms in the entire universe. We would have to study in detail the structure of these chains and proteins in all species—millions of which exist in the world—and in all individuals. Such determination of the sequence of amino acids for each species would be a great task. But it would be a study of nature, too; another step forward to a more complete understanding of the world. Such a task, if it is feasible at all, would consume hundreds of years. The task should consist in very detailed research not necessarily pertaining to the fundamental mechanisms underlying the laws of nature. In fact, it is doubtful if anyone will ever do it.

O. Don't you think that in the course of such research facts could be revealed concerning the very fundamental mechanisms of life which, in turn, would lead to the necessity of changing the general theories? After all, isn't that exactly what the development of theories in science is all about: some new facts, not fitting the accepted conceptions, make people look at things in a new way and often change a theory.

P. Yes, it has happened so and it still does. However, we know the world better and better and comprehend that the growth of our understanding has run along specific tracks of development. We don't know if it'll be so forever, if we will ever reach the ultimate knowledge. But I can tell you for a certainty that, in the foreseeable future, we are not going to fall short of interesting questions. The world is by no means dull or boring for scientists. And, quite luckily, there are going to be many interesting jobs for imaginative scientists in the years ahead.

O. Is imagination an inherent attribute of a scientist? And, if so, in what sense?

P. It simply is one of the tools of a scientist. Without imagination a scientist will not discover anything. The essence of scientific discovery requires that you look at what all people see but you notice something nobody's seen yet. To look differently at things, you must have a lot of imagination.

O. How did you make your discoveries, and what part did your imagination play in your work?

P. Since 1952 I've been thinking about the role the anesthetic molecule, xenon, plays in pain-killing. No literature was available on the subject; I tried to do some experiments myself but to no avail. For a long time I used to think of the problem before I fell asleep; it would wake me up in the middle of the night. Finally, I gave up, put off the whole problem, and engaged in another. Nine years later I was reading an article on crystallic structures. While reading an idea came to my mind, and—quite surprisingly to me—it was not related to the article in any direct way; I suddenly discovered that I had just understood the very sense of anesthesia. I had learned what it was about.

Before that I had started thinking on the spatial structure of proteins. I wanted to find a simple pattern, as did many of my colleagues. But I couldn't; all my attempts failed. I caught a cold in spring 1948 and had to stay in bed for a few days. I was making some notes on a piece of paper, and when I finished I was about to fold it, but since I was lying down, I folded the paper differently than I would have done if I had been seated at a table. I sort of rolled the paper first . . . and just then a revelation occurred to me: a spiral. I realized that I could look at the relationship within a structure in a different way. It turned out to be simpler than I first thought, so it amazed me that it had taken me eleven years to make that discovery.

O. Are you suggesting that you made those discoveries by accident?

P. By no means; accidental discoveries happen sometimes, but not very often. A scientific proof can be found accidentally in research originally aimed at something else, but no one has ever formulated a general theory by chance. You can't "accidentally" come to what I call a new vision of reality. My discoveries have always resulted from arduous experiments, hypotheses, and all kinds of suppositions or assumptions; from a hard everyday work you might call the fertilization of the brain. The very moment of discovery may not be really expected, but it is not an accident either.

O. You mentioned different kinds of suppositions; can you foresee the development of science, or expect certain new discoveries?

P. Not in detail. You can foresee the general trend in the development of science. However, many discoveries in the history of physics, chemistry, or biology have been made unexpectedly. I don't mean they were made by chance; only that no one had foreseen them. It is easy, though, to make mistakes, if you go into details. I gave a lecture in 1950 on enzymes; no one knew the molecular structure of enzymes at that time. I said it might be known sometime around the year 2000; as it's turned out, we've already known it for quite a long time now. And today, in 1983, we know the structure of a hundred different enzyme molecules determined by X-ray diffraction.

O. Aristotle advised that all you have to do to find the answers to nearly all questions is just think. Francis Bacon contended that nature is not to be understood without experiments. You combine the attitude of both a thinker and an experimenter. How would you define the relationship between experiment and theory? Does a theory determine the framework of experiments that, in turn, confirm the theory? Or do experiments "create" a theory?

P. My son, also a scientist, once said that there were two kinds of scientists: thinkers and doers. The former, like British physicist John Desmond Bernal, "cook up" theories and methods of research; the latter do experiments and conduct research. These two spheres should never be divorced. You must both think and experiment. In science today we have many theories that can be experimentally confirmed. But we also have—especially in biology—many hypotheses, often not quite coherent (some even contradicting each other) that may never be validated without experiment.

I may have been so successful because I've always been a thinker and a man of action at the same time. I've made significant discoveries through experiments, but the experiments have always been preceded by lots of thinking—by new ideas and new concepts.

O. Do you have a "recipe" that would teach us how to produce new, or innovative, ideas?

P. It is simple: you just have to have a lot of ideas and give up only the ones you've proven false or irrelevant.

O. How can you have a lot of ideas?

P. You must not kill—or let anybody else kill—your exploratory drive, your natural curiosity. You must ask questions and seek for the answers. And not the answers your schoolteacher, or an author, or any other authority would find correct . . . You must be inquisitive.

You must feed your curiosity instinct because it gives you the greatest satisfaction.

O. Do you consider curiosity one of man's main characteristics?

P. Animals can be inquisitive, too. In a strange environment they may act as if an instinct of curiosity motivated their behavior. They try to learn what it is that surrounds them; they do it to orient themselves in the new environment.

O. Do you remember when and how you first realized your own sense of curiosity?

P. I've been interested in the world from childhood, and I realized it when I was about nine years old. My father was a pharmacist, and he used to show me simple chemical reactions. It made me interested in the laws of nature; the experiments I watched awakened my intellectual personality. I was twelve when I first got interested in chemistry so I went on with more and more observations and experiments. I learned the essence of light diffraction all by myself, and scores of other, already well-known, phenomena. I've followed that path ever since.

O. Has the sense of curiosity always been the main motivation in your research?

P. Yes, I think so. But speaking of motivation in human activity, I should mention a problem of a more general nature, a philosophical problem. Everybody should have an opportunity to live a "good life," and be able to develop his potentials. All people ought to be well nourished, clothed, economically secure, and educated according to their abilities and interests. They should be given a right to contribute to the development of the world, to admire its beauty, to travel, and develop their interests. In short, all people, as a result of their own efforts, have a right to be content and satisfied with their lives. Many people take satisfaction from feeding their intellectual inquisitiveness. I'm a scientist myself, and I take contentment and pleasure from my work. I'm happy if I make a discovery, even if it's not a big one. I recall how I worked on the structure of sulphur minerals forty-five years ago: I studied the arrangement of metal and sulphur atoms in minerals and finally I found out that I was able to "foresee" the structure of some of them. I did it in my notebook and only later made experiments; several structures proved to be exactly like I'd sketched them. It was such a joy . . . In such moments I was truly happy.

In general, I think, many people are curious about the world in which they live; scientific research is one of the ways to fulfill that curiosity.

O. How come some people have that curiosity and some don't?

P. All children ask questions, try to experiment, want to apply an intellectual order to their environment. However, not everybody has an opportunity to develop his potentials and his abilities.

O. Does everybody have an opportunity to live a "good life," to be educated, travel, admire beauty, and contribute to the development of the world?

P. No, and I've always wondered how many talents go to waste, how many people don't have a chance to develop, how many human beings are wasted because we're not able to solve fundamental problems—we cannot find a sociopolitical order that would be acceptable to all and serve the creative development of all people. Many people are prevented from contributing to the work of the world because of unemployment; this I perceive as a violation of their basic human right. And there are numerous similar problems that remain unsolved.

I think no one, especially not those who've won success, has the right to remain passive or indifferent in the face of these problems. Therefore, I never could afford to be only a scholastic or lab-confined scientist. Whenever I found it possible, I fought for the well-being of humanity, for peace and security in the world, for human dignity, and for the highest ideals of mankind.

2. Evgenii Feinberg

Evgenii Lvovich Feinberg was born in 1912, and graduated from the Department of Physics at the University of Moscow in 1935. He earned his Ph.D. in physics in 1938, and undertook research at the P.N. Lebedev Institute of Physics of the Soviet Academy of Sciences. He later taught at the Higher School of Engineering and Physics, where he still works.

Dr. Feinberg's main area of interest is the physics of waves—acoustics and radio-physics in particular. He presented the results of his research and experiments in his book Spreading of Radio Waves over the Surface of Earth *(1962). He has also conducted research on cosmic radiation and the physics of elementary particles.*

He is also interested in the more general problems of the validity of scientific theories and the theory of knowledge and cognition. In his work he attempts to bridge a gap between physics and humanities or, more generally, between science and art and culture.

Dr. Feinberg is a member of the Soviet Academy of Sciences. For his scientific achievements he was awarded the Red Banner Order and the Order of Merit.

Wiktor Osiatyński: Do you think that modern physics offers us a physical image of the world?

Evgenii Feinberg: The concept of the physical image of the world is fairly popular nowadays, while, in fact, I myself don't quite understand what it means. Is it an image that today's physics produces? Or does it mean that physics may have enough tools for a complete description of the world in all its aspects since, as it is supposed, we are living in the "age of physics"? Or can this concept mean yet something else? I'd say that we have today a common method of approach to the outside world. For modern science makes it possible, in a methodologically similar way, to explore different domains, sometimes dramatically different, such as physics and biology.

O. Do you mean similar principles underlying hypotheses and experiments?

F. More than that. What I have in mind is, generally, the common theoretical approach. I want to point out that the basic cognitive categories—as, for instance, the concepts of correctness, chance, or proof—hold an identical validity in all disciplines of science.

O. Does it apply to the social sciences and the humanities, too?

F. It depends on how we understand them. I think, however, that natural sciences, social sciences, and the humanities are bound together at a much more basic level. What they have in common underlies all forms of cognition that are usually ignored because we tend to exaggerate the intellectual, or formal and logical, qualities of science. What I have in mind is intuition, usually associated with the arts rather than with science.

O. Are you speaking of an intuitive nature of hypotheses, or finding answers and solutions to scientific problems?

F. Not only that. What you mentioned covers a narrow meaning of intuition as a kind of supposition or conjecture. Any guesswork within each creative process always has an intuitive character. There may be conjectures that can be proved logically or experimentally.

For example, Francis Crick and James Watson had "intuitively" guessed that DNA had a double-helix structure. Later, they proved it experimentally. The same with each discovery. After it is proved, the initial, intuitive idea may be forgotten. It is no longer necessary. It becomes just a detail in a scientist's own biography. In a paper describing the scientific nature of a discovery, the fact of the intuitive guesswork leading to it is of no interest to anyone. Only the validity of scientific proof and its logic are important.

O. Then intuition serves as an aid in our otherwise strictly logical search for truth?

F. Essentially, yes. However, there is another kind of intuition that plays a more significant role in scientific cognition. It is a direct recognition of truth, not based on logical proof, not even requiring to be proved.

O. Such direct insight may happen in the arts or humanities, but can it be possible in the natural sciences?

F. Why not? I'll give you a trivial example. Let's take a theorem: the world does exist objectively. Can you establish a logical proof for that statement?

O. But it's not a scientific statement . . .

F. Of course it is. It certainly is a part of science. In many disciplines it even has a fundamental theoretical and cognitive meaning. I'll give you another example, unquestionably belonging to science: the principles of Euclid. The one, for instance, saying that only one parallel line can be drawn through one point. I can accept such an axiom and base whole geometry upon it. But you might ask how my geometry would be related to the world we lived in. We might try to experiment looking for a simple, limited plane, where Euclid's postulate proved true. But then comes the Russian mathematician Nikolai Lobachevsky who takes another assumption: that through one point there can be drawn an infinite number of parallel lines. Upon this ground he formulates another, also logical but completely different, geometry. Although he was not able to prove his idea, we today know that the geometry of Lobachevsky is correct and useful in the domain of immense dimensions.

My point is that the very same assumption underlying all natural sciences—namely, that truth can be proved experimentally—is, in fact, a synthetic intuitive proposition not to be proved logically or experimentally.

O. Do you mean that the fundamental principles of logic, and all disciplines of science based on it as well as all axioms, have an intuitive character?

F. Principally, yes, but only in such disciplines as mathematics or logic where, after making initial assumptions, a uniform construction of the whole can be completed; also in some natural sciences in which intuitive hypotheses can be experimentally proved. But in everyday life the situation is different, as it is in social and political sciences, the humanities, aesthetics, ethics, and the like. Here, it is not possible to prove anything or even test experimentally. Most of the time no proof can be found to support our hypotheses. Several equally valid judgments and opinions can be formulated. When a mother thinks about whether to punish her child or not, she has no logical reason to act one way or another. If someone arranges furniture in a house, or buys flowers for his girlfriend, he makes decisions beyond logic.

O. Does it mean that we usually make our decisions intuitively?

F. Yes, all except the ones belonging to a few narrow domains where we can demonstrate experimentally the particular ideas that, by the way, arise mostly from our intuition.

O. Are all the arguments that have seemingly led us to a decision or a judgment only rationalizations made after making an intuitive decision or judgment?

F. Essentially, yes. Arguments usually confirm and enforce intuitive judgments.

O. Why do we have to confirm and enforce our qualitative judgments and opinions?

F. Because we believe we have to. The essence of intuition lies in a multitude of possible judgments. If we want our judgment to prevail, we try to enforce it by argumentation or back it with a recognized authority.

O. Such an authority today is science, isn't it? Is this why most intuitive judgments in humanities, or, even more, social sciences plead their scientific character?

F. Maybe; we're living in the age of science, after all. In those disciplines we use logic, although it is so tightly intertwined with intuitive guesswork that the two are hard to separate. The seemingly logical moments are very often pointed out to support the intuitive judgments with a broad, scientific authority.

O. Once even science itself needed to be backed with a higher authority . . .

F. Yes, for millennia, religion had granted authority to all theories. Even the ones belonging to natural sciences; for instance, a theory of the universe's origins needed a religious enforcement. The development of exact sciences, and the rise in prestige of science in general, put an end to it. In other fields, though, an authority to support our theories is still needed. Especially in ethics. Can you, for instance, logically prove that one should be good? Or can you find proof to the contrary?

O. There is no way to do it. It is even hard to tell what's good or bad.

F. Absolutely; it is religion that has done it for us for a long time. I think art does the same, and it may explain its continuity, popularity, even necessity of existence.

O. Art in the role of religion?

F. Not in the role of religion, but in a similar role of enforcing, with its authority, the validity of synthetic judgments escaping all proof.

O. In what way can art do that?

F. I'll give you an example. There is a question with no logical answer—what's more important: the love of two people or the prestige and dignity of a family? One can argue about it, but cannot give any positive answer. Now, go and see Shakespeare's drama *Romeo and Juliet*; you will know, somehow, what is otherwise impossible to prove. There is a conflict between logic and intuition in every truly great work of art. The solution of the conflict usually means the triumph of what's intuitive.

O. Really? Don't Romeo and Juliet die? The heroes of tragedies governed by intuition are usually defeated.

F. That's true. But that is what the triumph of intuition is all about. Both sides are right in a true tragedy; only their reasons are contradictory. One is a reason of logic and rationality; while the other is a reason of intuition and irrationality—in a word: of humanity. A hero's death usually means the symbolic death of his adversary. It shakes the audience, thus confirming the domination of intuitive reason over the discursive, logical one.

O. Is art able to "assist" science where science cannot establish any logical or experimental proof? Can art enforce an unprovable scientific theory?

F. Not exactly. In fact, art can be helpful, but in another sense. Science's successes nowadays result in a fetishization of rationalism and, generally, of all that's logical or rational. People begin to think that truth is only what they can prove rationally, while art can provide the authority of an intuitive cognition of truth. In so doing, it indicates the limited nature of logical cognition, and enforces an authority of intuitive cognition in general, including also intuitive cognition in exact sciences. It points out that even science is not based on logic only. Breaking the monopoly of logical analytical reasoning, art trains us in inspiration, which is necessary to exercise science. For if science were based on sheer logic, it would wind up at a dead end.

O. Is the only purpose of art the enforcement of the authority of unprovable intuitive judgments?

F. It is the main purpose, but not the only one. Besides this cognitive function, art does other things, too. Its power of emotional influence plays an immense ethical role. It offers evident aesthetic experiences. It also is a specific means of communication among people. And, first of all, it introduces order and harmony—both in the individual and group life, the latter being especially chaotic by its very nature.

O. Wasn't that one of the traditional purposes of science, to put the outside world into order?

F. That's right. But science fulfills this purpose because of intuition, not logic. Here again, an analogy between art and science strikes—in this nonlogical, intuitive aspect. Compare the statement of Stravinsky—"The phenomenon of music serves solely to introduce order into everything that exists"—with what Einstein once said—"The main task of a physicist consists of the discovery of the most general, elementary patterns from which one could logically draw an image of the universe. One of the ways to perceive the laws is intuition, which helps to see order, hidden behind the obvious manifestations of various processes."

O. Since you brought it up, tell me professor, does modern physics really help to see that hidden order? Doesn't the discovery of more and more elementary particles rather blur the picture and make the chaos increasingly unpenetrable? Isn't it so that, from the time of Werner Heisenberg's principle of uncertainty,* physics has become increasingly chaotic?

* The uncertainty principle, or indeterminacy principle, states that "it is impossible to determine with arbitrarily high accuracy both the position and momentum (essentially velocity) of a subatomic particle like the electron. The effect of this principle is to convert the laws of physics into statements about relative probabilities instead of absolute certainties." (*The New Columbia Encyclopedia*, 1975)

F. It may seem so but it's not true. Our difficulty in understanding the law of uncertainty results primarily from the difference in proportions between man and electron. We want to describe peculiarities of the electron and explain them in categories corresponding to our own human scale.

O. Isn't it feasible?

F. Thanks to the uncertainty principle, it is. Uncertainty does not mean ignorance. This principle is a law of knowledge. We know that the subject of cognition is so complicated that, if we want to describe it in categories of situation, velocity, speed, and other coordinates, we have to do it extremely carefully, adjusting our method of description to the specific properties of the electron. This is the law of cognition. Quantum mechanics, in general, lets us know how probable is a given fact. Our incapability to say exactly where an electron falls results not from our ignorance but from the very complexity of the electron itself, for an electron possesses no property such as being able to fall at any determinable place with any determinable speed.

O. Since such property is quite ordinary in our own scale, we are bewildered with the peculiarity of the electron.

F. Yes, but here again you've touched the topic of our conversation: intuition. Lev Landau, an outstanding Soviet physicist, once remarked that it was quite astounding and beyond comprehension that people have discovered these peculiarities of the electron at all. They are totally foreign to the scale of human life or activity, aren't they? They don't fit our receptors and the measurements we are used to. Isn't it astounding that scientists have guessed—conjectured indeed, for no logic led to it directly, nor experiments that were yet to be designed—that the atom was so specifically built. Landau saw in it evidence of the staggering power of the human mind. It's too obvious to disagree. This is why it cannot be ruled out that we may yet discover many more equally extraordinary facts, phenomena, or patterns.

O. Speaking of that, what do you think, professor, of phenomena we still cannot explain, termed generally as parapsychological? Do you believe they will ever be explained in scientific, physical terms someday?

F. The problem is there are so many different phenomena. Some belong to science even now; some don't. And still others may be related to what we have yet no idea about.

O. Telepathy, for instance, is often said to be a phenomenon whose physical interpretation seems quite probable. The nature of telepathy may involve some waves that we haven't found yet.

F. It is extremely doubtful that there still would be undiscovered, completely new kinds of waves . . .

O. How about some unknown receptors catching usually ignored signals transmitted by the recognized waves?

F. That sounds a little more probable. Currents detected in the brain suggest that radio waves may be emitted there. Although they are very faint, some extremely sensitive receptors are conceivable. The waves may grow more intensive under emotional stimulation and such stimulation can be transmitted. It is very unlikely, though, that there could actually be transmitted any information couched in concrete terms.

O. We may not be aware that we all possess such power of extrasensory perception . . .

F. It's hard to say anything for certain. In fact, some arguments seem to support such a possibility. Psychologists have long noticed that there might be unconscious judgments or perceptions occurring beyond consciousness. For example, there were people who "lost" their hearing through war trauma. Detailed examination proved that they could actually hear, that is, the brain received the sound signals. However, they did not realize the fact, for there was no higher integration of the signals at the level of consciousness. It means that, generally, there can be a stimulation of an organ of the body without one's conscious realization of the fact.

O. Such a person is just not aware of receiving information?

F. Right. It may be so, but the problem is rather too complex to draw any concrete conclusions. However, telekinesis—the act of putting material objects into motion by psychic power or thought—seems quite improbable. I may admit the existence of very sensitive receptors facilitating extrasensory communication between people, but inanimate objects lack receptors, consciousness, energetic or motoric power that might enable them to carry out my "order." To put an object in motion by means of thought, I'd simply need more energy. Well, these two examples show that parapsychological phenomena ought not to be sacked all together or considered all as one.

O. But you cannot rule out that man may have powers we are not able to predict, can you?

F. No.

O. Especially in view of the remarkably rapid and dramatic changes of our knowledge in the last decades. Physics itself has reached the theory of relativity, principles of uncertainty and complementarity, quantum mechanics, and scores of other revolutionary discoveries in a very short time. What is the influence of those discoveries on our general understanding of the world?

F. I see nothing extraordinary here. The twentieth century has witnessed dramatic discoveries. Well, let us think how it was one, two, or three hundred years ago? What did people say then? It appears people have always believed that some extraordinary things happened during their lifetimes. A French physicist wrote in the early nineteenth century that the discovery of electricity was the utmost achievement of the cognitive powers of science. He supposed that no step forward was ever possible after that; further generations of scientists would only have to confirm previously revealed truths. Remember, he wrote this before there were motors, lamps, or telegraph. They just had a voltaic cell, but they said science had already reached its limit . . .

O. This is what makes a difference. Today, despite magnificent discoveries and applications, no one thinks science has reached the peak of its possibilities. Rather on the contrary . . .

F. It's true. This is what the theory of relativity and quantum mechanics have taught us. I think the most important effect of the relativity theory was the acknowledgment of the infiniteness of cognition. Or, in other words, that science has no limit whatsoever and never will.

O. Linus Pauling hopes that we may someday know all about everything.

F. I don't agree. I think that an understanding of the world in terms of dialectic logic is quite correct. I don't mean a vulgar meaning of dialectics, but a dialectic theory of knowledge being but an integration of logic and intuition. This theory says that the development of science does not consist, contrary to what many scientists used to believe, particularly reductionists, of determining another figure past the point or measuring more and more precisely what was already well known. The development of science is an ever renewed, dramatic breakthrough in our understanding of the world. Therefore, what's most important in science is that there will never be any finite, absolute truth. We will always be able to find something smaller than the smallest particle and something bigger than the universe. Even in our own scale there may be something beyond any current suspicion.

And last but not least, we ourselves are continually changing, shifting our own points of view. Therefore, quite fortunately, there will always exist a broad field for the development of science, as well as for intuition, underlying all human feelings and thoughts.

2

On the Macrocosm and the Microcosm

Is there intelligent life outside earth? Is extraterrestrial expansion a human destiny? What cosmic forces created our planet? How will they shape the future of the universe? How do these forces operate on the basic level of elementary particles? Is randomness or causality the basic principle of nature?

These and other questions are addressed by Iosif Shklovskii and Robert Hofstadter. Shklovskii, a Soviet astrophysicist, helped to originate international research aimed at the search for life in the universe. Now, he categorically rules out the possibility of life outside earth. He also offers his theories on the history of the universe from the Big Bang to the distant future, stressing the necessity of man's expansion into the universe.

Hofstadter, a Nobel Prize winner in physics, explains the microcosm of elementary particles, presents fascinating prospects for the application of high-energy physics in medicine, and discusses the nature of truth in physics. In so doing, Hofstadter comes to share Feinberg's conviction about the limited abilities of science, while Shklovskii's forwardness brings to mind the optimistic reductionism of Pauling.

3. Iosif S. Shklovskii

Iosif Samoilovich Shklovskii was born in 1916 and graduated from the Department of Physics of Moscow University. In 1938 he took a job at the Institute of Astronomy at the same university. Since 1968 he has been the director of the astrophysics department at the Space Research Institute while continuing his teaching at Moscow University.

Astrophysics and, in particular, the evolution of stars constitute the main area of Shklovskii's scientific interests. The theory of ionization of the solar corona and research on radiation in the galaxy and on the origins of cosmic radiation are among his achievements of the greatest significance.

Iosif Shklovskii has published more than 250 articles, papers, and monographs. His major books, including Intelligent Life in the Universe *(coauthored with Carl Sagan, 1966), have been translated into English.*

Shklovskii is a member of the Soviet Academy of Sciences, a foreign member of the National Academy of Sciences and the Academy of Arts and Sciences in the United States, and a member of the Royal Astronomic Society of the United Kingdom. He has been awarded the Lenin Prize for his research in astronomy and astrophysics.

Wiktor Osiatyński: Professor Shklovskii, there has been more and more talk lately of the ties linking man and space, of the dependence of the evolution of life on earth on the fate of the universe, and to what extent the entire history of outer space contributed to the emergence of the human being. Some see in it an opportunity to overcome the grievous isolation of man in the universe.

Iosif S. Shklovskii: I don't understand what you are talking about. Do you mean man was created by God?

O. No, what I mean is that we've been influenced by the universe perhaps more strongly than it seemed to us.

S. Do you really suggest some extraterrestrial intervention? Humanity as a culture is a little more than ten thousand years old. I assure you positively that nothing has ever arrived here from outer space.

O. But humanity is just a particle of a continuous and long history of the planet . . .

S. I see. Your point is that this trivia, man, emerged on earth, and earth is part of the solar system, and the solar system is part of the galaxy and the universe. It is rather a shallow philosophy. I prefer speaking of concrete things.

O. All right. Is there life in outer space?

S. No, at least not in our galaxy; nor do I believe in the existence of any rational, technologically advanced life anywhere beyond it. I believe that civilization is a rarity; it has developed exclusively on earth. When it comes down to it, we are unique.

O. What about other forms of life?

S. There may exist nonrational forms. It cannot be known for sure, for there is no way to prove it. I think, however, that in our galaxy there is no addressee of our communications and appeals.

O. Then why are we looking for other civilizations? Why are we sending all sorts of "space letters"?

S. It is useless, sheer stupidity. If there existed some advanced civilization we should have perceived signs of its activities long ago. So enormous is the speed of technological progress that a civilization equalling ours should be able to conquer the neighboring part of space in a matter of three hundred years, and in a period of ten centuries it could control the entire solar system in which the planet belonged, or even reach other galaxies. If there existed any civilization older than ours by only a thousand years—and in cosmic categories it is practically close to zero—then it would have spread beyond the original planet long ago. Such a civilization could have gained control of its own solar system and reached as far as our sun. However, nowhere are traces of such activities to be found. It means we are alone.

O. Can it be that the other civilization doesn't want to conquer the universe? Has it perhaps pursued another way?

S. No, that's impossible. There are people who say that civilization can evolve, as it were, locked up within its own boundaries, spending its energies only inwardly with none whatsoever emitted into the surrounding outer space. But it is physically impossible; it contradicts the principles of thermodynamics.

O. Do you mean that should there exist another civilization, it would have to evolve exactly like ours?

S. Yes; after all, technological progress is but a very recent development. Science is only 350 years old. Over this short span of time man has progressed from nearly no knowledge to his present level; from barbarity to a highly developed civilization. It means that if the human potential keeps doubling every ten to twenty years, our civilization will spread over the entire solar system in the next three hundred years.

O. In what way? Will traces of our activity, like waves we emit or space probes, spread through the solar system?

S. It is human beings who will travel literally all over the solar system. Space cities have already been designed, and today's space technology makes it possible to build a colony for ten thousand people to live comfortably in the orbit of the moon; not astronauts but ordinary human beings. It could be done in some ten to fifteen years at a cost of $100 billion, which is just three times more than was spent on man's landing on the moon. And in fifty years we will be able to build a space colony for thirty to forty million people.

O. But will it pay to do it?

S. That's quite another question. I've been saying it's possible. I think, however, that it is not up to man to ask whether to explore the universe or not. It will be his only choice, for it will be his only way to survive. Now, you see, we have had an energy crisis here on earth. And just one lunar orbit colony could supply enough energy to satisfy the needs of all the United States. Solar energy, transferred into microwaves, would be transmitted to earth. Or take pollution: threats of pollution from energy generating plants or from chemical experiments can never be completely eliminated. Therefore, projects involving the threat of pollution should not be carried out on earth but, instead, somewhere in space.

O. To make space polluted instead?

S. There is enough room out there. The cosmos is not easy to litter. My point is that with the present rate of development, within the next millennium, human beings will certainly move out all over the solar system. We will construct space cities. Then the problem of overpopulation on earth will be solved, as will energy and environmental problems. It seems to be a technological necessity. If a catastrophe does not erase humankind from the earth before, it will be inevitable.

O. You see expansionism as the only destiny of man, don't you professor?

S. The history of humanity is the history of expansionism. No steady development is possible without expansion. To stop expanding would mean death. But expansion does not have to be strictly territorial. It can involve energy or any other kind of activity. All parameters defining our development double every ten to twenty years. But our planet isn't big and human potential is gigantic. Man has transcended the potential of the small planet that gave birth to him.

Therefore, he must expand. The expansion will be very rapid. From the cosmic perspective, a thousand years is but the twinkle of an eye.

O. You said man came out of barbarity 350 years ago; what is barbarity and what is civilization?

S. I am speaking only of technological progress. Ancient man knew almost nothing; motion was a mystery to him. Even ancient science did not understand motion.

O. But then, ancient people were able to make good use of it, however little they knew about the principles of motion.

S. They were only using the power of their slaves' muscles. That is precisely why their evolution was so slow and limited, and why it ended with the collapse of the ancient world.

O. They simply were defeated by barbarians even more barbaric, more ignorant, just more motionally efficient. Or maybe, to satisfy his needs, ancient man needed only the power of his muscles?

S. Do you mean that man may be developing anomalously and, therefore, he should not struggle for expansion? Is that what you suggest?

O. Yes, I find it possible. Why do so many people, especially humanists, seem to be frightened by prospects of expansion, pollution of space, and technology? Or even by people with such a clear, precise vision as yours, professor?

S. These are not really serious fears; they often result from ignorance. It is not man's expansion that poses a real threat, but the unlimited technological development here, on this planet. It is only lately that we have started to understand this. On the other hand, someone who does not deal with space professionally cannot realize the dimensions of outer space. There is plenty of room out there. The entire envisioning of space will be artificial, made by man himself.

O. Where will we get the energy and materials to create it?

S. We will use solar energy; it is available over our entire solar system. And our building materials can be taken from Jupiter, or from asteroids.

O. That sounds like fantasy or science fiction.

S. Well, soon it will not be fantasy at all. This direction of our development is a necessity. To not follow this path means retardation, stagnation. A steam engine that is not used rusts.

O. Now I understand why you exclude the existence of other civilizations. If they existed, they would have developed in the same way and would have already reached us. Or they would "rust." Could they actually be "rusting" now? Perhaps at a certain level of technological progress, like the use of nuclear energy, some inner force destroys civilizations.

S. There is such a theory, but I don't think it is widely held. It might be possible for some civilizations to overcome internal problems, but we have found no evidence of their activity in space.

O. Perhaps they all perished.

S. That wouldn't change my answer to the question of whether there exist technologically advanced civilizations or not. They do not exist. Either they never existed or they have perished.

O. It can affect, though, our way of thinking about progress and expansionism. Perhaps we should consider the limits beyond which a catastrophe lurks. Do you think that intelligent life has emerged, more or less accidentally, only on earth?

S. Yes, I think so. I've already mentioned that I don't rule out definitely the existence of more primitive forms of life on other planets. So far we have not found any. American scientists ruled out the possibility of the existence of life on Mars; not even bacteria were found there. Some microbes may exist somewhere, we can't know. It seems a very remote possibility to me. Could life spring up at any place where chemical evolution reached a proper level, then it would appear on Mars, too. I think, though, that the emergence of life resulted from the coincidence of a multitude of factors. Maybe only on earth did these favorable circumstances occur just once . . .

O. However, the latest reports of research based on the findings of the Viking space probes do not rule out the possibility of the existence of primitive forms of life on Mars. Let us assume, however, that you are right and that—as you put it—the search made by the Viking probes was superfluous. Does that mean that when we search for traces of life on other planets and do not find any, our quest is totally useless?

S. Of course not. It is not useless because now we can be certain that life exists nowhere in the solar system except on earth. Mars is the only other planet where favorable conditions exist. It is ridiculous to think of life on Mercury or Jupiter or Venus. Since life does not exist on Mars, it means that it exists only on earth. It may exist in other solar systems, but we won't be able to experiment out there for some time yet.

O. Don't you think, professor, that it is worthwhile to undertake projects like the Viking probes not only to find out if there is life somewhere else, but to better understand ourselves: our life, our origins, our uniqueness, our desires and needs?

S. I don't know. We should calculate and compare costs involved and profits gained, and they are often incalculable. I was absolutely positive that the Viking probes would find no traces of life on Mars, but then the Americans are rich so they can afford such experiments.

O. In what terms do you estimate the benefits of space research? Only in practical and technological terms or also benefits of a philosophical nature?

S. Both.

O. What are then, in your opinion, the most significant philosophical effects of the past two decades of space research?

S. I believe man's place in the universe has become clearer. We've been taught at school that we inhabit a small planet, but no one seemed to acknowledge it. Rather, we have believed in empirical experience telling us that the dimensions and resources of earth are nearly limitless. The beginning of the space era has awakened people to the notion that our planet is not very big at all. Moreover, another important outcome of the space era is the fact that we haven't found anything basically new in the entire solar system. Whatever the astronomers had known before about the planets, the sun, and the whole system has only been confirmed. The space flights, of course, helped us to establish certain technical details. On Mars, for example, we have located the biggest volcano in the whole solar system; it has a diameter of 500 km and it is 25 km high—and you can't see it from earth. It is interesting but by no means basic. We've already explored from earth all the dimensions, temperature, magnetosphere, and other characteristics of the planets. And space flights have only confirmed our suppositions. They became the empirical test of the validity of our knowledge of the solar system—knowledge based on indirect reasoning. This, in turn, helps us to check the validity of our conjectures about more distant regions of the universe, which the spaceships will not reach in our lifetime. We can also check our theses about the history and evolution of the universe. In short, space programs have confirmed the validity of our science and the scientific methods we apply. That is quite a lot, isn't it?

O. You mentioned the history and evolution of the universe. Most scientists today believe in the hypothesis that the universe sprang up from an eruption called the Big Bang. People often wonder what was there before the Big Bang.

S. You want to know what was there when nothing was there?

O. I don't know. I simply think that the concept of infinity in time and space is a problem that can be posed by man but cannot ever be solved.

S. I think you may be right, but only to some extent. The notion of time is not as fundamental as it seems to be. There is a very simple answer to the question: what was before the Big Bang? Before it, time as such did not exist at all. It's hard to imagine it now, but let us try. The universe is, say, the size of an electron, 10^{-12} cm. The specific gravity of that particle is 10^{120} g/cm^3. Under such extreme circumstances, the concept of time is meaningless, especially in that there are no changes by which one could perceive the passing of time. It is the general theory of relativity that helped us to learn how fantastic were the forces of gravity before the Big Bang, so we cannot even apply the terms of time and space to that situation. No time or space as we know them were there. When we ask, "What was before," the very word *before* implies time. And we do not realize that "before" time could not have existed at all. Time can actually occur only "after" . . .

O. Can we then say, as did Kant, that time and space are categories created by the human mind for man's own convenience?

S. No, man did not create them. They exist objectively. They sprang up at a certain moment in the evolution of the universe. But once everything was different, and time didn't exist. In physics you have phenomena that a hundred years ago seemed fundamental but now have lost all meaning. For example, an electron seemed to circle an atom nucleus along a predetermined orbit. But the notion of an electron orbit turned out to be senseless, for the motion of an electron is so complex that it cannot be described in simple terms of velocity. The same with the universal application of notions of time and space. Once—as Gogol wrote in his *Diary of a Madman*—a day was timeless.

O. And what will happen in the future? Will time and space cease to exist once again?

S. They will not. The universe—our universe—will expand infinitely and no force will stop the process of its expansion.

O. You mean the universe is not going to stop expanding and start contracting again?

S. No; the principles of the future development of the universe depend on its average density. Modern astronomy helped us to measure the actual density of the universe. It is 10^{-31} g/cm^3. There is only one atomic nucleus in one cubic meter. Were the density of the universe twenty times as big as it is now, then, in a few dozens of billions of years, the universe would stop expanding and start contracting all over again, until it became just a microscopic point. However, since the mass is not dense enough, nothing can stop the process of expansion of the universe.

O. Wasn't the critical point reached when the universe was twenty times smaller?

S. No, because this critical value changes along with the expansion of the universe. The number of atomic nuclei is strictly determined and it is 10^{80}. This number is the critical value. This is how our universe is built and its very structure predetermines its future.

O. I doubt one can ascertain so categorically and authoritatively the density of matter or the number of atomic nuclei in the universe, since both these values are still debated and uncertain. Let us assume, though, that you are right. Does that mean that there will never be an "end of the universe"?

S. Right, there will not. A very extraordinary phenomenon occurred at the origin of the universe and nothing like that is likely to ever happen again. The universe will expand infinitely. That is, at least, what today's science says.

O. And how about the future of our solar system? May there at least be "the end of the sun" someday?

S. Of course that may happen. Each particular unit of the universe has its own history. There was a time when there were no galaxies, no stars, no solar systems, no planets, no chemical elements. There was only homogeneous plasma. This plasma started taking form. Galaxies emerged from the plasma and as it condensed the stars were created. Thermonuclear reactions within the stars led to the emergence of chemical elements, and so forth. The planets emerged and, then, life. The universe has developed from the simple toward more and more complex forms. Our sun, from a cloud of matter, has become what it is now and it happened approximately five billion years ago. The planets were forming simultaneously . . .

O. What will be in the future?

S. Within the next four to six billion years the sun's energy will start to run out, although it will not reach point zero. The sun will expand to become a red giant; it will shine a hundred times brighter; its outer layer will reach earth or even Mars. Then, clouds of matter will separate from the red giant to create what we call a planetary nebula. The central part of the sun, however, will contract and will become a small object we call a white dwarf. Nothing will ever happen to it again. Practically, it will exist eternally.

O. Will it ever disappear?

S. No, sometimes a white dwarf's electron coat breaks, but that will not be the case with our sun. It is too small. The critical mass of a white dwarf is 1.2 that of our sun. So, if the sun's mass increased only 16 percent, it could seize matter from space and a catastrophe would occur. The white dwarf would turn into a so-called neutron star and collapse. However, the mechanism of how these stars spring up and why some white dwarfs collapse is not quite clear.

O. But nothing like that will happen to our sun.

S. You don't like that idea, do you? It is not enough that the sun will turn into a white dwarf.

O. I really don't care. Since when the sun becomes a white dwarf around which our planet will orbit—cold, no atmosphere, deserted, and extinct—there will not be any humans either.

S. That's not necessarily true. It will not happen for billions of years and man may be able to create his own, new atmosphere as well as his own, new sources of energy. Man's potential is boundless. After all, you need just a millennium to conquer the entire solar system. And for the sun to turn into a white dwarf takes several billion years.

O. Does that mean that man will be able to alter the sequence of those natural processes?

S. No, these processes can't be stopped or changed. People can simply adapt themselves—they can create an artificial environment where survival will not depend on the sun, only there will be new artificial energy sources.

O. Is it possible that mankind might outlive our solar system?

S. Why not? The potential of the human mind is immense. If mankind continues developing at the present rate, people may take over and change the entire galaxy in a few million years. Man may be able to create space cities around every star. And it can happen very soon indeed, for what's five or six million years to a galaxy for which one turn around its axis takes two hundred million years? But man must learn how to use his potential. Mankind can practically exist forever if no catastrophe destroys him.

O. What kind of a catastrophe do you have in mind? An internal or external one?

S. The very same that has haunted the minds of politicians all over the world, the internal one, which can destroy our entire civilization. Man has limitless technological potential, but he is still very immature in his social and moral spheres. And these shortcomings can trigger a catastrophe; they can destroy civilization from inside.

O. So maybe it's a pity that such an imperfect creature is, in your opinion, so unique in the universe and may even become the master of the universe?

S. You haven't understood much from what I said, I'm afraid. When I spoke about the uniqueness of man, about the necessity to reach out beyond our planet, you seemed to be scared of the very word *expansionism.* You didn't take into consideration that, instead, realizing the necessity of expansionism can change man himself. It can make him morally better, more responsible for his actions.

O. Because as masters of the universe we take responsibility for the universe?

S. Because we assume the responsibility.

4. Robert Hofstadter

Robert Hofstadter was born in 1915 and received his M.A. and Ph.D. degrees in physics from Princeton University in 1938. In 1946 he became an assistant professor of physics at Princeton University. In 1954 he was appointed professor of physics at Stanford University.

Hofstadter has concentrated his research in the high-energy physics of elementary particles. He also conducted research projects for NASA concerning the origins and nature of energy in the universe.

In the last few years, Dr. Hofstadter has become a pioneer in the field of angiography through the use of synchrotron radiation. His contributions have been particularly useful in the preventive diagnosis of heart diseases.

In 1958 Dr. Hofstadter was elected to the National Academy of Sciences, and in 1961 he was awarded the Nobel Prize in physics for his "pioneering studies of electron scattering in atomic nuclei and for his thereby achieved discoveries concerning the structure of the nucleons." In 1970 Hofstadter was elected to membership in the American Academy of Arts and Sciences.

Wiktor Osiatyński: In your research, you study the smallest particles known to man; you also study physical laws valid for the smallest distances we can measure. What is the smallest particle?

Robert Hofstadter: We don't know. In 1955 my colleagues and I concluded that the particle then considered the fundamental and indivisible element of all other things did not necessarily have to be the smallest particle known at the moment. Very complicated experiments led us to the discovery of a complex inner structure of that particle; we even calculated how electric charges were distributed in it.

O. As far as I know, the consequences of your discovery went far beyond pure physics.

H. Yes, in a sense. It changed the traditional approach to the composition of the atom and opened a question as to whether there will not always be another level—where particles even smaller than the ones we already know, examine, and study, exist.

O. But it cannot be an indefinite process, can it? Don't things contain a certain finite number of particles, even the smallest ones?

H. Not necessarily. The chain of particles we consider the fundamental units of nature may not have an "end." It is not a matter of nature itself but rather of the development of tools for researchers to use. By "tools" I don't mean only physical techniques, but intellectual tools: new ideas, hypotheses, questions, and doubts.

My argument derives from the history of science. Whenever man looks for something smaller than he's already found, he finds it. It happened to me. Since then, science has made another leap forward. Although no one has seen a new, smaller particle, many theoretical arguments suggest that the particles we consider elementary really consist of even smaller elements, such as the renowned quarks. No evidence yet proves directly that quarks exist, but, upon this hypothesis, many theoretical conceptions can easily be validated.

In the last few years, for example, using the Crystal Ball—an experimental device for electron and elementary particle studies, resembling an accelerator—we have done a lot of work on a subparticle called charmonium, which is a combination of a charm quark and a charm antiquark. When we first talked, in 1975, it was hardly known, but since then there has been much progress in understanding the dynamics of behavior of elementary particles, including interactions and decays. All these are perfectly consistent with the quark hypothesis.

O. Can one say that contemporary physics would be inconsistent without the quark hypothesis?

H. I think that's probably the case, even though free quarks haven't been seen.

O. Why is it that nobody has managed to see a free quark? Is it unobservable because it is so small?

H. The electron is also very small, but a free electron is observable. Nobody knows exactly why we cannot see a free quark, but there are theories which postulate that you shouldn't be able to see it. The interaction is such that every time you want to separate the quark, something else happens. Free quarks don't appear because they bond with other things. In the last decade, however, there has been a development in the whole science of quarks, and I am not a particular expert on it anymore.

O. Is it true that your interest has recently switched from physics to medicine?

H. To some extent but not wholly. In fact, my colleagues and I are trying to apply the methods of advanced physics to medicine. (Incidentally, my colleagues Dr. E.B. Hughes and Dr. E. Rubenstein, are even more responsible for the results than I.) One of these methods—coronary angiography—is particularly suitable for observing the coronary artieries, which supply blood, oxygen, and nourishment to the heart. Since the heart is constantly beating, one cannot see the blockages and narrowings of the lumen of an artery by an X-ray. The picture is blurred. Doctors, however, need to see the arteries before a bypass operation. Mass examination of apparently healthy people to see if they have developed arteriosclerosis would also be useful.

O. Do I understand that your method of coronary angiography—when established and introduced into medical practice—would be able to provide a clearer picture of the arteries?

H. In the standard method now used by physicians, one can get a sharp picture by using a solution of iodine and a catheter that can be put into the artery in the arm and then inserted into the heart. After the injection of iodine you can see the arteries very clearly on an X-ray. The difficulty is that it is a dangerous procedure. Two or three people in a thousand die during the examination and from 1 to 4 percent suffer some damage later. So it is not a technique that one would use for mass examination. Our procedure at Stanford, if it is successful, means that you don't have to use a catheter. You just inject iodine, let it be carried through the veins, and then take an X-ray with synchrotron radiation, the same machine that physicists use to study elementary particles.

O. Why isn't such a picture blurred?

H. Synchrotron radiation provides much more X-ray intensity than an X-ray tube. But also the machine is tuned only to iodine, so when we take the picture we don't see the bones or the heart itself; in fact, we don't see anything but iodine, that is, the interior of the arteries. Of course, it is more easily said than done, and there are various problems to be worked out. We are now building at Stanford the wide beam needed for this purpose, and we hope to apply this method to the first human being in 1984. We were among the first ones to start this type of project, but now that it appears to be successful, we have some competition from Germany, England, and the Soviet Union.

O. Can you tell me how you became involved in these studies? It's quite different from what you had been doing before.

H. Not too different. And I had good reasons, too. I think that it is a very interesting field and it's directly helpful to people. But I also have a daughter who has not spoken since birth. Without new diagnostic techniques, it is not possible to know what is wrong with her. For a long time, I and others have suspected that there was something anatomically wrong, that certain areas of her brain were being fed improperly. But she has been examined by all available methods and nothing seemed abnormal.

O. Is there a possibility of using your method to look at the brain?

H. I think so. In fact, the brain in some ways is easier to examine than the heart because there is less motion in the brain. With our technique of injecting minute amounts of iodine we can look not only at the cerebral patterns but also at the metabolism of the brain when it carries out certain functions, even such complicated ones as thinking. Such a picture of the brain could be much better than anything the psychologists can base their hypotheses on today.

O. I see now that it may have a revolutionary meaning for psychology, neurophysiology, and other brain-related disciplines. But let me ask a personal question. Did you start to think about it because you desperately wanted to find out what is wrong with your daughter?

H. That's partially correct. For years I have been interested in medical research with that aim in mind. And now it looks like my hopes may be satisfied by using this technique or something similar to study the brain. It is rather surprising, considering its original proposed application to the heart; the heart does not have an obvious relationship to the brain. I hope that in the future this method may be useful not only for such endeavors as brain operations but also for, say, understanding schizophrenia.

O. Some people say that basic research has an inadequate practical impact. They would finance only research that can solve, say, the mystery of cancer. Your example shows that one can never predict practical uses of basic research.

H. Yes, I think that our example is, if not the first, one of the first applications of high-energy physics and instrumentation to medical technology. The high-energy physicists would probably be very happy about it because it shows that what they are doing has practical uses.

O. Did you think about such uses when you first became interested in elementary particle physics?

H. Not at all. It was pure curiosity which put me on that particular scientific track. I was very young when I first heard of the concept of the atom; it stirred in me a desire to explore it; for me it was a fundamental problem not only of a physical but of a philosophical nature.

O. Thc problem of learning "what things are made of"?

H. Right. I wanted to know it; if I didn't, I wouldn't be able to put into order thc chaotic universe. In my youth I felt inspired by the scientific research of such great scholars as Ernest Rutherford, Marie Curie, and Albert Einstein. They all studied elementary laws of physics; they explored the foundations, as it were, upon which the whole structure was erected. I also developed an interest in these problems. Mathematics attracted me, too, as did the logical premises of the existence of phenomena. Thus, my curiosity found direction.

O. Have you satisfied your curiosity?

H. I'd rather be spared such satisfaction, because then I'd have nothing to do. Fortunately, it's not going to happen to me or to anyone. Each new answer brings new questions—this is what's so wonderful about science and what gives it sense.

Of course, I hardly understand anything. In fact, I can learn and comprehend very few things. But whenever I want to understand something, I try to get through to the roots of the problem. Some think that questions about fundamentals are simple, because they deal with problems considered as obvious. However, I've always wanted to know if what's obvious is also true. When I was young I believed that I would be able to determine that; I'm not so sure anymore. Youth gives you strength, energy, and faith.

O. You speak about checking whether what's obvious is also true. Don't you think that a scientist—even in such an "empirical" discipline as physics—who tries to put things in order and formulate new hypotheses, is not only an observer but also a creator of the universe?

H. Yes, especially if he happens to be right. If he is not, then it is of much less significance.

O. What does "to be right" mean?

H. If someone has an idea that can then be confirmed through experiments, the idea is "right" or true.

O. There are scientists who contend that, even in physics, the notion of truth cannot be applied.

H. Without this notion, it wouldn't be possible to understand things or put them in order. I strongly believe there is truth in physics, limited, however, to the boundaries of our comprehension and experimental fields.

O. And within the limits of certain assumptions.

H. Right, but these assumptions are constantly verified. Whenever we find an assumption to be fallacious, we discard it.

O. That suggests that science may be a continuous and logical process, a consequence of collected facts and observations. However, a question arises, is the hypothesis itself a logical result of already acquired knowledge? Or is it perhaps a new creation, an almost supernatural manifestation of some creative power? What is, in your own experience, the impetus for hypothesis and experimentation?

H. It's simple and quite natural. A question comes first—for instance, where are the elementary particles? Then you design an experiment and carry it out. You don't have to be very imaginative to do that.

O. Even if you deal with an almost entirely new vision of the universe? How about the particles you study with the Stanford Linear Accelerator, and, recently, with the Crystal Ball in Hamburg, Germany? There are no such particles—or rather, there is no way to observe such particles—in nature. Man had to design and construct facilities to observe the behavior of the particles.

H. But some particles were discovered by accident. I think that the role of an accident in science can hardly be overvalued. Accidental discoveries are usually the most important ones.

O. But such "accidents" don't happen to everybody. They happen to those whose minds have been appropriately prepared, enabling them to see the significance of an accidental discovery. Sir Alexander Fleming discovered penicillin accidentally, but it was no accident that it was he who did it, and not somebody else.

H. Right; however, things have changed since then. All kinds of research and experiments are conducted today and hypotheses are not created by individuals anymore; they often result from scientific efforts undertaken in several research centers at the same time. And even more often, a scientist cannot tell what the consequences of his discovery will be. In many fields, scientific research doesn't rely on individual effort but, rather, collective endeavor.

O. But even under those circumstances, individual scientists may collect necessary data to produce a hypothesis.

H. It happens, but more and more often a hypothesis and a set of experiments are designed by a whole team of researchers. And they all take part in the observation and the interpretation of the results.

O. What is the relationship between observation and interpretation? Isn't observation itself a form of interpretation? A scientist makes selective observations, doesn't he—for he wants to find facts to confirm the assumptions and hypotheses he has made.

H. You've just touched a fundamental problem, which bothered Niels Bohr. He claimed that no one could be a "pure," "neutral" observer; that an observer affected things he was supposed to study.

O. Is that why a researcher cannot be sure of his measurements?

H. Yes. Werner Heisenberg defined what we know as the uncertainty principle, related to measurements and tests. Our experience tells us that his principle is true.

O. As far as I know, Einstein never accepted the conceptions of Bohr and Heisenberg.

H. That's right. Einstein could not refute what Bohr said, and he had to consent because Bohr's theory was confirmed experimentally. However, Einstein hoped to find another explanation for the imprecision of results. He didn't want to accept the philosophical conclusion of Bohr's theory that physical phenomena were random. He believed randomness was not inherent to nature and probability did not have to be a fundamental physical concept, nor a philosophical one.

O. Did Einstein mean to eliminate randomness from nature?

H. I think that was his approach. He clearly tended toward causality. But acceptance of either randomness or causality as a higher principle defines an essential philsophical difference between two schools of modern thought, not just two approaches to physics.

O. But don't you think these two approaches can be just two complementary models or kinds of descriptions of the universe? That, in general, two seemingly contradictory theories can be true? Like a view of a room from two different corners: the room is the same, but its descriptions vary and complement one another. Like two models of the physical description of the universe—wave and molecular—that, in fact, complement one another although their dissimilarities have been so heatedly stressed.

H. Physicists have never seriously talked of the dissimilarities of the wave model and particle model of the world. It's a trivial misunderstanding, resulting mostly from nonprofessional popularization. If you accept the uncertainty principle, then the wave and particle models not only complement one another, but they can be easily reduced to one model. I think, however, that the difference between an assumption of randomness and causality is much deeper. These two approaches may be found to be consistent in the future, but nothing suggests so far that they will not always contradict one another.

O. Then how could Einstein have eliminated the randomness, included in Bohr's theories, and replaced it with causality?

H. By finding an unknown interrelation between particles that would put into order what now appears random. For example, besides the well-known forces, say, electromagnetic ones, there also exists weak interaction. We understand its essence to a limited extent only. Therefore, it is possible that in some cases, such weak interaction—or even an interaction that we haven't discovered yet—can influence all other interactions and cause the imprecision of experimental measurements. The discovery of such a mechanism could help us put into order what now appears random.

O. Do you think that will be possible? Which approach is a more valid one, Bohr's or Einstein's, in terms of present scientific knowledge?

H. If I had to choose between the two conceptions I would opt for

Bohr's—that is, for randomness. Stronger arguments speak for it. But from the philosophic, or even aesthetic, point of view, this theory is not palatable. Could it be possible that everything—the universe, the earth, the human being—might have emerged by sheer chance? To tell the truth, in spite of all I know about science, I'd like to believe that it is Einstein's theory that will someday prove true.

3

On Evolution and Mankind

When did life emerge? How did it develop? Why did certain species suddenly disappear? What were man's origins and how did he evolve? How will we survive?

These questions are addressed by Leonid Tatarinov and Paul Ehrlich. Tatarinov focuses primarily on the evolution of life and the emergence of man, while Ehrlich presents his views on the difficulties facing mankind today.

Tatarinov, contrary to Shklovskii, doesn't rule out the possibility that life may have originally emerged in various forms, of which only one, known to us, has persisted. He also refutes an argument that evolution operates by chance, and elaborates his own view on the reasons for the sudden disappearance of dinosaurs and other species. In addition, he disputes the thesis that all livng forms fit perfectly into their environment. He argues that no life form fits perfectly, and evolution can be best explained as an attempt of living forms to adjust to a changing environment. In so doing, he downplays the importance of a biological purpose to evolution.

Population biologist Paul Ehrlich approaches the question of evolution from a different stance. Humankind is imperiled, he says, and his perspective raises a question of evolutionary progress. Ehrlich, like Tatarinov, categorically rejects the very notion of progress in evolution.

In addressing the ecology crisis, Ehrlich directly links environmental problems with overpopulation, lack of energy, diminishing renewable resources, and an inadequate world food supply. He speaks strongly against nuclear energy and for a more egalitarian distribution of goods between rich and poor nations. He argues that even small changes in everyday life in the rich countries could save a great deal of energy and resources. But Ehrlich does not see the political willingness for introducing changes or much public interest in solving ecology crises. He admits that mankind has the ability to help earth survive, but feels strongly that it will perish if people do not use their potentials.

5. Leonid Tatarinov

Leonid Petrovich Tatarinov was born in 1926. After graduating from the Department of Biology of Moscow University in 1949, he worked as a researcher in that department. He then went to work in the biology section of the Foreign Literature Publishing House in Moscow, and undertook scientific research at the Paleontology Institute of the Soviet Academy of Sciences. Since 1975, Leonid Tatarinov has been the director of this Institute, serving at the same time as a deputy secretary of the Soviet Academy of Sciences.

Dr. Tatarinov is interested chiefly in paleobiology and, more specifically, in the evolution of invertebrates. For many years he has conducted comprehensive paleobiological research in Mongolia, and has edited two books on the subject.

Wiktor Osiatyński: When did life first appear on earth?

Leonid Tatarinov: It is not known exactly. It seems, however, that it was much earlier than we thought twenty years ago. In the early fifties, paleontologists found evidence of life forms as far back as five hundred to six hundred million years. A. I. Oparin, the founder of one of the theories on the origins of life, believed that the first forms of life emerged approximately 2.7 billion years ago; the developments of the last decade helped to establish evidence of life in the oldest sedimentary rocks in southern Africa, which reaches back nearly four billion years. Thus, in the paleontological theory the duration of life has nearly doubled. However, as far as the very origins of life are concerned, we have only begun our quest. Besides, paleontology cannot provide an answer; we hope to find it rather through developments in biochemical research.

O. So life was an early phenomenon in the history of earth. What did the first living forms look like?

T. I don't know. We can say very little about the process of the transformation of inorganic matter into the first living organisms. What we can do, however, is try to reconstruct the extremely difficult and slow change from the first life forms into those forms existing closer to the present. The most difficult stage in the development of life was obviously its very beginning. It was only 2.7 billion years ago that favorable conditions for photosynthesis first emerged. Processes of energy exchange without participation of oxygen are thirty times less effective than with it; therefore, the first organisms were not only very primitive, they were also extremely inactive. In the first period of the evolution of life, amounting to nearly a half of its entire history, the organisms were just one cell, lacking a fully formed nucleus. The fully formed nucleus and procreation by cell division, which today prevails in all of nature, appeared only after the emergence of photosynthesis. It is likely that the preliminary process of energy exchange without oxygen, which occurs now even in humans, is a relic of that first stage of evolution.

O. Could it mean that life, from the very beginning, has evolved along just one, constantly improving, line?

T. Not necessarily from the beginning. A relatively great diversity of forms of exchange of energy can be found among the simplest types of organisms. Even today, many bacteria use different kinds of energy exchange than the more highly developed forms of life.

O. Does that mean that, at the beginning of life, there could have been several diversified forms of existence, and only after a time, some proved more successful than others?

T. That's quite likely. And it is possible that what is today common to all organisms is the result of a long process. From the biochemical point of view, the organisms living presently—bacteria aside—are all alike. They differ in their visible forms, activity, roles played in nature's circulatory system; but they have an identical biochemical composition on the molecular level. This fundamental biochemical composition developed through the entire first half of the evolution of life on earth.

O. Is it possible that for two billion years life might have tried to adapt itself to existence, that it searched for mechanisms of survival and only when such mechanisms were developed did an accelerated evolution begin, resulting in the emergence of many diversified forms of life?

T. You may be right. Anyhow, during the first two billion years, the most effective, fundamental principles of biochemical processes were worked out; these are the principles upon which life has been based ever since. However, we still know very little about the actual genesis of these mechanisms. I believe biologists may be able to explain it soon. Paleontology has attempted to reconstruct the course of evolution of higher forms of life, particularly life during the last few hundred million years. From the study of evolution in this period, we have already been able to draw a rather general picture of the increasing complexity of life forms.

O. Can you, from this general picture, draw any conclusions on the direction of evolution? On the purpose of the growing complexity of life? Can mere survival and evermore successful adaptability to the environment and the continuous proliferation of life be the purpose of life?

T. Essentially, proliferation is a characteristic of life as a whole. Formerly, life existed in the water only; now it dwells on the land, too. This, though, seems to have limits. For it is known that the earth became saturated with life as early as the Jurassic era, more than 150 million years ago.

O. What do you mean: "the earth became saturated with life"?

T. Together with biochemists, we've attempted to measure the total mass of all organisms living on earth in various periods. It appears that, since the Jurassic era, the total mass of life—including microorganisms, fauna, and flora—has not increased. There were some mass fluctuations, but in principle, the mass has not exceeded the limits determined in the Jurassic period. Presently, it is somewhat smaller.

O. Which kind of life-mass prevails today?

T. You'll be surprised: next to the trees in the forests, which are in the greatest abundance, are plankton and organisms living in the soil.

O. How about ourselves?

T. Humanity makes for a very small fraction of the mass of life on earth, even though it is growing all the time. Of course, it is at the expense of other forms of life. In general, ever since the Jurassic era, evolution has consisted not in an increase of the mass of living organisms but, primarily, in replacing some forms of life by others.

O. Can you define the principles of such replacement? Which organisms perish and which survive?

T. If you don't take into account the simplest forms—viruses or bacteria—then, primarily, less-active forms give way to more-active forms that are less dependent on the environment.

O. And this all happens as a result of spontaneous mutations that are then culled by natural selection?

T. It occurs to me that evolution is not as disorderly as most theoreticians suggest. Most scientists assume that mutations are more or less haphazard, don't depend on the environment, and that it is only as a result of natural selection that better-adapted forms emerge. If, however, this were the case, each particular adaptation should be unique; while, in fact, many mechanisms of adaptation recur in various organisms at quite different stages of evolution. We don't know the reasons of such recurrence, but solution of this problem may become a remarkable contribution of paleontology to a better understanding of the essence of life.

O. Can paleontology tell anything yet about the principles of adaptation to the environment? After all, the five to ten million species existing now are just a particle of 1 percent of all organisms that have ever existed in the history of earth. Paleontology explores those forms that have not survived. Why did some species evolve while others failed to adapt?

T. The unadapted ones were once able to adapt, weren't they? And, conversely, those we consider today to be perfectly adapted, may in time—measured not in terms of thousands but millions of years—become inadequate.

O. If the conditions change? Or because of a change of the species itself?

T. A change of environmental conditions would be of vital significance. And these very conditions would result, to a great extent, from biological changes. Thus, there may emerge new groups of organisms that may be more successful in the struggle for survival than the old ones; I think this is a major reason why some species die out. Although many contend that the extinction of a species results from its "intrinsic" maladaptation or lack of flexibility, that answer seems very unlikely from the point of view of the theory of evolution. You often hear that dinosaurs died out because of their large size and small brains, yet even the dinosaur evolved according to the principles of selection and adaptation. Of course, a change of the environment, such as the rise of mountain ranges during the Cretaceous period, which, in effect, drained the great seaways and the vast swamplands and caused tremendous changes in climate and food supply, might have caused a substantial decrease in their ability to survive. But, I believe they became unfit only when some other, better-adapted organism, characterized by a greater energy, flexibility, and a bigger brain, appeared on earth—namely, birds, which were more successful in the struggle for survival than the dinosaur.

O. Irrespective of the reasons of extinction, evolution did eliminate the less adapted species. For the very fact that some groups of fauna and flora were dying out testifies to their maladaptation, and that some others have survived proves their adaptation. Can paleontology define any criteria of adaptation? Or, more generally, any criteria for evolutionary progress?

T. It is a complex question, including a wide dispute and many misunderstandings. A popular opinion, reflected in your question, holds that all species now alive are perfectly and ideally adapted. I don't think that is true, or at least, it seems to me an oversimplified idea. No single being and no single species is ideally adapted. They all suffer from diseases, clash with their environments, and are exposed to sudden death. I think the living species are adapted only to the degree that enables them to survive. In order to survive, they may resort to various adaptation mechanisms: for some it's their high reproduction rate; for others it's a decrease of their dependence on the environment; and still others survive because they rely on those sources of nutrition and energy that are ignored by other species.

O. When you study processes of evolution, can you trace the directions of change of the adaptation mechanisms? Aren't higher forms better adapted to the environment than more primitive organisms?

T. To the changes of the environment, rather than to the environment as such. This is what evolution is all about. The opinion that all living species are ideally adapted to life is very recent; it derives from the turbulent history of genetics and biochemistry in particular. In fact, from the biochemical point of view, it is hard to find differences of adaptation; a virus is biochemically no less adapted to survive than the more complex species.

But biochemists study what has survived, ignoring the fact of how long it has survived and in what kind of environment it can survive. If, however, we look at the entire process of evolution occurring in nature, we may notice that, in the course of billions of years, all organisms have become increasingly complex. The growth of complexity has "improved" the adaptation to the environment, or more precisely, to its changes. You can create a constant environment only in a test tube or in a laboratory. In nature, everything changes, if only the time of day or season.

Let's take the history of vertebrates: the primitive forms could not have been active in winter because they did not have a stable blood temperature. The increased complexity that led to the warm-blooded birds and mammals resulted in the ability to be continuously active and resistant to environmental changes, which eventually enabled those species to survive under a variety of conditions.

O. Do you mean that evolution may be directed toward an increased complexity of organization, serving as a defense mechanism for an organism against alteration of the environment?

T. Right; it's sometimes called a growth of independence from the environment—in the sense of independence from both the "outer" and "inner" environment. A virus or a bacterium are completely dependent on their genetic programs, while other beings are relatively independent. This independence, in turn, increases the possibility of adaptation to the changes in the environment. Claude Bernard, a nineteenth-century French physiologist, defined this ability as an increase in the "freedom of life." This premise of a growing independence from the environment influenced the concept of evolutionary progress.

O. If I have it right, this progress can be seen on the physiological rather than biochemical level.

T. It probably occurs in both, but it's been only recently that we started looking for biochemical mechanisms of evolution, while physiological changes have been long a subject of our observation. It was discovered long ago that lower forms are organized in a simpler way, while the higher ones are more complex and that this complexity increased their adaptability.

O. Does this adaptability result from the growing complexity in itself?

T. Organization can never be disorderly, by definition. It essentially consists in subordination to a certain pattern. In the unicellular organism, it is principally an invulnerable genetic program. The more complex forms of life require that the cells act in harmony with each other. Hence, there developed a need for decreased rigidity of the genetic program of each individual component of these organisms, and a control and programming center must emerge within the organism itself. In effect, one of the major characteristics of evolution is a continuous increase of the role, and dimensions, of the central nervous system. It is exactly why some organisms have gradually freed themselves from environmental dependence. And man, whose brain reached the highest level of development, can all by himself create the environment he considers most suitable.

O. How did man become Homo sapiens?

T. It's more difficult to answer such a question now than it would have been thirty years ago, when rather simple and conventional boundaries marked the perception of man's evolution. From the nineteenth century, the following order had existed: it was known that in Australia and Java there had been Pithecanthropus; Neanderthal man had been in Europe, Asia, and Africa; and our direct ancestors lived in other places. But lately, this whole order has been shattered, for it was discovered that many different anthropoids had existed—which made the early history of man more complicated. In effect, we are now at a point where new discoveries result in growing doubts about our old answers.

O. Can we at least tell where and when the ape became man?

T. From every present indication, it happened in Africa. But man as we know him today inhabited vast areas of central and western Africa, southern Europe, and large parts of Asia. Anthropoids inhabited all areas of the planet.

O. Do you mean that ape turned into man in Africa and that these first primitive humans migrated and populated all the available lands?

T. Yes, but it was a very slow process. No ape turned into a human being overnight. At the beginning, there were the first humanlike creatures who originated many other humanlike beings. But all archaeological traces of these creatures have been found in Africa. If we assume that the process of the evolution of man started 3 to 3.5 million years ago, then for the first 2 to 2.5 million years the process was going on in Africa. Anyway, the fossils from those early periods have been found only in Africa.

O. Why is it believed that they are fossils of humanoids? Don't we assume that it is a symbolic system of communication, or more precisely language, that distinguishes humans from other primates? Did the first African man use language?

T. Who knows? We can only study the shape of his skull, which in fact is quite different from the ape's. We may compare it with the skull bones of contemporary man, too. But can we rule out that ancient man had a spoken language judging by a slightly different bone anatomy than ours? What we can do, however, is study the devices used to make fire and various tools made of the bones of animals that primitive man utilized as a source of nutrition. The ability to make tools indicates that man was different from apes at least in two aspects: he was capable of abstract thinking, and also of a collective, purposeful activity.

O. Did the African primitive man use tools?

T. Yes, they were simple tools, but made purposefully.

O. Can you say that the first primitive man was the original of all races existing now?

T. It is almost certain that one of the first anthropoids was the forefather of humankind. The first anthropoids appeared two to three million years ago; races, however, emerged only a few hundred thousand years ago. The preceding millennia abounded with continuous changes. When contemporary human beings developed, they populated lands from eastern China to western Africa. They lived in sparsely populated communities and had nearly independent cultures. This is about all we know. The situation is even more unclear because different kinds of humans overlap in history: some more primitive and some more advanced humans must have existed at the same time. The more primitive ones could have originated the other, more advanced "breed" of humans, skipping, as it were, other intermediary forms.

O. You are speaking of primitive and advanced humans. What is the criterion of these qualitative terms? Had the biological evolution of the first man been linear, leading in a distinct direction?

T. The only clear direction was a slow but continuous development of the central nervous system and the brain cortex in particular.

O. Because of selection?

T. In humans, selection was not the only important factor. The brain also developed as a result of increased use: manufacture and perfection of tools and language. But selection must have also contributed to man's evolution by eliminating the individuals with low brain development and retarded intellectual power. Only one humankind exists now, but there might have been several types of primitive man. It may be that man's major competitors in the past included some other kinds of humans. And the one who survived may have conquered them.

O. Do you mean there could have been a universal war among the various humanoids and the winner later originated all the different races as we know them now?

T. Today, only one kind of human exists; within it, we have distinct races. Anatomically, all races are hardly different. We see features, but there are very few anatomical differences, and there are only slight dissimilarities of the bone structure.

O. Are there any differences among the human races that would predetermine intellectual or other potentials?

T. That is a difficult question. It is popularly accepted that all races belonging to humankind have equal potentials to develop, that anthropological differences do not affect the social abilities of man. Some misunderstandings have arisen because of quite evident differences in physical appearance; on the other hand, however, we seek to overcome former racial prejudices. What modern science says is not that there are no different races, but that the differences do not, of themselves, determine intellectual or social abilities and that all races can fully and equally participate in human activities and contribute to the development of humanity.

O. You said we could speak of progress in nature based on the study of evolution. Can we also justifiably speak of the purpose of evolution? Of the purpose of life?

T. It depends on how you approach this problem. If we assume life was preprogrammed by someone, say by God, then we might speak of the purpose and meaningfulness of life. Today we believe, however, that life and evolution are an effect of the activity of earthly spontaneous forces. We can hardly find any sense or purpose in the activity of such forces, for the very notion of spontaneity contradicts purposefulness. How could you speak of a sense of purpose of life for bacteria, grass, or even of a crow? They don't even possess any mechanism enabling them to inquire about the sense or purpose of life. Only man asks such questions. And only man is aware of a problem with the purpose of life. Social purpose, for that matter. Therefore, I think that you can speak of the purpose of life of an individual only in terms of his or her society.

O. Why do humans ask about the sense and purpose of existence?

T. Because of the development of their brains and intellect. Man can think in terms of the past and future. As one American paleontologist said, man is the only animal who knows he is a product of evolution, and who can learn how life has changed over the generations. Man can also ponder how his life may change in the future.

That is why all his activities are judged in terms of possible effects. What he does is not spontaneous or accidental. His activities are purposeful and orderly, and they are aimed at the introduction to and maintenance of a premeditated order. Hence the perpetual question about the purpose of human life. However, if you consider it in terms of the entire evolution and history of life, such questions about the sense of life appear meaningless. It is just like asking a question about the reason for the existence of water, lands, or why rivers flow . . .

O. Can we be in the position of a drop in the river, but the one that is able to look back and think: why does this river flow?

T. Maybe; man and his ability to think resulted from evolution. If it were not for evolution, there would be no man or his inquisitiveness concerning the purpose of life. It is because of evolution that man can think. He is also aware of the past and he thinks ahead, wondering about the future. A question about the purpose of life arises. Man has to try and answer it to find an order in the surrounding chaos. May it not be this urge that brings meaning and purpose to his life?

6. Paul Ehrlich

Paul Ehrlich was born in 1932 and graduated from the University of Pennsylvania in 1953. After taking a doctorate at Kansas State University in 1957, he went to Stanford University and, in 1966, became a professor of biology.

Ehrlich's main interests include population genetics, theoretical problems of population biology, and relationships between population growth and social and political problems. He has conducted research in various regions, including Alaska, the Arctic Sea, India, New Guinea, Solomon Islands, East Africa, and Antarctica.

He is the author and coauthor of many books covering a wide range of biological and social problems, including The Population Bomb *(1968) and* The End of Affluence *(1974). Dr. Ehrlich is active in the international environmental and antinuclear movements.*

Wiktor Osiatyński: You've contributed valuable research to population biology, genetics, and the protection of man's natural environment; you have written and lectured on the dangers of overpopulation and on the necessity of birth control. Doesn't your research contradict those theories held by other biologists that the number of individuals within a species is the main proof of biological progress and adaptation?

Paul Ehrlich: Such theories are sheer nonsense. That assumption results from the fundamental error in the notion that the idea of progress can be applied to evolution. Evolution simply occurs over time, it doesn't follow any specific direction. If we accepted that the number of individuals within a species is the criterion of progress, we would have to conclude that, say, mosquitoes were on a higher level of evolutionary progress than man.

O. Your latest book, *Extinction* [1981], deals with the causes and consequences of the disappearance of species. Is there any fossil trace suggesting that a species might have become extinct because of overpopulation?

E. No proof, just suppositions. In nature, things are usually well balanced. When a population grows too fast, the death rate increases so that the number of individuals in that population declines to "normal."

O. You said the notion of progress cannot be applied to evolution. Doesn't that mean that progress reveals itself by the growth of an open part of the genetic program, by the increase of the freedom of choice of the individual, and by liberation from the "slavery" or "limits" of the inherited genes? Isn't this how most biologists understand the notion of progress in evolution?

E. That is a retrospective and an anthropomorphic description. In the literature on progress in evolution, what pertains to humans is usually considered developed; and what is found on the lower level of the evolutionary scale is considered primitive. Moreover, if we were bacteria, we could say that evolutionary progress consisted in the completed genetic preprogramming—typical for bacteria, and not in openness of the genetic program—as is the case with man. For always, when a program is open, the bacteria might reason, there may follow such horrible consequences as cultural evolution, which can result in scores of unnecessary questions and existential anxiety, or even in a nuclear bomb or total destruction of the species.

O. You advise greater relativity in defining progress?

E. Not necessarily. Everyone can judge things as he or she wants, but an individual evaluation will always depend on the point of view. These are not real problems though. After all, does it make any difference if evolution advances or not? The fundamental problems concern what's going on now and what the results of it might be in the course of the next few generations. What will happen to humankind and to the other species that are closely interrelated with man's own existence? How can we preserve all existing forms of life, yet give human life a new quality at the same time?

O. But shall we not solve them? Aren't we the very first species with the power to decide on our own fate for better or worse?

E. Yes, we have that opportunity. However, no opportunity is realized automatically. We have the power, but we can be destroyed with that power. The question is, how can our power be directed to serve humanity? This is probably our most important task for the near future. If we fail in this, we are likely to perish as a species. I think such an outcome is much more likely than it usually seems to be.

O. Do you mean we might perish because of the soaring birth rate?

E. That's what I am afraid of. I even tell my students now that I can't see any other way out but through a spontaneous biological reaction—a higher death rate. In 1968, when I was writing *The Population Bomb*, I was more optimistic. Today, the world's population grows at the same rate as then, but the world's resources are being used up much more rapidly.

O. Do you think that the problem of overpopulation and scarcity of resources is really universal? Doesn't it differ from India to the United States to Sweden? Shouldn't the birth rate be slowed down only in certain countries?

E. To apply such categories is wrong; in fact, it is dangerous. Overpopulation is a universal problem, particularly in view of the exhaustion of natural resources and the resulting energy shortage and scarcity of food. From this universal perspective, overpopulation becomes a greater problem for such countries as the U.S. and Sweden than for India. In fact, thinking in terms of ecological problems, one has to consider how each individual affects the world's resources and the natural environment of man. From this point of view, each child born in the U.S. will use fifty times more resources than will a child born in India. The latter, for example, will use little oil and probably no aerosol that destroys the ozone layer of our atmosphere. While his birth affects the living conditions in India alone, the birth of a child in America or in Sweden affects the condition of the whole world, including India.

O. Then overpopulation is not of itself evil. It becomes a problem only in relation to the scarcity of resources, energy, and food.

E. No problem is evil by itself, in total isolation. The problem of population has always had to do with resources, energy, and food. Everybody has always had to eat, clothe himself, and keep warm. This is not new. What's new is reaching the absolute, where the world's population will exceed the energy and resource potentials of the planet. Taking into account the presence of lethal nuclear power, one can expect the worst—if these problems are not solved somehow first . . .

O. You speak of nuclear power as being destructive from the perspective of a possible nuclear war. But nuclear energy may also serve beneficial purposes as an almost inexhaustible energy source.

E. Nonsense, and dangerous nonsense, too. Nuclear technologies are too dangerous to risk using for energy production. And I mean not only an accident that might bring about a catastrophe but also of how radioactive waste will affect the environment and the hardly clear but obviously dangerous effect of nuclear technology and radiation on the human organism. The money spent on nuclear power plants might be used much better in maintaining the existing energy resources by developing new, safe technologies, such as solar energy, and by protecting our natural environment.

There is also another problem, bearing even more significance than how nuclear energy is used. Who advocates the development of nuclear energy? Nuclear physicists who, trying to clear themselves of the feeling of guilt for the bomb, tell the world that this energy can be beneficial to mankind. Who else? Politicians, economists, and profit-greedy businessmen obsessed by the mania for unlimited economic growth. They want nuclear power plants as a source of huge amounts of cheap energy. What will they use this energy for? They will use it to exploit our planet till the end, with no regard for the inevitability that such exploitation will result in the total destruction of the environment of the whole world.

O. But the world wants to develop. The hungry want to have enough food and have access to the goods that are available to the rich. Nobody has the right to deny them this. And you need energy to supply these goods and services.

E. Certainly, but you don't necessarily need an unlimited growth of energy consumption. What is necessary, however, is social and political moves to foster a more balanced and equal distribution of resources. It is widely believed that economic progress, similar to that in the U.S. since the end of World War II, will automatically solve the problem of poverty in undeveloped countries. It's nonsense. The last thirty years prove that the economic growth resulted mainly in a further advancement and enrichment of affluent societies and in increased poverty and dependence of the poor. Today, these affluent societies must realize that sharing their wealth with poor nations is not only their moral duty, but lies in their own interest. We should protect and distribute the existing resources more carefully rather than endlessly increase their consumption. On the other hand, however, the real energy crisis in such countries as the U.S. does not consist in a shortage of energy but, primarily, in its excessive use and waste. Energy use in our country could be easily decreased by 30 percent or more.

O. How could such a change be carried out? In *The Population Bomb* you appealed for a mass movement for such change—one that could influence our political leaders . . .

E. Yes, but today I have no such illusions. Governments, corporations, and other major bureaucratic organizations have proved extremely reluctant to meet the demands for change. They don't seem to do much to improve the situation, and they often make it worse. Hence came our proposals in the book, *Ark II*, which I wrote with Dennis Pirages in 1972. We wanted to bring the problems of environment, resources, energy, and population policy to the attention of as many people as possible so that people would deal with these problems out of self-interest rather than letting the professionals do it. The government should take care of fewer but more important things that the individual cannot cope with alone. A change in social consciousness could have helped to improve the situation. So would, of course, organizational and economic changes. If no one polluted the environment, there would be no problem. If raw materials and energy were more expensive, a tendency to waste them would decrease.

O. How effective are, in your opinion, the efforts aimed at changing social consciousness? After all, these efforts have been taken by a large group of people of significant authority.

E. People still know very little about ecological problems, I'm afraid. The average person believes that air pollution is what environmental problems are all about. It is widely held to be a potential threat somewhere off in the distance, and it is not taken very seriously. People don't realize how serious the risk is of having the entire environment of our planet destroyed, or of the decrease in the genetic diversity of agriculture. Often, people do not even know where the food they eat comes from. They have no idea that without a natural ecosystem, we could not exist at all. The majority perceive the problem in terms of an alternative: either I'll have more pollution in my town and will be able to watch television and drive my car, or I'll have clean air but then I'll have to lower my standard of living. They naturally choose the former. However, such an alternative is false.

O. Can't your students and readers of such books as *The Population Bomb* change people's minds about overpopulation?

E. When *The Population Bomb* was first published, I was blamed for scaring my readers. So, in 1971 I wrote *How to Be a Survivor,* a book hardly anyone read. In 1974, *Ark II* was published; it attempted a profound analysis of the situation of modern societies, and it suggested some necessary changes. It was also completely ignored. *The Population Bomb,* however, was a great success. I wonder if people might not just like it better if somebody scares them instead of suggesting what they could do to help themselves. It's much easier to go home and fix a drink than trouble one's head about such things.

O. But in *The End of Affluence* you were offering some constructive advice: you told people to take care of themselves and their own future, to grow vegetables and fruits and prepare themselves for the inevitable "end of the affluence."

E. Yes, in time I became more skeptical about what governments and organizations can do. The government here blocks most environmental actions. For instance, during the energy crisis, the permissible pollution standards were modified in order to save energy spent on water- and air-cleaning devices. If the government does nothing and responds to no pressures, there is only one way left: to take care of one's own life.

O. Is that possible at all in a complex society characterized by such a complexity of labor division? Can everybody "take care" of himself all by himself?

E. No, only very few can. But everybody can become more independent than he or she is now. Independence can be defined largely by what we consider needful or necessary. If one believes he or she needs frozen food and electric air-conditioning, one is more dependent than someone who can live without these things. Of course, this is no long-term strategy to help our species to survive. But let us assume that our civilization has only ten years more. Wouldn't we play around and drink wine rather than fight hopelessly with politicians and bureaucrats?

O. Gallows joy. Wouldn't it be better if we tried to change something? Why do you think governments ignore demands of change?

E. It's to their interest. Maybe not to the government's as such, but to the interest of the hidden power structure. Strong special interest groups want to keep the status quo from which they gain profits. And the government is too weak to oppose them, and also is not reasonable enough—to put it mildly—to change anything. The government is anxious for the support of the elite and for votes and won't take a stand on important problems.

O. And in this situation, isn't it the value system predominant in society that plays the most significant role?

E. It certainly is. But people here think only in terms of production and its volume. A steel corporation executive is concerned about increased production and how to attain the highest possible profit whether or not it results in a wasteful use of resources. The growth of production is the supreme goal and the highest value.

O. How many changes would be required in the life of an average person to change this value system oriented on production and consumption only?

E. A few, but not as many as it is normally assumed. So enormous is the waste of energy in the U.S. today that even without any major change in our life-style, we could save much energy. Standard of living and quality of life are, contrary to popular understanding, two different notions. It requires wisdom to improve the quality of life while simultaneously decreasing our GNP. An improved public transportation system would surely add to the quality of our lives, if only through the saving of energy . . .

O. But you don't want to return to the "idyllic primitivism," do you, professor? You are fond of being well-off and having a comfortable life, and perhaps this is the reason for your fears. Aren't you afraid that you may be deprived of all the things you like?

E. Yes, I like to live comfortably, and I want everybody else to live a comfortable life, too. The problem is that we haven't the means for everybody to live comfortably, especially in the face of the population explosion. The point is that the size of the population determines what we should do to preserve the world in which we live. If I am asked what kind of world I'd want in the future, I always ask back, "For how many people?" If I were an airplane designer and a customer came to me to order a plane in which each passenger could do whatever he or she might wish, I'd ask him to tell me, "What does that mean, 'to do what one wishes'? How many passengers is the plane to accommodate?"

This example relates to our present situation: we must turn our planet into a "craft" that will be able to accommodate an ever-growing number of passengers. They will increase to millions and billions. So I am not sure that such an accommodation is feasible at all. Therefore, for years I've suggested limiting the birth rate. For this, along with other changes, is the only way for mankind to survive.

PART TWO

ON MAN AND HIS ENVIRONMENT

4

On Brain and Mind

What is consciousness?

Despite different views on the emergence of life and on evolution, all scientists interviewed in the preceding chapters agree that the most important feature distinguishing human beings from other animals is consciousness. But do we know what consciousness is? How is it related to memory and motivation? How does memory operate? What is the mechanism of the perception, storage, and retrieval of information? Are we a tabula rasa at birth? Why is decision making so painful a process? What are our main driving forces? Can we control emotions?

These questions are discussed in detail by Konstantin Sudakov, who explains the so-called functional system theory of the brain, and Karl Pribram, who presents his original holographic theory of memory storage and brain operation. Each of these theories stresses different problems, but both scientists point to the same crucial mechanisms in the functioning of the brain and mind, to the role of motivation and emotions in perception and decision making.

Sudakov defines consciousness as a person's ability to assess most adequately his situation and his needs and to undertake on this basis a purposeful activity. The two most important components of consciousness are memory and motivation. Referring to the decision-making process, Sudakov stresses that it is not the capacity of the brain that distinguishes human beings from other animals; it is man's ability to liberate himself from all unnecessary alternatives.

Sudakov also deals with emotions, particularly with the impact of negative emotions on stress and physiological disturbances. He points out that the fluctuations of emotions seem to be a more general characteristic of nature.

Karl Pribram offers a detailed explanation of his original holographic theory of the brain, in which concrete memories are stored in various parts of the brain with each cell containing complete information. He holds that the mind is not a tabula rasa at birth; instead, he believes it has already been endowed with perceptive categories that allow it to construct images of the surrounding world.

Pribram also discusses the objectivity of our perceptions and comments on the philosophical consequences of the holographic concept of the brain. Like Sudakov, Pribram emphasizes the role of motivation and emotion in human life, and points to our limited ability to control emotions.

7. Konstantin Sudakov

Konstantin Viktorovich Sudakov was born in 1932 and graduated from the Institute of Medicine in Moscow in 1956. He went to work with Pyotr A. Anochin, an outstanding Soviet neurophysiologist and founder of the so-called theory of functional systems. In 1966, Dr. Sudakov took over the chair of physiology at the P.A. Anochin Institute of Physiology in Moscow.

He has further developed the theory of functional systems, attempting to integrate all processes occurring in the brain. In particular, his work focused on problems of motivation and emotional stress. The most noteworthy among his numerous works include Cybernetics of the Living *(1968),* Biological Motivations *(1971),* Emotional Stress and Arterial Hypertension *(1976), and* Systemic Aspects of Neurophysiological Behavior *(1979).*

Dr. Sudakov is a member of the Soviet Academy of Medical Sciences.

Wiktor Osiatyński: What is consciousness?

Konstantin Sudakov: It may sound strange, but the notion of "consciousness" has not been precisely defined. Despite heated discussions on the meanings of consciousness, we still do not know what it is. I can, therefore, only speak of what we, in our research, understand as consciousness. Our working definition is that it is one's ability to determine adequately one's situation and social environment, to evaluate one's inner state, one's biological needs and the results of one's actions, as well as to undertake, upon this basis, a purposeful activity. When, for instance, an anesthetized person becomes unconscious, he loses the ability to adequately evaluate a situation, his needs, or his attitude toward other people.

O. Can you say that the ability to take stock of one's own needs and situation, and the power to foresee the consequences of one's own actions, are the main elements of conscious activity?

S. Yes, in a sense, you can. The proper evaluation of one's activity and its result seems to be the fundamental, albeit not the only, quality of human consciousness. For conscious activity involves other important factors, too, such as motivation—both genetically predetermined biological motivations such as hunger, thirst, and fear, and, for humans, the higher social motivations. However, motivation hardly functions in isolation from other factors; it is related to experience and memory. Memory works effectively only when there is motivation to remember. If there is no motivation, or if it is too weak, memory works much less effectively. The more effectively one satisfies one's own needs, the better one remembers the best way to achieve them.

O. Do you mean that motivation serves as a kind of thermostat for the whole body?

S. Right; you can say that motivation is a crucial part of any purposeful activity.

O. But if we speak of purposeful or conscious activity, a question arises as to whether the two factors you mentioned, motivation and memory, work above the threshold of consciousness?

S. We cover a broader system here, in which both conscious and unconscious elements intertwine. For instance, motivation itself can be subconscious.

O. And memory?

S. Memory can be both conscious and unconscious. Most of your automatic reflexes as well as acquired responses occur on the basis of your memory without conscious realization of it.

O. Why, then, did you say that motivation and memory were the main elements of conscious activity?

S. They are prerequisites, as it were. No activity, conscious or unconscious, would be possible without them. These two factors may be followed by others, typical of conscious activity only, including analysis of a situation and decision making.

O. And what constitutes decision making? Is it the synthesis for the motivations and information coded in the memory?

S. It is not only that. I think decision making consists primarily of elimination of all superfluous alternatives. The human brain has great powers. Many people believe it is these powers—that is, the brain's capacity and an astronomical number of synapses—that comprise man's genius or exceptionality. Of course, it is not true. The human brain is remarkable primarily because it is able to disregard all superfluous information in order to fulfill the biological or social needs of an individual. However, because of the immense amounts of information and conflicting motivations, the decision-making process is extremely important and often very difficult.

O. Is decision making a conscious or emotional act?

S. I don't think it's quite right to juxtapose conscious activity and emotional reactions. Emotions accompany all kinds of processes—both conscious and unconscious. Motivation itself is an emotional and subjective experience. Memory, too, is relatively highly dependent on emotions. So is the process of decision making; in fact, in this process emotional factors play an especially significant part. That is why making a decision is often extremely difficult emotionally, and that is why we want so badly to satisfy what we desire most. Evaluations of the results of an action, both a conscious one and an unconscious one, have an emotional connotation, too.

O. How does this emotional connotation change depending on its results?

S. If the desired end is reached, a biological or social need is satisfied, an award in the form of a positive emotional reaction always follows. However, if we fail in reaching our goal, a negative emotion is set off. This emotion, in turn, triggers an "inquisitive response" or a question that Pavlov put in a nutshell: what happened? Why did the action fall short of the goal? At this moment a reevaluation of the situation is done, a new decision is made, and an action is undertaken—all bent on reaching the desired result.

O. What happens if all attempts to reach the goal fail?

S. In physiology we call it a conflict situation. Negative emotions grow more intense, mobilize the whole body, and spur the person on to a more concentrated and intensive action.

O. But such a renewed action doesn't always bring about the desired result either, does it?

S. If the conflict is severe and involves a very important need that cannot be satisfied, then a situation develops verging on pathology. We call it emotional stress. If it persists, it may lead to disorders of the heart and circulatory system, to strokes or heart attacks, liver and stomach disturbances, and many other diseases. Animals kept under emotional stress die.

O. Does emotional stress occur in all of nature?

S. Not really. Stress can be forced upon animals in special experiments. In nature, conditions generally do not exist for prolonged conflict situations. There are simple patterns in the biological environment: either an animal escapes danger, or it satisfies its needs, or it doesn't survive. An animal would never crouch at the burrow of its prey, say, for a year or two, causing the latter to experience a continual agitation. But man quite often creates grievous stress situations for himself. The continual presence of such a situation may result in peculiar "emotional circles" created in the nervous system; with time, they become fixed and permanent. Thus begin neuroses. A person becomes unable to estimate adequately the results of his actions; his or her consciousness diminishes considerably. On the physiological level, however, permanent, continuous stress causes chemical changes that result in a disorder of the self-regulation mechanisms which control all the individual functions of the body.

O. But while we all suffer today from a certain degree of stress, not everybody is afflicted with a serious disease. Why? Moreover, why does one get ulcers, another high blood pressure, and still another, say, eczema?

S. In different individuals, similar negative stimulation may affect the functions of the internal organs in different ways. It may cause a disorder in the circulatory system, it may affect the stomach. It seems to depend on the individual's health in general; stress affects the most vulnerable or impaired areas. In the case of an improper diet and bad eating habits, it may be the stomach and alimentary canal; in the case of lack of proper physical exercise, it may be the heart and circulatory system. Emotional tension causes excessive endocrine secretion. The effects of this secretion may differ, depending on the hereditary constitution and the overall condition of an individual. These relationships should be thoroughly studied, because a considerable number of evermore dangerous diseases result from the processes occurring primarily within the nervous system. In most cases, medicine treats the effects rather than the causes of the actual disease. We should encourage research in the still neglected domain of the physiology of emotions. On the other hand, we should control our own emotions in order to avoid the negative effects of emotional stress.

O. How can one avoid such effects? How can one control emotions that, as you say, so strongly influence all the functions of the nervous system?

S. First of all, people should be aware of the dangers of prolonged emotional responses; responses should be transient and episodic in character. This means that one should always try to interrupt and redirect a fixed negative emotion. There are at least a few ways to do it. The easiest way is through physical exercise. Intensive physical workouts diminish the negative effects of painful psychic emotions. In the course of our research we have discovered that active and strained muscles send signals to the very brain cells that are engaged in the negative emotion. While stress causes a change in the chemical processes occurring in these cells, physical effort brings the cells back to the former chemical state; thus the cells "free themselves" from the tension. One can also try to replace the negative emotion with a positive one, such as the satisfaction one gets from a job well done.

O. Is it better to suppress or express one's emotions?

S. It is definitely better to reveal them. There is an old saying: a good cry will do you good. It's true, a cry is an outlet for emotional tension or excitement.

O. It is believed, however, that an emotion can be choked down even in the most upsetting situation, if a person remains calm and controlled.

S. This is quite a widespread view, but I'm afraid it's not true. In fact, there are two different negative symptoms of emotions. One group includes such things as changes of facial expressions, body and limb motion, a changed way of speaking, abnormalities in breathing, or just a "good cry." These symptoms can be controlled to a degree. Thus a person can express the outward manifestation of an emotion and keep, so to speak, a poker face. However, very few people can suppress such symptoms of emotions as a change of heartbeat, the rhythms of blood circulation, changed functioning of the sweat glands, or contractions of the nonstriated stomach and intestine muscles, since it is hardly possible to keep control over the functions of these organs. Even when the external symptoms do not outwardly show, it is obvious that each emotion will affect the uncontrollable functions of the internal organs. Persisting emotional stress causes biological reactions affecting these organs and, by gradually bombarding them with nervous impulses that result in destructive effects, causes the diseases I've already mentioned. The discharge of an emotion through an outward reaction prevents, at least to a degree, these processes.

O. But all you're talking about has to do with elimination of the negative consequences of actual and revealed emotions. You have also mentioned, however, the possibility of controlling and directing the emotions. How can one do it? Does one have to have a special education or "emotional training"?

S. Yes, it appears that emotions can be as subject to training and direction as are our physical systems. And as with physical exercise, emotional training ought to be started in childhood. This kind of education should teach a child how to combat prolonged negative emotions and replace them with stronger social or personal motivations. Any strong motivation is a good remedy for the fomenting negative emotions that we face every day. After all, a person deeply absorbed in doing something he or she perceives as fascinating or useful is much more immune to negative emotions than a person who has no goals. I think that this attitude might serve as a guidepost leading us to control our own emotions. Unfortunately, these problems still need a more precise theoretical outline, not to mention their practical application in education or everyday life.

O. Would it be possible to somehow eliminate all negative emotions? Could we live without them?

S. Categorically no. I've already said that both the positive and negative emotions are important elements of any purposeful activity. Emotions have developed in the course of evolution as a means of evaluating our needs and their fulfillment. Without emotions no person—meaning body and mind—could function normally. Without fear, we soon would die out, as we would without hunger. In fact, in less dramatic cases, the reduction of emotional tension immediately results in a considerable deterioration of performance and, consequently, in less satisfactory effects of purposeful activity; strong emotions, conversely, provide in general for a more successful activity.

O. Do you mean that we are, in a sense, doomed to the harmful influence of negative emotions?

S. We are doomed to nothing. Negative emotions serve us well, provided they are of a temporary and passing nature. That's all. They become dangerous only when a painful emotional tension persists. The effects of such a situation accumulate and, sometimes, lead to an irreversible disease. If, however, negative emotions are of a transient nature and do not last long, and moreover, if they alternate with positive emotions, then they are no threat to the individual. In fact, it has been confirmed experimentally that if, for a time, only negative emotions are produced in an animal, it eventually has a stroke; and if another animal is exposed to treatment producing only positive emotions, he, too, winds up with a stroke. However, if an animal is subjected to negative and positive emotions alternately, no change in the animal's well-being occurs: the animal feels well and reacts properly even in the most dangerous situations.

That's how life goes. You succeed, and are overcome with positive emotions; you fail, and feel unpleasant emotions that motivate you to try harder to achieve success. The instability, or variableness, of emotional feelings seems to be the general pattern of nature, reflected in our nervous systems. This pattern must not be broken.

8. Karl Pribram

Born in 1919, Karl H. Pribram obtained his doctorate in medical sciences from the University of Chicago in 1941. Since 1946, he worked under the tutelage of Karl Lashley at the Yerkes Laboratory of Primates' Biology. From 1948 to 1951, Pribram conducted research at the Yale University School of Medicine. He has been professor of psychology and neurophysiology at Stanford University, California, since 1959.

Dr. Pribram's research focused on the neurophysiological bases of memory and the processes of learning, motivation, and emotion. Plans and Structure of Behavior, *the book he published in 1960 (coauthored with George A. Miller and Eugene Galanter), launched the so-called cognitive revolution in brain and mind research—the shift of scientific interests from behavior to thought.*

He has published several dozens of works on neurophysiology, neurosurgery, anatomy of the brain, and experimental psychology. His best-known book, Languages of the Brain *(1971), is a compendium of facts and theories on the brain's functions. In 1976, Pribram's book on neurophysiological grounds of psychoanalysis,*

Freud's Project Re-assessed, *was published. Presently, Dr. Pribram is working on a popular book about the brain and its functions.*

In 1966, Dr. Pribram published the first paper suggesting that the brain deals in interactions, interpreting frequencies and storing images like the hologram, and that memory is not localized but dispersed throughout the brain. This new theory, which Pribram has been developing ever since, known as the holographic, or holonomic, hypothesis of brain functions and memory, is considered his greatest scientific achievement.

Wiktor Osiatyński: What is your theory really about? And how did you come to it?

Karl Pribram: One of the fundamental achievements in neurophysiology has been the discovery of the direct relationship between certain parts of the brain and the body functions that are controlled by the specific parts of the cerebral cortex. By stimulating certain specific areas of the brain, a reaction occurs in the corresponding parts of the body; stimuli applied to different parts of the body result in the stimulation of the corresponding nerve cells in the brain. It is called the principle of localized representation, which became one of the axioms of modern brain research.

K.S. Lashley discovered in the 1920s that partial damage to the brain did not prevent a person from performing functions controlled by the missing parts of the brain. It seemed to contradict the principle of localization. It did not mean, of course, that the brain was not affected by the damage; when one of the projection areas was destroyed, it disrupted functions of the sense organs it controlled. It did not disturb, however, higher-level function, such as memory for specific events. It appeared that the remaining, undamaged parts of the brain could take over the functions of the damaged parts. Scientists today interpret this phenomenon as proof that the structures responsible for memorizing and remembering things are not located in any single part of the brain, but have to be distributed over large areas of the brain.

O. What is the pattern of this distribution? Are the different elements that are necessary for recognition of a complex visual image located in different parts of the brain?

P. That is exactly what we didn't know at first. If, as some suggest, the different elements necessary to constitute a single visual image are distributed in different parts of the brain, then the damage to one of these parts would effectively prevent the reconstruction of the whole picture. It would lack a necessary element because that part of the brain was cut off. But, as I've already explained, the incomplete brain is able to "remember" and to reconstruct the whole picture and all elements constituting this complex function. It was the hologram that came to rescue us from this unfathomable puzzle.

O. Isn't this notion taken from optics, or more generally, from physics?

P. Right; the hologram is a record of information encoded on film when light is reflected from or refracted by an object. The photographic plate is exposed to light from two sources: light from a coherent light source that illuminates the photographic film, and light reflected from the object. The apparently meaningless swirls that occur on the plate do not resemble the original object, but the image can be reconstituted when the film is illuminated by a reasonably coherent light source. Once the film has been developed, any piece of it can be made to reconstruct the entire image.

O. Now I see the analogy. A damaged holographic film can be used for the reproduction of a whole picture, and a damaged brain is able to "remember" the complete information. But can you use the hologram as a model for how the brain might store memory?

P. It's a very complicated explanation, so I'll only give you the simplest part of it. There is indisputable evidence that the visual system is sensitive to the temporal frequency of sound waves. In a similar fashion, recent experimental results have shown that the visual system responds to spatial frequencies—that is, the alternations of light and dark across space. Such sensitivity to frequencies has been proven both on the cellular level in animals and in experiments involving humans. Thus, temporal and spatial information received by receptors is separated into frequency components. Because of overlap of the stored information—that is, the storage of frequencies in adjacent cells—the brain can decode these stored traces into a recollection of a complete image. The decomposition and recomposition are the inverse of one another and precise mathematical descriptions of these processes have been obtained. These mathematical descriptions have little common-sense relationship to the world as we perceive it.

O. Does the holographic theory contradict the traditional concept of anatomic localization of the brain function?

P. No, rather it extends the theory. Local regions of the cortex remain responsible for retrieving the stored information. On the other hand, the holographiclike system in the brain is responsible for storing and distributing information so that several distinct retrieval processes can activate the same memory traces.

O. How, then, can a local lesion or partial damage to the brain sometimes result in the inability to retrieve memories?

P. We have to make a very important distinction. What is distributed is the memory storage, not the retrieval mechanisms. The latter are localized and can be separately damaged by brain injury.

O. Do we know the principle on which these retrieval mechanisms operate?

P. Each bit of stored information produces a pattern of electrochemical events that can be stored. If the input, transformed into the frequency domain, is similar to a stored pattern, the body receives a strong signal to which the entire network of interconnected cells responds. In this way sensory patterns are recognized.

O. How, then, is learning possible? Especially at the very beginning? Does it mean that the brain is not a tabula rasa?

P. Of course not. If, at the moment of birth, the brain were a blank tablet, we would never be able to recognize or learn anything. Basic reflex responses and perceptual sensitivities are inborn. They are like elementary building blocks that are used to develop our inherent abilities.

O. Is the process of cognition based on direct perception of an objectively existing world, or do we "construct" it from these building blocks in response to external or internal stimuli?

P. It is an eternal philosophical problem and a question at issue in neurophysiology. In 1966, James Gibson proposed an ecological model of perception; it was based on direct perception: the perceived information is contained in the physical universe and affects the perceiver. A holonomic model, on the other hand, is of a "constructive" character: sensory information is transformed, coded, and stored, and the brain reconstructs images when subsequent sensory stimuli that more or less match the stored code affect it. So the images result both from this match between information stored in the brain and from sensory information.

O. Has this constructive nature of brain functions found confirmation in any experiments?

P. Yes, many times. I think everybody could find it in his or her own experience. I may mention one interesting experiment. If you display a solitary point moving horizontally (————) and another moving in a semicircle, thus:  , and then show these together, you will see a moving wheel!

O. So what is it that we perceive? How is it related to the real world? Can we ever know what the real world is really like?

P. I've already pointed out the "constructive" nature of the perceptual process that arouses doubts as to whether or not a complete, as we call it "objective," knowledge of the physical world is possible. Similar doubts have arisen in modern quantum physics, where it is equally hard to establish to what extent a researcher describes reality, and to what extent he may affect it by the techniques he uses. Physicists from the times of Niels Bohr and Werner Heisenberg have attempted to define a basic order in the microcosm. In 1971, one of Albert Einstein's pupils and collaborators, David Bohm, suggested that a holographiclike model might define such a basic order. A hologram looks random, haphazard, but is not. Thus the probabilistic, haphazard organization of the basic order noted by Bohr might reflect its holographic nature. Bohm attempts to reconcile models of classical physics, quantum physics, and the holographic model.

O. Does this mean that there exists a holographiclike reality?

P. Certainly. That's precisely what modern physics deals with. One could call it the frequency domain, in which particles create waves of specific frequencies to compose this holographiclike reality. Space and time become enfolded in the frequency domain. Thus, proximal and efficient causality upon which most scientific explanations depend are suspended. Instead, transformations, complementarities, synchronicities, symmetries, and dualities must be called upon as explanations.

O. If the "real" world is a hologram, how, then, can we know anything about it?

P. First, I didn't say that the real world is a hologram. What I said is that one aspect of the world, one order, is holographiclike. Second, and this is the essence of the idea, we can know this aspect of the universe, because the brain itself operates on holographiclike principles.

O. Our images of the world don't seem to be holographic; we don't see frequencies but real objects.

P. That's because the brain transforms the frequencies of objects into images, as well as vice versa: the frequency code within each neuronal receptor field is transformed back into the image mode by the retrieval and motor mechanisms of the brain. What I'm saying, in short, is that the brain, operating in part with the holographiclike principle, is a part of the universe that is also partly holographiclike in nature.

O. So the brain is neither creating nor merely receiving reality?

P. I think that the brain generates its own constructions and images of physical reality. But at the same time it generates them in such a way that they resonate with what really is there.

Let me give you an analogy that I like. Radio and television programs are carried by sets of waves that exist in the frequency domain. If you took a slice of the airwaves at any moment in time, the cross section would resemble a hologram. To decode this frequency-carried information into auditory and visual images, you need a tuner. The same thing occurs with regard to sensory information. Our senses tune to certain frequencies in the spectrum of frequencies available; our eyes to visual frequencies, ears to auditory ones, and so on. So, in answer to your question, there must be a matching of our brain and sensory apparatus with the reality beyond them.

O. And when we are tuned to waves we become a part of the frequency domain?

P. It is an important aspect of the holonomic model that an organism is no longer sharply separated from what lies beyond the boundaries of its skin.

O. This continuity is based on the fact that both the brain and the universe operate on the same holographiclike principles. Since time and space are enfolded in the frequency domain, don't we have occasional access to this domain during extralinguistic, timeless, and spaceless forms of conscious experiences? Don't spiritual experiences and mystical states allow us a direct access to the frequency domain?

P. Possibly; moreover, it seems to me that the frequency domain is "spiritual" precisely because there is no clear separation of the self in space-time from more encompassing orders in the universe.

O. You mean that the world is spiritual in its essence?

P. No; I mean that in our access to more encompassing orders we are expressing our spiritual nature. Moreover, I think the fact that scientists both in modern physics and in brain research are, for the first time, admitting the study of spiritual values is of crucial importance. For spiritual values are precisely what we desperately need in our highly technological civilization.

O. It seems that the holographic model may explain many psychic phenomena as well. Parapsychologists have searched, without success, for a form of energy that may take part in telepathy and other psi phenomena. But if these events take place in the frequency domain, transcending time and space, there is no need for energy. They are potentially simultaneous and everywhere, so they don't have to be transmitted.

P. I want to be very clear about this. Parapsychology is not my field, and I don't know anything about extrasensory phenomena. However, the holonomic domain offers the beginnings of an explanation for such phenomena—if they exist. I am not saying that they do. I am also not saying that they don't. It's just not my field of expertise; I haven't looked into it.

O. Why, then, in most of what I've read about your theory, is this very aspect emphasized so strongly? I remember reading several times that Pribram's theory explains telepathy, clairvoyance, and psychokinesis. Does it mean that your hypothesis is being distorted by those who challenge the dominant paradigm of contemporary science?

P. I'm afraid that often my views, as those of others, become distorted when adopted by others. For example, there is no basis for any explanation whatsoever of psychokinesis. Holonomic theory doesn't help. Generally speaking, my work has little to do with parapsychology.

I deal with classical neurophysiology. I deal neither with parapsychology nor with quantum processes occurring in the brain. I've said only, and I want to emphasize that I myself treat the holonomic model as a scientific hypothesis, that the ordinary way brain cells interact is in some respects mathematically similar to the way quantum events interact. I am dealing with a classical neurophysiology.

O. Even so, it sounds like quite a new neurophysiology.

P. That is because much of traditional neurophysiology is framed exclusively within the space-time domain, neglecting this other side of reality, which is framed in the frequency domain. And I don't say that the traditional approach should now be suspended. Both approaches are indispensable.

Let me say this another way. In the spring of 1983, one of the great physical chemists of our time, Ilya Prigogine, gave a speech in Vienna in which he stressed the importance of research in physics within the space-time domain. He said that physics has dealt with static (timeless) phenomena for decades, and it is time to study dynamic processes. My answer to Prigogine was that we biologists have been studying our phenomena in a space-time frame for centuries, so it's time for us to pay attention to the frequency domain. Of course, not exclusively. Both perspectives are equally necessary.

O. How significant can the holonomic model be for brain research in general?

P. It goes some way to explaining the organization, functions, and incredible capacity of the brain. The model not only helps explain the fact that information is stored in many parts of the brain, but also other characteristic processes occurring in the brain. Its phenomenal storage capacity, for example. As with holographic memory, the brain can store hundreds of millions of bits of information in a single cubic centimeter of the brain. Further, an explanation is possible for the rapidity with which recognition occurs.

O. And what is the impact of your model on classical psychology?

P. Until recently, psychology has been primarily an analytical science. The results of specialized research have not been related to each other. Psychologists still seem unable to come to a convincing conclusion about the relationship between learning and memory, attention and decision, emotion and motivation, and these to one another, and to various electrophysiological manifestations of brain processes. It's as if physicists could not understand the relation between planets and moons, or between solar systems and galaxies. I believe the holonomic theory, plus the research comprising different brain functions, may be a useful instrument of integration if applied to the sciences dealing with brain, mind, and spirit.

O. Speaking of behavior and what determines it, in your book, *Languages of the Brain,* you included motivation and emotions in the category of feelings. What is the difference between emotions and motivations?

P. A motivating feeling occurs whenever we deal with the outside world; while emotions, as William James put it, ordinarily stop at the skin. Emotional feelings are handled internally.

O. Can we effectively master our feelings and have them rationally controlled?

P. Violent patients can be calmed down with drugs, which change chemical balances in the brain.

O. But can you change your "dark mood" all by yourself?

P. If we knew how to do it, life would be easier. It certainly requires much effort. In order to overcome a negative feeling state, I may have to make great efforts myself and I may need outside help, as well: that is one of the things which psychoanalysis and group therapy attempt. Sometimes they succeed, sometimes they don't.

O. Are these feelings and values that affect our "conscious" activities transitory, or are there any neurophysiological premises suggesting a universal nature of certain values?

P. You shouldn't forget that we all have similar brains, therefore our cultural values must have been preprogrammed similarly, too. In fact, this is what the oldest and most enduring ethical principles have been based upon. What's good for me is usually good for all; what makes me suffer, makes us all suffer.

O. We say that man is both rational and emotional, logically farsighted and instinctive. What is a human being really like?

P. You just said it: man is complex. Sometimes, for didactic purposes, we "separate" human attributes. But then they must be put together again, for in life all things are intertwined.

O. What would be your definition of a human being as opposed to other species: rational being, creator of tools, Homo symbolicum, political being . . .

P. Creative being. One who always has something to do; who has to continually reorganize the world.

O. Don't animals do that, too?

P. In another sense; animals act to satisfy their instincts and needs, and always, for millions of years, animals have done it the same way. Man looks for something new, constantly changes things.

O. Why?

P. Because that is the way his brain functions. Man simply has to.

5

On Experimental Medicine

Pribram and Sudakov pointed to the role of emotions in our everyday lives. In this chapter, the relationship between emotions and health are discussed in more detail by Sergei Anichkov and Norman Shumway. Anichkov is involved in general studies in the field of experimental medicine; Shumway successfully continues heart transplant operations, refining them into a normal medical practice.

Anichkov explains the concept of experimental medicine as a discipline based on the universal character of life processes. The aim of experimental medicine is to apply the results of experiments on animals to the treatment of human beings. Anichkov also presents his own research on the impact of drugs on the central nervous system, showing that some drugs—and even stress and anxiety—can change the genetic material of a cell. In a discussion of the relationship between modern and primitive medicine, Anichkov explains that despite its durable achievements, traditional medicine was a very costly trial-and-error reasoning that was based on simple observations. Experimental medicine, by contrast, is based on theory and aims at establishing the complete chain of causation. Shumway shows the importance of establishing the chain of causation correctly as he explains the logistics of heart transplant operations. He reveals the practical problems—both medical and personal—of this, one of the most advanced experimental practices in modern medicine.

9. Sergei Anichkov

Sergei Viktorovich Anichkov, who was born in 1902, first attended the Military Academy of Medicine in what was then Petrograd and later went to study at the University of Kazan. He served as a paramedic and then fought as an officer during World War I. In 1918, he completed his studies at the Institute of Medicine and started working as a researcher at the chair of pharmacology of the Military Academy of Medicine in Leningrad, where he obtained a doctorate in 1922. Two years later he was nominated to head the chair of pharmacology. During the Stalin purges of 1937, he was sent to Gulag, where he initially worked as a physician and was subsequently downgraded to a pharmacist. In 1945, he returned to Leningrad and resumed his scientific activities at the Institute of Medicine. In 1948, Dr. Anichkov became the director of the pharmacology department of the Institute of Experimental Medicine in Moscow.

Dr. Anichkov devoted his research to pharmacology and, in particular, to the influence of pharmaceutical substances on the central nervous system. For remarkable achievements in this field he was awarded the honor of Hero of Socialist Work. In 1976, he received the Lenin Prize for his research on the influence of physiologically active substances on the nervous system.

Since 1950, Dr. Anichkov has been a member of the Soviet Academy of Sciences.

Wiktor Osiatyński: Tell me, what does the field of experimental medicine embrace? Cannot the word itself give rise to quite unsavory suspicions?

Sergei Anichkov: Do I understand that you have in mind experiments on humans? I must dispel your fear. An honest, conscientious scholar or doctor never performs such experiments. The field of experimental medicine first sprang up in the nineteenth century with Claude Bernard, an outstanding French physiologist and pathologist, as one of its pioneers. The entire science of modern times is, as you know, based on the experimental method. However, the experimental method was introduced into medical science relatively late: only when it was discovered that the pattern found in all forms of life is more or less the same was it adopted. Ever since, experiments on animals have been carried out extensively, and their results used in research on the causes or origins of diseases, studies of immunity, and new methods of medical treatment. In fact, experimental medicine has served this purpose remarkably well. Take infectious diseases: the successes in this field derive from research on animals artificially infected with the same bacteria or viruses that cause the diseases in humans; then, the effective means to prevent or fight the disease must be found and, in many cases, they are.

O. It is true that all life is based on the same pattern, but isn't it also true that humans differ substantially from animals? To what degree are the results of experiments on animals applicable to humans?

A. All discoveries of experimental medicine provide only a very general pattern of biological processes. From the medical point of view, the decisive significance is that the new discoveries can be used to treat humans.

O. Suppose you've done a series of experiments on animals, which results in discovering a substance that may prevent or cure a disease in humans. Then, you administer the substance to your first patient. Isn't this an experiment, too?

A. Any activity involving people implies risk. In practice, however, the researchers usually test a new method or drug on themselves or on volunteers. If the effects prove satisfactory, scientists have not only a right to apply it but also the moral obligation to make the treatment available to everyone.

O. But if an experimenter or his collaborators are healthy, how can they tell that the proposed remedy will bring the expected results in sick people?

A. If it is necessary to test a new drug on a sick patient, progress in medicine is facilitated by the hopefulness of the terminally ill and their invincible desire to live. Such patients and their families beg the doctors to try the new drug or method. In this sense, the first operation under anesthesia, the first kidney transplant, and all first applications of new remedies can be considered experiments on humans. But isn't that true of every activity of man? The first bridge might have fallen down, as might have the very first skyscraper. Implicit in all first trials is risk. But without risk there would be no progress.

But speaking of experimental medicine, I'd like to make the point that while experiments on animals may involve arbitrary changes of dosage, samples taken at will, and the administration of all sorts of drugs regardless of whether the animal will suffer, die, or survive, it is never so with humans. Here, we always act on the fundamental principle *primum non nocere*—first, do no harm. A new remedy is used only if it can help a suffering or hopelessly ill person. And it is done with the utmost caution. Experimental medicine in general has to do primarily with animals. No sensible person doubts that our successful struggle against the most dangerous diseases depends on these kinds of experiments.

O. What are the main lines of research of experimental medicine today?

A. The experimental method is used in every medical discipline and in all natural sciences in the scientific exploration of life. Experiment, in fact, is what makes modern scientific medicine different from ancient medicine, which consisted solely of observation of the subjective reactions or feelings of a patient.

O. What is the main purpose of experimental medicine? Is it the quest for more effective methods of diagnosis and treatment and for new, more potent, drugs?

A. Our main, so to speak, human, task is, of course, the improvement of applied medicine, which is not possible without theory. However, the theoretical part is also increasingly dependent on experiments. What is the significance of today's theories? The significance is that we can experimentally reach the innermost levels of life. Electronic microscopy, stereochemistry, the ability to separate components of the cell, and many other achievements make it possible to work at the molecular level and study physiological processes at this lowest level of modern biology.

O. Isn't a person or even an animal or a plant a composition of cells that constitute a singular entity? Do the conclusions drawn from the examination of even the innermost level correspond to the principles of the organism's functions as a whole?

A. Of course not. That is why the analysis of the organic processes occurring at the molecular level must be combined with the study of all phenomena occurring in the entire body, and with the interrelationships of these phenomena and the very complex process of regulation. All organic phenomena, including the most complicated and least observable biochemical processes, are controlled by the nervous system, which also determines the attitude of the organism to its environment. It is research into the nervous system and all factors affecting it that chiefly interest us at this institute.

O. Your personal interest, professor, has to do with the influence of pharmaceutical and physiologically active substances on the nervous system. What does this influence entail? What did you discover in your research?

A. You can influence the entire organism and all its functions through the nervous system: you can affect thermal processes and energy exchange, circulation of the blood, and even the endocrinal system. We examine the effects of various stimuli. Thus we study the effects of caffeine, narcotic drugs, and alcohol on intracellular exchange and functions of the brain. We manipulate various substances, looking for new combinations that would affect the nervous system in a desirable way. We have found, for example, a drug that, by affecting the nervous system, is useful in resuscitation; it is very helpful in keeping newborn infants alive. I could also mention a number of drugs helpful in the treatment of neuroses or mental diseases.

O. You said that all occurrences in the organism could be influenced through the nervous system. Is that really so? Some reactions, we are told, are genetically predetermined and protected against any outside influence. Can they, too, be affected by the nervous system?

A. I guess you are talking about the genetic mechanism. That is still a question. The functioning of the genotype of the somatic cells can definitely be influenced. We already know that nervous agitation itself can change the DNA or RNA of the cell, which of course affects its reproduction.

For several years now, my institute has carried out research on how neurotropic drugs affect, through the nervous system, the genotype contained in cells or in tissues. It appears that irritation of the nervous system results in a considerable change in the body's energy exchange and in the genetic mechanism itself. A short but towering rage, stress, or even momentary tension may cause similar effects.

O. It is popularly believed that cancer may be a result of such an impairment of the genotype. Can irritation of the nervous system initiate the growth or cause the metastasis of cancer?

A. The latest research, both in the Soviet Union and in the United States, proves that disorders of the endocrinal as well as the nervous systems may have a carcinogenic influence. It was also proved through experiments with animals that the mortality rate in cancer patients dramatically increases if the disease is accompanied by stress. The relationship between cancer and stress, however, still awaits scientific explanation.

O. You said that by affecting the nervous system you could influence the physical condition of the body. Suppose my arm hurts for no apparent reason. Is it possible to influence my nervous system to get rid of the pain?

A. Of course. I may simply give you a pain-killing drug that doesn't affect the source of the pain directly but which works on your nervous system. Or I may apply psychotherapy.

O. But if we still don't know why my arm hurts?

A. It doesn't matter. Every occurrence in your body is controlled by your central nervous system. Hence, a sensible influence on this system may bring a desirable result.

O. Isn't that the method used by Filipino healers and many others considered quacks by official medicine? They don't know the cause of a malady either, but they can sometimes heal their patients.

A. I cannot discuss it as I have never witnessed anything like that. I have only heard about it. However, from all I know about the role the nervous system plays in the organism, I cannot deny that such "magic" might be effective indeed. The quacks, or the healers, intuitively treat their patients with suggestions. This affects the nervous system, which, in turn, influences the general health of a patient. I think that the successes of healers are enhanced by the fact that they tend to treat a person as a whole being while modern medicine, very unfortunately, approaches man as if he were a collection of organs and systems.

O. If you acknowledge, at least partly, the effectiveness of "magic" medicine, then questions arise. Where is the line drawn between magic and science? What is the difference between modern medicine and folk medicine? Wasn't the gathering and testing of herbs old-fashioned medical experimentation?

A. It is true that almost all of folk medicine is based on the use of plants or herbs. Modern scientific medicine has adopted many of these substances. In fact, very few diseases today are cured without them.

O. Therefore, since they have long been effective, the differences I've just asked about seem to be insignificant.

A. Not necessarily. I think the main difference lies in that folk medicine, contrary to what you have just said, was not based on experiments but on observations. Experimentation derives from theory, while observation is simply a method of trial and error, with haphazard and usually very expensive results. Folk medicine, of course, boasts of remarkable achievements, which have served humanity extremely well, but these were not derived through experimentation.

O. In experimentation, do you have to design the conditions and do your designs have to result from previously formulated theories?

A. A complete theory is not indispensable; it may be an operational hypothesis. An experiment doesn't always confirm a hypothesis, but there is a theoretical framework within which we carry out the experiment. Let us go back to modern experiments with herbs. We experiment with herbs today not to learn how to heal sick people, for we have known how to do it for millennia, but to provide the theoretical framework for the old methods.

O. So the theoretical framework makes the difference between magic and science, doesn't it?

A. The theoretical framework is not the point. After all, some theory has always been there. For instance, ginseng root. It was believed to be an effective cure because it has an anthropoidal shape. Wasn't this a theory, imperfect as it may be? In my opinion, progress in medicine consists primarily of the perfection of theories, establishing more and more causal relationships; of the growing knowledge of natural processes; and of the possibility of experimental testing of our theoretical suppositions.

O. Even so, the two methods have something in common. You say it is the recognition, whether based on a theory or just on an "intuition," of the significance of the central nervous system.

A. Right; for in the course of the last thousands of years, man himself has not changed significantly. What has changed dramatically is our knowledge of man. The nervous system—and, in particular, the emotions—has always, both formerly and today, played a decisive role in the constitution of man. Alas, we act too often as if we underrate the importance of emotions.

O. What is the role of emotions? In everyday life, one can judge it by oneself; but what is the role of emotions on the physiological level?

A. Strangely enough, these problems are still relatively unexplored, though from every indication, emotions are positively vital. In our experiments we provoked, through irritation of a certain part of the hypothalamus, negative emotions in animals. Thus we caused a stroke, or aggravation of a malady, or cancer. Conversely, it can be assumed that positive emotions ought to positively influence our health.

O. How can you provoke a positive emotion? Not experimentally, but naturally, in everyday life?

A. I think it is directly related to the environment. Poor living conditions lead to increased negative emotions. There must also be a self-control over the emotions. And one can learn to control one's emotions, at least to a degree.

O. How?

A. What is necessary is reflection and awareness of oneself. The awareness of what one wants, what one really needs, and how to get it. And finally, in order to produce positive emotions, one should think of pleasant things as frequently as possible.

O. Do you actually know what is pleasant for you?

A. Yes, the work. I've known it for a long time and that is why I do what I do.

10. Norman Shumway

Norman E. Shumway, born in 1923, is the head of the Department of Cardiovascular Surgery at Stanford Medical Center in California. In December 1959 he became the first person in the world to perform a heart transplant in a dog. For the past twenty-four years, Dr. Shumway has been conducting research on the mechanism of rejection of transplanted organs. His research contributed to the development of the technique of transplantation that made it possible to transplant hearts in humans. Norman Shumway performed his first human heart transplant operation on January 6, 1968.

Today, under the leadership of Dr. Shumway, Stanford Medical Center is the world's leading center for both the number of heart transplantations and the length of postoperative survival time, as well as the first center to have initiated the combined heart and lung transplantation operation. It is the only center in the world to have long-term survivors of the combined heart and lung operation.

Wiktor Osiatyński: How many heart transplant operations have been done at the Stanford Medical Center?

Norman Shumway: So far [June 1983], 267, plus fourteen heart-lung operations since March 1981.

O. That's 267 transplantations in fifteen years. Has the number increased in recent years, as compared to the number of such operations done at the beginning?

S. Yes, although our facilities limit the number to two heart transplantations a month. Each requires a lot of work, personnel, and money. We simply cannot afford more than two in a month. We did twenty-four heart transplant operations last year [1982], plus three more heart-lung operations.

O. How do you select your patients? Haphazardly?

S. Absolutely not. In general, there aren't too many candidates for heart or heart-lung transplant operations. Heart patients are mostly old people who've already lived their lives and don't want to go through all the agonies and problems of transplantation. Others can be helped in other ways, too. Therefore, the number of patients we consider for heart transplantation who have been waiting for their donors is never more than six or seven persons at a time. So this is not the problem. For when we find a donor, he or she has a certain group of blood; it usually corresponds with the blood group of no more than just one patient; so in practice, it's easy to decide whose turn it is for the operation.

O. Is it only a blood group that tells you a heart is "right" for one person and "wrong" for another?

S. No, not only that. But these are quite simple technical problems that are easily taken care of; what you often need is just an X-ray.

O. What happens if more than one of the patients-to-be has the donor's blood group?

S. We choose the one who is most ill. The relevant factors always determine our decision as to who should get the donor's heart, so no real problems are involved. But I guess I know what's on your mind. I want to assure you that our decision has nothing to do with how rich the patients are or with any nonmedical reason.

O. It means that your decision is haphazard only in the sense that the donor is haphazard. You just learn that a heart will be available and this determines your choice of a patient.

S. Right. Only this.

O. Who are the donors? Accident victims and people who died of other diseases?

S. Mostly victims of accidents or, occasionally, suicides. People who die of other diseases cannot be heart donors because of medical reasons. The heart of a person who died of brain cancer was transplanted in St. Louis, Missouri; the very same kind of malignant tumor developed in the brain of the heart recipient so he died soon afterward. You have to be careful; a sick person's heart is often too weak to function normally in a new body. Also, we never take a heart from someone who dies of a drug overdose because it sometimes causes the so-called reversible brain death: at first the brain does not respond to stimuli—it is dead; then, after a time, a sudden recovery happens. So we cannot know whether what happens is a real, final death of a person, or not.

O. And how is it with the victim of an accident? Can medicine say absolutely positively that someone's chance for survival is totally lost?

S. It used to be recognized as death when the heartbeat stopped and blood ceased to circulate. But it's happened to us that we would make a heart resume its heartbeat three or four times a day. Today, the moment when the brain ceases to work is legally recognized as death. It is right from the medical point of view and it also helps to make decisions in all kinds of transplantations of both heart and kidney . . .

O. How long, after the heartbeat stops, must you wait before you can consider the brain dead?

S. It is not my determination. Normally, a donor is first examined in neurosurgery here. When three neurosurgeons, after a thorough examination, declare that the donor's brain is functioning no more, we may take over. We never make decisions on the donor's death. That is the realm of neurosurgery.

O. For how long is the heart of a dead person viable for transplantation?

S. If it's not kept "alive" very carefully, it can be only a few hours. The dead brain sends no messages to the rest of the body and all organs stop functioning, and you can't transplant a dead heart, can you?

O. How can you keep the heart alive in a body with a dead brain?

S. First of all, the dead donor must get artificial respiration so that oxygen could be forced through his lungs. The dead brain cannot send messages and the person cannot breathe, so a ventilator must be used to keep the heart alive in a body with a dead brain.

O. Then you select a patient and the transplantation is made?

S. You forget the next most important thing: we must have permission from the next of kin of the deceased person. Regardless of what the law says, we consider the permission of the family a crucial thing. No transplantation has ever been made here without such permission.

O. Only because of possible legal complications?

S. Definitely not. It's simply a question of human dignity. Human beings should not be treated as things.

O. Do people often say no?

S. Not often, but it happens sometimes.

O. On what grounds?

S. On religious grounds, occasionally. Sometimes people want to bury their loved ones with their bodies intact. According to some religions, mostly Eastern, no part of the dead body is to be removed. Generally, however, people understand that the bodies of their loved ones could be useful and help to prolong someone else's life.

O. Sorry for asking you this, but have you ever encountered financial claims from a donor's family?

S. Never; not even the slightest hint about money.

O. I ask you about this because a fear arose years ago that people might want to "sell" bodies of their loved ones . . .

S. It never happened. Human nature is not as bad as it often seems to be.

O. Did you think of any ethical problems years ago, when you still experimented on animals? If so, which of your reflections proved significant in practice and which haven't?

S. So many medical problems are connected with transplantation that we've never had enough time for problems of an ethical or social nature. We make a point of two things I've already mentioned: first, the donor's death must be declared totally independently from all members of the transplant operation team; and the second is the permission of the donor's family. Following these two principles we have never had any legal or ethical problems.

O. But such problems arise elsewhere.

S. Right, because these principles are not always applied. For instance, transplantations were performed without permission from families in South Africa; similarly, in the United States, in Virginia, a transplantation was once done without permission of the donor's family, who couldn't be traced down at once. Next day relatives came up, embittered because they had not been asked for permission. We think such seemingly immaterial details are simply a question of human dignity; we respect the principles and, therefore, we can carry on our program while nearly all others had to be discontinued.

O. From what you said it appears that both the dignity of a deceased person and his next of kin are at stake. The relatives just want to be asked for permission and usually they give it.

S. Not only that. In most cases their spirit is sort of lifted up since there can be some use of a tragic situation. I recall the first transplant operation I performed. In December 1967 I appealed to all medical doctors that I was able to use the heart of a person who had died as the result of an accident. On January 6, 1968, Virginia White, forty-three, had a brain blood effusion, a stroke. When doctors told her husband that the patient's condition was terminal, he asked if they knew of any medical research in which the victim of such a case would be of use. I was called by the doctors, but the initiative had been taken by the deceased's next of kin. In many a case the families have found it helpful that their tragedies could contribute to a humane purpose.

O. How many centers are performing transplants?

S. Besides Stanford, other centers where transplants are performed regularly are at the University of Pittsburgh, the University of Arizona, the Downstate Medical Center in New York, the Medical College of Virginia, and now, of course, at the John Hopkins Hospital in Baltimore.

O. How many quit?

S. Once there were nearly a hundred medical centers in which transplants were undertaken.

O. What were the main reasons some of them quit? Did they ignore the principles of ethics?

S. First of all the lack of success. Their patients just died. Our success may not be very big, but it's still bigger than anywhere else.

O. What is your average postoperative survival time?

S. We have 107 patients out of 267 who are alive now. One patient has lived for more than thirteen years after the heart transplant operation. Eighty percent live as long as a year after the operation. You can compare it with the first year of our program, when a year-long survival time applied to only 22 percent of heart recipients. Five-year survival is now averaging 50 percent. You can see how the technique has progressed.

O. Can you tell what would be the survival time of your patients without transplantations?

S. We've had some patients who were ready for a transplant but never had a matching donor; their average life span is four to six months.

O. When the first human heart was transplanted, there was much discussion about the transplantation of the hearts of animals, especially pigs.

S. Research in this line hasn't gone far yet. There is little chance that a pig's—or, for that matter, a sheep's—heart would be of any use to humans. The difference in genetic programs is too great. It's hard enough to fit a part of one human to another; to match an animal's organ to a man is virtually impossible.

O. Eight years ago you ruled out the possibility of constructing an artificial heart for humans. What do you think now, after the operation on Dr. Barney Clark?

S. The results of that procedure speak for themselves. I think it will be a long time before our results of the transplantation of the heart and both lungs can be matched by any type of artificial organ implants.

O. And in what direction will the further development in heart transplantations go now?

S. I think the research aimed at the solution of a problem of tissue diversity in different individuals will be crucial. Once we solve this, we'll be able to transplant tissues with less immunological problems, which cause rejection of a transplanted heart by the body of the recipient. Our results have improved greatly with the use of the new drug cyclosporine, and we will continue to work toward solving the rejection problem.

O. There will be no more rejections?

S. Not as many as before. Now, when a patient is prepared to take a transplant, he is made vulnerable to all kinds of infections.

O. In transplant deaths, how often was an immunological problem the immediate cause of death?

S. Probably in 20 percent of the cases. Patients die of infections; infections are a part of the rejection problem because it has so much to do with the immunological barrier of the individual. In transplant cases we administer drugs to diminish the patient's natural resistance to foreign cells or tissues; in effect, the patient becomes a victim of an infection that, otherwise, could be easily fought down by a healthy person; now, a parasite, a virus, or a common cold can cause death. If we manage to solve this problem, we'll be able to transplant tissues without such a high risk of rejection.

O. Heart transplantation can hardly be compared to, say, appendix surgery. A patient cannot be sure that he or she won't die during the operation. What is the patient's approach at the moment of making their decisions?

S. The decision making is done before we first meet. They come from all over the country, sometimes even from abroad. Their doctors tell them that they have not much longer to live and that hardly anything can be done to help them. So we don't see the patients when they make their decisions. They come here after they have already made up their minds.

O. Have you ever met anybody who'd been offered a chance of a heart transplant and refused it?

S. Never. When I meet my patients, they are determined to undergo a heart transplant operation.

O. Who are they? What do they have in common?

S. All kinds of people—middle-aged, mostly in their forties—who want to live and accomplish something before they die; they are active and full of energy, and they understand that we offer them their only chance for survival.

O. We all know we'll die someday, but we don't know when it will be. This uncertainty makes it possible to live a normal life. The prospect of a transplant operation makes one's own death apprehensible. A doctor says, "You have three to four months more to live." Can you, professor, restore a person's uncertainty as to when he or she might die? Is it possible to achieve this through a transplant operation?

S. I believe so, especially in view of the latest developments in immunology, which increase the patient's chances for a longer time of postoperative survival. As I've said, we have one transplant patient who is still alive more than thirteen years after the operation. I don't think it will be long before our patients will live even longer.

O. How much longer?

S. I don't know. It's just that uncertainty you found so important, didn't you?

O. How does a patient feel when he or she is taken to the operating room? Does it occur to him that he may never leave it alive?

S. Hope is probably the strongest feeling among my patients. It was they who decided that their lives, such as they had been, were not worthy to carry on, that they had suffered enough; therefore, they consent now to the risk of transplant surgery. It is something a healthy person can hardly understand at all. But if someone is really seriously ill, and there is a chance he or she may feel better, such a person will take even a greater risk.

O. What is the first postanesthetic reaction after a successful transplantation?

S. Patients don't talk much. They only say they feel well; they seem to be happy they're still alive. But they discuss nothing. I think they don't even go into much thought about how close they were to death.

O. Is there a feeling like: well, I took the risk and I succeeded. My life is saved.

S. Yes, there is something of the sort.

O. How long does such a feeling of hope and satisfaction last? Have any of your patients whose life you prolonged come back to you, again under a critical condition?

S. Of course, many times.

O. What were their feelings then? Were they grateful for the year of life you gave them, or were they disappointed that it was not enough?

S. They never complained in any way. What they mostly showed was hope once again. After all, one wants to live and believe in one's ability to survive, especially if one has already escaped death. In fact, we've done a second transplant operation in four cases, and soon, we may transplant a heart for the same patient for the third time. We seem to cope quite successfully with the immunological barrier, especially with the new drug cyclosporine. There is a continuing progress in this line; we get to know the human body better all the time. We may be able to make heart transplantations several times, prolonging the life of our patients even more.

O. If not life, then at least hope—and it is equally important, isn't it? It can actually be the greatest ethical success of transplantations once disputed over so heatedly and with so many reservations. What, in your opinion, were the reasons for those discussions?

S. People were afraid of the possibility of using donors who were not really dead. People suspected that doctors, and especially transplant surgeons, would perform transplantations just for their own renown and prestige. I don't like to talk about it, but I think that in many a case, especially at the beginning, such fears were justified.

O. Do you find them irrelevant today?

S. I believe so.

O. Is it because transplantations have since become a normal medical procedure and are nothing extraordinary anymore?

S. Right; we perform transplantations today that the media don't even mention.

O. Don't you think that all those discussions could have resulted, to a considerable extent, from the fact that the notion of "heart" has played an exceptional role in human culture?

S. Yes, I do. Poets have always attached a special significance to the heart. Some thought that the "soul" might dwell in the heart. The heart is a vital element of our emotional language. We speak of heartache, of heartburning hatred, heartbreaking affection, of heartfelt or openhearted emotions, and so on.

O. Aren't you afraid that the very fact of successful heart transplant operations, just like bone surgery, can change that poetic and cultural significance of heart?

S. I hope not. The word *heart* is still being used in its poetic meaning, even by cardiac surgeons. And it probably always will be.

O. So there must be something exceptional about the heart?

S. Of course there is. After all, it's the only organ in the body that "does" something. All the others simply are there. The heart is the only part that functions all by itself.

(All photos by Wiktor Osiatyński)

Linus Pauling

Evgenii Feinberg

Robert Hofstadter

Iosif S. Shklovskii

Karl Pribram

Konstantin Sudakov

Noam Chomsky

Guram Ramishvili

Willis Harman

Igor Bestuzhev-Lada

Fritjof Capra

Sergei Semenov

6

On Language and Culture

For biologists, the distinction between human beings and other animals is the ability to create and use language. But what is language? How does human language differ from animal communication? Do we think in language? Is language rational? Is language a learned capacity? Or, is the capacity to learn language biologically inherited? Was there a universal language? What is universal grammar? Are differences among languages really so great and so important as we usually assume? What are the social roles of language? What is the role of language differentiation? What is the relationship between a linguistic group and a nation?

In addressing these questions, Noam Chomsky and Guram Ramishvili reveal drastically different attitudes toward the human symbolic word and language. Chomsky explains his concept of universal grammar and points to the similarities among different languages and cultures, while Ramishvili stresses differences among languages and the uniqueness of each language-based culture.

Chomsky begins with his conviction that linguistics can be helpful in understanding what distinguishes human beings from other species. The analysis of language can provide us with a pattern useful in studying others, specifically human pragmatic structures. According to Chomsky, all these structures have a similar, genetically transmitted, biological base.

Ramishvili doesn't speak against universal grammar. He points out, however, that Chomsky's concept is relevant to grammar and phonetics only and does not apply to the cultural role of language. This role seems to Ramishvili the most important aspect of language, for it was not created exclusively to satisfy biological or communication needs. Language is a driving force in the development of uniquely human spiritual values.

Ramishvili's concepts are related to the needs of his own nation: the Georgians living in the Soviet Republic of Georgia. At the time of the interview, Georgia was undergoing upheavals caused by the proposed change in the constitution of the republic. Formerly; the constitution recognized Georgian as a national and official language in the republic. The change would give an equal status to Georgian, Russian, Armenian, and other languages in use in Georgia. The national identity of the Georgians, imperiled by an attempt at Russification, was at stake. The demonstration by half a million Georgians in the republic's capital, Tbilisi, finally prevented a change and Georgian continues to be the official language of Georgia.

11. Noam Chomsky

Born in 1928, Noam Chomsky joined the staff of the Massachusetts Institute of Technology after receiving his Ph.D. in linguistics from the University of Pennsylvania in 1955. In 1961, he was appointed professor in the Department of Modern Languages and Linguistics and in the Research Laboratory of Electronics. Since 1976 he has been an institute professor in the Department of Linguistics and Philosophy.

In 1955, while a junior fellow of the Harvard Society of Fellows, Chomsky completed his doctoral dissertation entitled Transformational Analysis. *Some of the major theoretical viewpoints of the dissertation appeared in the monograph* Syntactic Structures, *which was published in 1957. Ever since this publication, his concept of transformational grammar has been analyzed by several authors and dozens of panels, and discussions of his theory have been held in many countries. Among his books are:* Aspects of the Theory of Syntax *(1965),* The Sound Pattern of English *(coauthored with Morris Halle, 1968),* Language and Mind *(1969),* Studies on Semantics in Generative Grammar *(1972),* The Logical Structure of Linguistic Theory *(1975, based on a manuscript of, 1955–56),* Reflections on Language *(1975),* Language and Responsibility *(1979),*

Rules and Representations *(1980), and* Lectures on Government and Binding *(1981). These tracts have won Noam Chomsky great renown both within the linguistic community and among the popular readership.*

Noam Chomsky also writes and lectures on contemporary social and political problems. His major books on these issues are: American Power and New Mandarins *(1969),* At War with Asia *(1970),* Problems of Knowledge and Freedom *(1971),* For Reasons of State *(1973),* Peace in the Middle East *(1974),* Political Economy of Human Rights *(coauthored with Edward Herman, 1979),* Radical Priorities *(1981),* Toward a New Cold War *(1982), and* Fateful Triangle *(1983). These books offer an insight into Chomsky's radical, though not revolutionary, approach to contemporary politics.*

Noam Chomsky has received seven honorary degrees at universities in the United States and abroad. He is a member of the American Academy of Arts and Sciences and the National Academy of Sciences.

Wiktor Osiatyński: You represent an anthropological approach to linguistics. Do you think linguistics can contribute to the understanding of the philosophical problems of human nature and culture?

Noam Chomsky: My feeling is that a human being or any complex organism has a system of cognitive structures that develop much in the way the physical organs of the body develop. That is, in their fundamental character they are innate; their basic form is determined by the genetic nature of the organism. Of course, they grow under particular environmental conditions, assuming a specific form that admits of some variation. Much of what is distinctive among human beings is a specific manner in which a variety of shared cognitive structures develop.

Perhaps the most intricate of these structures is language. In studying language we can discover many basic properties of this cognitive structure, its organization, and also the genetic predispositions that provide the foundation for its development.

So in this respect, linguistics, first of all, tries to characterize a major feature of human cognitive organization. And second, I think it may provide a suggestive model for the study of other cognitive systems. And the collection of these systems is one aspect of human nature.

O. Language, then, is a key to human nature?

Ch. In Western scientific thought of the last several centuries there has been a tendency to assume that human nature is limited to the immediately observable physical structure of the organism. And that for other aspects of human nature, specifically for behavior, there are no genetically determined structures of comparable complexity to the directly observable physical organization of the body. So human physical structures and intellectual structures are generally studied in different ways. The assumption is that physical structures are genetically inherited and intellectual structures are learned.

I think that this assumption is wrong. None of these structures is learned. They all grow; they grow in comparable ways; their ultimate forms are heavily dependent on genetic predispositions. If we understood, as we do not, the physical bases for these structures, I have little doubt that we would find structures in the brain for social interactions, or language, or analysis of personality—a whole variety of systems developed on the basis of a specific biological endowment.

O. Do you mean that all our behavior is innate, genetically determined?

Ch. No, but the basic structures for our behavior are innate. The specific details of how they grow would depend on interaction with the environment.

O. Supposing linguistics could describe one such structure. Would the findings apply to all our intellectual activities? Do we think only in language? Or, do there exist nonlinguistic forms of thinking, too?

Ch. The analysis of linguistic structures could help in understanding other intellectual structures. Now, I don't think there is any scientific evidence about the question of whether we think only in language or not. But introspection indicates pretty clearly that we don't think in language necessarily. We also think in visual images, we think in terms of situations and events, and so on, and many times we can't even begin to express in words what the content of our thinking is. And even if we are able to express it in words, it is a common experience to say something and then to recognize that it is not what we meant, that it is something else.

What does this mean? That there is a kind of nonlinguistic

thought going on which we are trying to represent in language, and we know that sometimes we fail.

O. I've read several times that we think in language, but "feel" in nonlinguistic ways.

Ch. I know that it's false of me, at least if "language" refers (in my case) to English, and I assume that it's false of everyone else. I don't think you would have any trouble at all in deciding that you are thinking of some event and then visualizing it happening with its consequences, and constructing a rational analysis of it without being able to verbalize it adequately in anything like its full complexity.

O. You used the expression "rational analysis." Do you believe that all our thinking is rational and linear?

Ch. I don't think all thinking is a kind of rational structure. But I don't think it is correct to identify the rational-nonrational dichotomy with the linguistic-nonlinguistic dichotomy.

O. Can language be nonrational?

Ch. Yes; so those are two dimensions that do not correlate. It's true that language is in a sense linear but that is as obvious as perceptual space is three-dimensional.

O. As I understand, language has an innate biological basis. Its use, however, is social. What do you think of the social functions of language? Is it primarily an instrument of communication?

Ch. I think a very important aspect of language has to do with the establishment of social relations and interactions. Often, this is described as communication. But that is very misleading, I think. There is a narrow class of uses of language where you intend to communicate. Communication refers to an effort to get people to understand what one means. And that, certainly, is one use of language and a social use of it. But I don't think it is the only social use of language. Nor are social uses the only uses of language. For example, language can be used to express or clarify one's thoughts with little regard for the social context, if any.

I think the use of language is a very important means by which this species, because of its biological nature, creates a kind of social space, to place itself in interactions with other people. It doesn't have much to do with communication in a narrow sense; that is, it doesn't involve transmission of information. There is much information transmitted but it is not the content of what is said that is transmitted. There is undoubtedly much to learn about the social use of language, for communication or for other purposes. But at present there is not much in the way of a *theory* of sociolinguistics, of social uses of languages, as far as I am aware.

O. What, then, in the field of linguistics, are the greatest achievements?

Ch. I think the most important work that is going on has to do with the search for very general and abstract features of what is sometimes called universal grammar: general properties of language that reflect a kind of biological necessity rather than logical necessity; that is, properties of language that are not logically necessary for such a system but which are essential invariant properties of human language and are known without learning. We know these properties but we don't learn them. We simply use our knowledge of these properties as the basis for learning.

O. Do we genetically inherit this knowledge?

Ch. Yes, we must. In fact, by universal grammar I mean just that system of principles and structures that are the prerequisites for acquisition of language, and to which every language necessarily conforms.

O. Does it mean that this genetic basis of language is universal?

Ch. Yes, that's right. But we are only one species. You can imagine a different world in which a number of species developed with different genetically determined linguistic systems. It hasn't happened in evolution. What has happened is that one species has developed, and the genetic structure of this species happens to involve a variety of intricate abstract principles of linguistic organization that, therefore, necessarily constrain every language, and, in fact, create the basis for learning language as a way of organizing experience rather than constituting something learned from experience.

O. Would such knowledge also be helpful in understanding human nature?

Ch. It would, in two respects. For one thing, it is by itself a part of a study of human intelligence that is, perhaps, the central aspect of human nature. And second, I think, it is a good model for studying other human properties, which ought to be studied by psychologists in the same way.

O. Do you mean that psychology could benefit from linguistics? Could you explain how?

Ch. One thing that you and I know is language. Another thing that you and I know is how objects behave in perceptual space. We have a whole mass of complex ways of understanding what is the nature of visual space. A proper part of psychology ought to be, and in recent years has been, an effort to try to discover the principles of how we organize visual space. I would say that the same is true of every domain of psychology, of human studies. To understand, for example, how people organize social systems we have to discover the principles that we create to make some societies intelligible.

O. I understand that we could have a kind of universal grammar of nonlinguistic forms of human behavior as well. But if, as you say, our behavior and language are heavily guided by universal principles, why, then, do they differ so much all around the world?

Ch. I don't think they differ so much. I think that as human beings, we quite naturally take for granted what is similar among human beings and, then, pay attention to what differentiates us. That makes perfect sense for us as human beings. I suppose frogs pay no attention to being frogs. They take it for granted. What interests a frog are differences among frogs. From our point of view they are all more or less the same, from their point of view they are all radically different.

Similarly with us. For us, we are all very different, our languages are very different, and our societies are very different. But if we could extract ourselves from our point of view and sort of look down at human life the way a biologist looks at other organisms, I think we could see it a different way. Imagine an extrahuman observer looking at us. Such an extrahuman observer would be struck precisely by the uniformity of human languages, by the very slight variation from one language to another, and by the remarkable respects in which all languages are the same. And then he would notice we do not pay any attention to that because for the purpose of human life it is quite natural and appropriate just to take for granted everything that is common. We don't concern ourselves with that, all we worry about are differences.

O. Would this extrahuman observer think the same way about our symbols, ideas, needs, and values?

Ch. Absolutely. I think he would be struck with the uniformity of human societies in every aspect. And there is more than that. Let's imagine again an observer looking at us without any preconceptions. I think he would be struck by the fact that although human beings have the capacity to develop scientific knowledge, it must be a very limited capacity because it is done only in very narrow and specific domains. There are huge areas where the human mind is apparently incapable of forming sciences, or at least has not done so. There are other areas, so far in fact one area only, in which we have demonstrated the capacity for true scientific progress.

O. Physics?

Ch. Physics and those parts of other fields that grow out of physics. Chemistry, the structure of big molecules—in those domains there is a lot of progress. In many other domains there is very little progress in developing real scientific understanding.

O. Isn't it because man wants to exercise control over the physical world?

Ch. I don't think so. I think it probably reflects something very special about the nature of our minds. There is no evolutionary pressure to create minds capable of forming sciences; it just happened. Evolutionary pressure has not led to higher rates of reproduction for people capable of solving scientific problems or creating new scientific ideas. So if, in fact, the science forming capacities evolved for other reasons, it would not be too surprising if those particular structures that have developed proved to be rather special in their nature, reflecting the contingencies of their evolution or the working of physical law.

O. Do you mean that we may be, by virtue of this accidental origin of science, capable of development of some disciplines of science and incapable of others? And that we are not conscious of that?

Ch. Yes, as human beings we are not too conscious of that because we naturally assume that our mental structures are universal. But I suppose an outside biologist looking at us would see something very different. He would see that, like other organisms, we have a narrow sphere within which we are very good, but that sphere is very limited. And that, in fact, the very achievements we can have within that sphere are related to lack of achievements in other spheres.

To construct a scientific theory from the data and to be able to recognize that it is a reasonable theory is possible only if there are some very sharp restrictive principles that lead you to go in one direction and not in another direction. Otherwise you wouldn't have science at all, merely randomly chosen hypotheses. Then, human genius may have limitless opportunities to develop in one direction, but at the same time this genius will not go in other directions. And those two considerations are related. The very properties of the human mind that provide an enormous scope for human genius in some domains will serve as barriers to progress in other domains, just as the properties that enable each child to acquire a complex and highly articulated human language block the acquisition of other imaginable linguistic systems.

O. What domains do you consider the most backward and neglected?

Ch. I think that we have basically nothing in the field of human behavior. Maybe that is just a condition of temporary ignorance. But it may be that we are simply not intellectually equipped to develop such a theory.

O. Do you mean that not only do we not have tools to develop such a theory but we are incapable of creating the necessary tools?

Ch. Yes, intellectual tools. Our minds are specifically adapted to developing certain theories, and we have a science if the theories that are available to our minds happen to be close to true. Well, there is no particular reason to suppose that the intersection of true theories and theories that are accessible to the mind is very large. It may not be very large.

O. Can we know, at least, how large it is?

Ch. It is a question of biology how large that intersection is. And if humans are organisms like every other organism, which they are, then we should expect that if there are some domains where real scientific progress is possible, then there are others where it is not.

12. Guram Ramishvili

Guram Solomonovich Ramishvili, born in 1923, graduated from the philology department of the University of Tbilisi in 1955. After earning a doctorate in linguistics for his dissertation on the philosophical and linguistic concepts of Wilhelm von Humboldt, Ramishvili became a lecturer at the University of Tbilisi. In 1970, he published a dissertation in German entitled The Problems of the Inner Forms of Language in Modern Linguistics. *In 1971, Ramishvili became the director of the general linguistics department at the University of Tbilisi. In 1973–74, at the invitation of the*

Alexander Humboldt foundation, Ramishvili was a Visiting Professor at universities in Bonn and Münster.

His interests have ranged primarily from the theory and history of linguistics to semantics and general problems of language as a cultural factor. His books—On the Energetic Theory of Language *(1978),* Language and Thought in View of Linguistic Research *(1979), and* The Inner Form of Language *(1980)—deal with the common elements of linguistics and the theory of culture, philosophy, and psychology.*

Another field of Dr. Ramishvili's research is the study of speech generation and recognition—the topic of his books Speech Processing Systems *(1981) and* Automatic Speech Recognition *(1981).*

Since 1975, Guram Ramishvili has been a member of the European Linguistic Society.

Wiktor Osiatyński: Language is sometimes said to be the borderline between nature and culture. Do you agree with this opinion?

Guram Ramishvili: Yes and no. It implies an opposition between nature and culture, and I doubt that's right. We should not speak of any such opposition—obviously not before language first developed, before the culture emerged. When it happened, though, the biological nature became increasingly dependent on culture. The creation of language meant an intervention of culture into nature, or an enrichment of nature with culture. In this sense, it was a crucial event, although it was only a part of the "natural" evolution of nature, being at the same time its continuation.

O. Are you referring to the biological or, more precisely, to the evolutionary necessity of the formation of language?

R. Not only. Johann Gottfried von Herder, the German philosopher and theologian, once said that language compensates for man's biological inadequacy. Nature has equipped humans less generously than animals to survive in a natural environment. In a purely natural environment, man, as a defenseless biological being, would probably lose his battle for survival with animals, while language and the entire culture based on it have helped man to survive. That is why language and humanity are just the same thing.

O. Was it language, or Homo sapiens, that developed first?

R. That question doesn't make much sense, I'm afraid. You shouldn't separate or put in order of precedence the three notions:

humanity, language, and society. After all, even at the time of the formation of language, man was already a member of a society. On the other hand, language is a precondition of social existence. Also, the concept of man without language is not only incomplete, it's just not possible. The concept of language without man is inherently contradictory. The "animal language" is just a metaphor. You know, "animal" in Georgian is *pirutgvi*. It means "unable to speak," or "mute." We also use different verbs referring to the "life" of humans and to the "existence" or "being" of animals. I think that this specific Georgian vocabulary may reflect a very significant difference between humans and other species.

O. If humanity and language are the same thing, how can you explain the multitudes of and differentiation among various languages?

R. There are several explanations. One is genetic: an analysis of the anthropological evolution, the differentiation of mankind, and the accompanying linguistic evolution. I believe, however, that culture itself offers a more convincing explanation. Culture is never schematic or created upon a single pattern. Everything goes to show that humanity, as a species, needs differentiation and a multitude of different approaches to the universe in order to experience the richness of the universe and its own immense potential.

The world itself is differentiated and ambiguous. If people looked at it from a single point of view, they would not be able to comprehend it precisely or even adequately. The differentiation of languages helped mankind to approach the world in a variety of ways and, because of that, to use more fully its intellectual potential through a mutual complementation of many different, linguistically predetermined, "images of the universe." This is why I find a comparative study of the semantic structures of languages to be a kind of semantic introduction to the general theory of human intellect.

O. Do you mean that comparative linguistics may help us comprehend more adequately reality itself and the variety of mankind's intellectual capabilities to understand reality?

R. Right, and not only that. Comparative linguistics, or even only a study of foreign language, has an immensely profound impact, extending far beyond communication as such. For a study of a foreign language involves a break of an original, "naive" model imposed by the mother tongue; it lends distance to one's own way of perception considered the only right approach to the reality. It helps to acquire a new perspective comprising different approaches to the world. It may serve, then, as kind of a linguistic condition of an extension of the sphere of cognition. In effect, the tendency to dogmatism, implied by the narrow, traditional approach, becomes less persistent, while democratization and tolerance—accompanying the processes of differentiation—tend to prevail. It might have been Goethe's message when he said, "Who knows no foreign language, cannot understand his own either."

O. Listening to what you said about the differentiation of languages, I thought about an analogy to the biological world; it is differentiated, too, isn't it? Without its differentiation it could not have evolved, or it would not have existed at all.

R. You may apply this analogy to humanity, but you must not forget about an essential difference between the genetically predetermined limitation of the biological species and an "openness" of the linguistic groups. There were, however, many cultures that did not survive; the differentiation of cultures, the existence of other cultures, made it possible for humanity as such to survive at all. I believe the multitude of linguistic groups is no accident nor any extravagance, but a necessary and creative differentiation. It is remarkable that in a tenth-century Syrian document, the tower of Babel is construed, contrary to popular interpretation, not as a punishment but as a necessity and humanity's last resort . . .

O. But it is commonly believed that if not for the tower of Babel and the confusion of tongues, the nations would have better and more easily understood each other.

R. There is a logical error in such a suggestion, I'm afraid. If there were no linguistic barriers, there would have probably been no nations. How could a nation exist without a linguistic discriminant?

O. Then, there would be very few nations in the world. There would not be so many of them in Asia or Africa, where numerous tribal linguistic groups have coexisted even though they've had no common language or culture.

R. In fact, it is likely to be the case. The populations of such countries are not to be spoken about as nations. But it is a very complicated problem, the whole range of the different nation-forming factors taken into account. Recently, the tendency has prevailed to consider a common statehood the major element of a concept of the nation. Small wonder, since history has proved that the state turned out to be an extremely strong nation-forming factor in many a country. In only a very few countries, like Poland or Georgia, has the notion of a nation coincided with the notion of a linguistic group. I believe it is the linguistic group that makes an elementary unit of the culturally differentiated humanity.

O. Do you mean language is an integrating factor for a group of people? Does language give the group an identity and a sense of distinction from other groups?

R. The point is somewhat different. One learns the language he or she hears as a child. But it is not only the child who "masters" the language; at the same time, the language "masters" the child who is learning it. It influences the cognitive processes of man and affects his consciousness. It is the same in a broader sense: language is not only a means to perceive the culture; it is also a factor contributing to the culture. Not only what we hear is important; what is silent in a language may be even more significant. Each of us, as a child, has learned to approach the world in our own mother tongues. Moreover, language is broader than logic itself. It is not only an intellectual act. The point is not that people who use the same mother tongue understand each other; because of the community of language, they feel identically, too. And this coincidence of perception, comprehension, and feeling determines the community—and simultaneously, the distinction—of a group using the same mother tongue.

O. What about the universal grammar considered by many modern theoreticians to be a fundamental basis of all languages? Doesn't it question the differences you've mentioned, or suggest the prospects of overcoming the linguistic barriers?

R. From a purely formal point of view, we may accept the existence of a universal grammar as a "deep structure" of all languages. It is revealed primarily in grammar and phonetics. But I am no expert in phonetics. Personally, I have no objection to phonetics as an important and useful branch of linguistics; however, I think there is more to linguistics than just phonetics.

A phonetician defines language as a system of physical signs used for the purpose of communication. It is true, but not adequate enough, for signs and communication also exist among animals. So this definition shows no distinction between humans and animals.

Once the borderline is clearly marked, an empiric acoustic act, which can be similar in humans and animals, will be seen in quite a different light. For animals, it will be a signal; for people, an element of a system of symbols. Phonetics, you see, doesn't distinguish between signal and symbol. Therefore, it cannot mark the borderline between man and animals. Moreover, formalized linguistics and semantic universalism, at their present stage of development, do not take into account that language is a means of categorization, selection, and cognition/perception of the world, and finally, that this perception of the world is different, depending on the language in which one has originally learned to understand the world. After all, whatever one means by the particular words one uses cannot be separated from linguistic or cultural denotations. You not only speak in Polish, you also think in Polish, and perceive the world and watch it in Polish, because this is how you learned to name things as a child.

O. And you did it in Georgian, didn't you, professor? Since now we are talking in Russian, aren't we both using a foreign language? How can this conversation be possible?

R. It is possible all right, although both you and I see it is not easy. Every now and again we have to clarify meanings of the terms we are using. But our conversation is carried on a "general cultural level," so to speak. It doesn't deal with perception of the world or with "feeling" it. We both know we are different from one another and we try to come to a mutual understanding. There is a general topic we both are familiar with, therefore we are able to understand one another. It would be far more difficult for us to reach a compromise in our everyday life, I'm afraid.

O. I think that the borderline between what's conditioned by the language and culture, and what you defined as general cultural level, is related to the way of life. In the more traditional agrarian cultures, it is the language that bears a greater significance, while in industrial—mobile and more universal—societies, characterized by advanced education, it is general cultural factors that play a greater role. Do you agree?

R. If I understand you correctly, your point is that intelligence is more universalistic. It may be, for education opens everywhere the same spheres of thought and experience. Moreover, the urbanized and industrialized systems are all alike, and social mobility draws people away from tradition. A simple farmer in a traditional society cannot even imagine that things may be called otherwise from what he was taught to call them. For him, there is an indivisible symbiosis between the things and phenomena and their denotations in his mother tongue. The words contribute to a harmony between the environment, man, and his life. He would not disturb this harmony even for an increased material wealth or decreased insecurity. He would not change his spiritual atmosphere so closely related to his mother tongue and his entire culture. In an urban environment, this harmony is, for many reasons, disturbed anyway. But here also, usually after a period of universalism, people tend to maintain their cultural and linguistic identity. As territory is a physical sphere of a nation, language is its spiritual sphere, said Wilhelm von Humboldt.

O. Which of the two spheres plays a more important part?

R. It is a complex question. There are nations that have survived even though they lost their territory and statehood. They survived because they've not given up their language. If they lost the language, they would have lost their heritage and cultural self-consciousness.

Territory unites people only in space, while language unites them also in time. An Austrian fin de siècle author, Hugo von Hofmannstahl, said, "When I open my mouth, thousands of the dead begin to speak." My language unites me with the dead and the ones to be born yet. Without language there would be no history, as is the case with animals. Language is not only the means of communication and expression of thought; it is a phenomenon of much greater significance, for it is to be traced as far back as the origins of historic cognition.

O. Why are the noncommunication functions of language ordinarily given so little consideration?

R. Because the communicative functions are most apparent and correspond to our common sense. It is so, moreover, because we are living in an overly pragmatic society. We want everything to be useful, even spiritual phenomena, like language. We seem to acknowledge only its practical purpose of communication, losing sight of its other functions. That way we are utilizing not only language but also man himself. We tend to turn everything into instruments, including ourselves. One can hardly miss a correlation between such an attitude and the problems of the spiritual life in the contemporary world. The instrumental approach to man is wrong, it should be opposed; so should the pragmatization of the spiritual—that is, nonpragmatic and not suitable to be used—spheres of human activity.

It must be emphasized that language did not emerge solely to help us satisfy some elementary biological or communicative purposes;

language is a creative power of culture; hence, it is a driving force of the nonmaterial progress of humanity and purely human values . . .

O. If a pragmatist asks you about the purpose of culture and all these nonmaterial values, what will you tell him?

R. That he is not too different from an animal.

7

On Human Values

For Ramishvili, there are the nonmaterial values that distinguish a human being from an animal. But what are these higher values? How can we find them? Who can change the dominant hierarchy of values? Should one impose his values on others?

These are the questions discussed by John Kenneth Galbraith and Nicolai Tchavtchavadze, who present complementary views on the dominant hierarchy of values and on the required changes in this hierarchy. Both agree that nonmaterial values should play a much greater role in human life and culture. An economist, Galbraith concentrates on the role of "educational and scientific estate" as an agent of value-change, while Tchavtchavadze, a philosopher, stresses the forgotten obligation of philosophy to shape human values.

Discussing the relationship between economics and civilization and culture, Galbraith argues that economists stress the need for continuous economic growth primarily to protect their own vested interests. This is the main reason for the failure of economics to understand new economic phenomena, like stagflation. Galbraith analyzes the role of the industrial corporation in controlling human beliefs and desires and shaping consumer values. Admitting the necessity for a drastic change in the dominant value system, Galbraith sees intellectuals as harbingers of change and comments on their social role.

Tchavtchavadze, in turn, hopes that philosophy can find values that might bring sense to human life. For it is a "philosophical attitude" that stresses the spiritual values more than material ones.

Tchavtchavadze speaks against the cult of science in contemporary societies. In its effort to find causes of every phenomenon and every act, science loses sight of the individual's responsibility, which acknowledges that an individual has a free choice of values. To answer that need, we should turn to a new, humanistic philosophy based on the recognition of human responsibility and on the respect for a unique personality of each individual.

13. John Kenneth Galbraith

John Kenneth Galbraith, born in 1908, is one of the outstanding American economists. During World War II he was the deputy administrator of the Office of Price Administration; after the war, he became professor of economics at Harvard University. From 1961 to 1963 he was U.S. ambassador to India, and in 1971 he was president of the American Economic Association.

J.K. Galbraith has written many books dealing with economics and social problems, including The Affluent Society *(1958),* The New Industrial State *(1967),* Economics, Peace, and Laughter *(1971),* Economics and the Public Purpose *(1973),* Money *(1975), and* The Nature of Mass Poverty *(1979). His writings also include a journal of his ambassadorship in India and, together with M.S. Randhana, a book on Indian painting. He is also the author of two novels:* The McLandress Dimension *(1964) and* The Triumph *(1968). In 1981 he published his memoirs,* A Life in Our Times, *and in 1983 his latest book,* The Anatomy of Power, *was published.*

John Kenneth Galbraith is a member of the American Academy of Arts and Sciences. In 1966 he became a member of the National Institute of Arts and Letters, and in 1982 was elected one of the fifty members of the American Academy of Arts and Letters.

Wiktor Osiatyński: An economic man and economic society are predominant ideals in the contemporary world. According to these ideals, the growth of individual affluence is a key to one's happiness, and the best way to solve social problems is the solution of economic problems. What do you think of the relation of economics to culture and civilization?

John Kenneth Galbraith: For a long time after World War II there were only two criteria of the economic success of a nation: the growth of income per capita and the distribution of the national product, the latter being stressed particularly strongly by the left. In the course of the last twenty-five years, a third criterion emerged. People asked how has the economic growth affected the quality and nature of human life? They now feel concerned that technological progress is accompanied by growing individual and social tensions, that life doesn't seem to be easier, that the growth of GNP results to a considerable extent from the nuclear arms race, and that the human effects of the arms race—and often economic growth in general—may have a really negative consequence.

In very recent times there has been a fourth concern. That is the recurrence of large-scale unemployment and extensive idle-plant capacity. This coincides, in turn, with the rise in the English-speaking countries of faith in monetarism, which works against inflation by producing unemployment. Perhaps one might add one further concern, and that is associated with the problem of large-scale organization. It is a common feature of both the Socialist and the so-called capitalist world that they are now struggling with the unsolved problems of massive organization.

O. Do you see any economic theory that could solve or, at least, comprehend all these problems?

G. The dominant tendency has been to avoid the role of the great modern corporation, and in some degree to think that there is some virtue in the economic policy of the nineteenth century. But we have seen that an effort to control the economy by controlling the money supply and allowing interest rates to grow to suffocating levels has produced the worst recession since the Great Depression.

O. But now, in late 1983, it seems to work.

G. I think it is quite possible that we will have a recovery. But if we have a recovery, it is because the administration is abandoning and will continue to abandon what has been called Reaganomics. It has already stopped the original efforts to control the money supply. It has already reduced interest rates. And it has initiated deficit financing on a scale that should be impressive to John Maynard Keynes, if he is somewhere watching.

So having abandoned Reaganomics, I would not be surprised that the economy would recover. I would only warn that with the recovery we will almost certainly have the recurrence of inflation.

O. Does it mean that inflation is still incomprehensible and unmanageable?

G. Until we have a willingness to have a much greater degree of planning, including an income policy, than has so far been the case. But I don't see such a willingness.

W. Do you imply a sense of misuse, or even abuse, of the science of economics?

G. Economics is misused by those who would like to solve all kinds of problems solely by the increase of the national product. And by those who would retreat into the past for solutions. As a criterion of economic efficiency they take the growth of production and the rate of employment as an absolute. And as a design for facilitating these they take the economic measures and the economic policies, or the absence thereof, that seemed to work in the nineteenth century. Almost irrationally they resist any other concerns. Additionally, they pursue their own group interest.

O. What is the group interest of the economists? Is it their ties with the existing system?

G. Not necessarily. Numerous economists simply want to maintain what has served them well in their textbooks and for their doctoral dissertations—what they have understood and taught. It's natural that people will defend interests connected with invested monetary capital; very few realize that one may defend one's intellectual investments even more strongly. After all, nobody wants to become intellectually obsolete. And more effort is needed to verify new views; the old truths are easier to guard. It is in this sense that I feel economic ideas are being misused.

O. Does such a misuse derive solely from the defense of the "intellectual investments" of economists? In your book *Economics and the Public Purpose* you claimed that economics maintained a set of obsolete images to protect the status quo.

G. I think these are two sides of the same coin. In more general and not necessarily pejorative terms, I believe that in every society there is a tendency to develop and maintain a set of beliefs that give validity, or legitimization, to the society, to justify its worthiness.

O. Why? Can you explain it or give an example?

G. It seems quite obvious that in a modern economic society it is the big corporation that enjoys major economic and also political power. However, neoclassical economics presents these corporations as helpless organizations, subordinate to market forces. The power remains in the hands of the state and the consumer; the corporations hold no power whatsoever. Such a conviction, taught as a basic assumption to hundreds of thousands of students each year, conceal the power of the corporations. If students were taught that the corporations have the power, they might get some inconvenient ideas. For instance, that this power should be limited, neutralized, or controlled. Therefore, I have no doubts that, perhaps even innocently and accidentally, neoclassical economics has become an instrument used to maintain the status quo. Teachers and professors keep repeating how important is a proper understanding of the society; in fact, however, there is much advantage in a wrong understanding of the society. I should say that the tendency to construe ideas to justify the existing reality is not peculiar to the capitalist society.

O. In each society there exists a variety of sources of power and authority. In your latest book, *The Anatomy of Power,* you distinguish between condign power, compensatory power, and conditioned power, which means control over the beliefs of people. The more cohesive these sources of power are, the more unquestionable, self-confident, and stable the power is. Considering this, how would you evaluate the power of corporations?

G. It extends over all the spheres you mentioned. Corporations, quite naturally, have compensatory power. They may have some degree of condign power deriving from their relations with the state. And they have great power over the opinions and beliefs of the people.

I do not want to suggest that economists intentionally repeat in their textbooks nonsense about the subordination of corporations to the market. It is an unintentional disguise of the reality.

O. Is economics the only source of corporate power over the people's beliefs?

G. Of course not. We discussed various functions of economics, and I pointed out that it plays a significant role in justifying the power of corporations. But the goals of corporations are also justified by the media as well as by the activities of the political parties and of the state.

O. Don't you think that there were some changes in the public perception of the corporation's role in recent years?

G. Two things have happened since we last met. One is certainly the acceptance of the enlarged social and political role of the corporation. And I would hope that I've made some contribution to that. Second, there has been some effect on the role of the corporation from the extreme economic difficulties associated with the revival of the competitive and monetarist doctrines under the Reagan administration.

Eight years ago I did not ever expect to see a recession as severe as the one in the early eighties induced by deliberate policy. It influenced, of course, the social image of the corporations and the quality of their performance.

O. But don't you think that the corporate world itself became more differentiated? I have a feeling that today some corporations are much more sensitive to social problems and more future oriented than before.

G. On this I would agree. The difference is between, on the one hand, corporations that are associated with the old mass-production industries, which involve simple repetitive processes and where the intelligence of management reflects the low level of demand placed upon it, and, on the other hand, highly technical enterprises—of which IBM is an example—where the problems of production force a much higher level of intelligence in management.

I would also add one other thing that was not much a part of my thinking when we first talked. That's the role of the bureaucratic dynamic in the corporation. By that I mean the tendency of the managerial structure of the corporation to expand by its own internal pressure and to become not only unwieldy in size but also to replicate itself. There is the tendency of all organizations to define intelligence in terms of whatever most resembles the people already there and wise policy as what is already being done. This is a problem that is also not unknown in the Socialist world.

O. Certainly; I can give you unlimited evidence for that, if you only need. But getting back to the conditioned power of corporations over the people's beliefs, cannot it be a result of the compatibility of the popular idea of happiness with the goals of the corporations? You wrote in *The New Industrial State* that people wanted the goods which were provided by the corporations; in this sense, a compatability exists, doesn't it?

G. I like an approach to economics that might be called a philosophy of the concrete. As long as we cannot see something, identify and measure it, we can only make suppositions and assumptions. Therefore, as far as people's desires and needs are concerned, I cannot say if they are autonomous or inherent. I am sure, however, that they are created and maintained by commercials, the system of education, and the whole set of social beliefs. These breed a competition for prestige measured by the quantity and quality of consumer goods. The competitive manifestation of the quality and affluence of consumption is a major social activity. The quality of a housewife is measured by her cooking and household management; the quality of a family by the nature of the house, garden, domestic pets, automobiles, and equipment. A major part of the social activity of people is in the competitive manifestation of the consumer's potential. Such an attitude is strongly supported: commercials appeal to social prestige —a "better" man is better dressed and he washes his shirts in a better detergent; a "better," more virile man is the one who smokes better cigarettes; and so on. Therefore, I would consider such a "consumption-for-prestige" attitude as conditioned ultimately by the production mechanism rather than as an inherent attribute of human nature.

O. Doesn't it apply to all industrial societies?

G. Not directly. However, in my travels, I've been surprised how many nations in the world do, or want to, imitate the United States's consumer standards. They want to catch up with us or even get ahead of the United States. They want to have the same number of cars, the same heavy traffic, the same problems we have here.

Some twenty-five years ago I had a seminar with an academic group in the Soviet Union. And one of the Soviet participants asked me, as one was often asked in those days, "Do you believe that we are going to catch up with you?" I said, looking down at the Moscow street, "Do you realize what your city will be like if you have as many automobiles per capita as has New York or Los Angeles? I am shocked that the goal of a planned economy should be to replicate the chaos of the unplanned economy." My Soviet friend was very much impressed by that but asked, "Then do you think, will we catch up with you in everything but automobiles?"

Well, I can only conclude that even in the Soviet Union this was an example of the way in which American values had been exported.

O. Are these values peculiarly American? Perhaps they are industrial values, in a more general and universal sense?

G. I don't deny that. I think there are industrial values. But I think we would make a great mistake not to emphasize our capacity to export our consumer values. It's a lesson in that matter to go to Japan.

O. Do you think Japan has accepted American consumer values?

G. I have no doubt.

O. Did it erase its traditional, nonconsumer values? I ask about it because I think that the level of consumption as the main, or the only, source of social prestige is a characteristic quality of American society. In other nations hierarchies of values and of prestige are not so one-dimensional.

G. You may be right there. I agree that in other countries individual prestige may depend on the level of consumption to a lesser degree than in the United States. There are differences here, too. As a result of the developments in the 1960s and early 1970s, the younger generation of Americans is less interested in amassing consumer products than their parents were, and there has been some drift away from the consumer ethics of earlier times. In the university community prestige and intellectual position count for more than affluence.

O. Do you mean that the cultural revolution of the 1960s left durable results in the realm of social values?

G. I have no doubt it did.

O. But the United States still remains the consumer society of the world. And stressing the peculiarity of your country I have in mind the amount of time spent by an average person to acquire and consume goods. In most countries of the world there are shortages of goods; people spend a great amount of time waiting, searching, and queueing for goods. In the United States there is an abundance of goods; shopping might take practically no time. Here, however, you have different prices in different places, or even at the same place at different times; people study advertisements, go to different shops, compare the prices, calculate. Doing so, they may use up their entire leisure time; they are constantly preoccupied with consumption, with the shopping, bargaining, prices, money . . .

G. In fact, making decisions on the distribution of one's income is a time-consuming occupation. Many years ago, when I lunched at the university faculty club, I used to spend five to ten minutes every day studying the menu. After a time, I decided to always order the same meal. I've been doing so ever since. I remember, while in the army, I didn't have to think what to put on in the morning. A uniform. People have come to simplify their lives, I think. Haven't you noticed, how uncomplicated are the typical outfits of young Americans today?

O. Yes, but I'm afraid it's just another fad that may also take much thought. Moreover, I wouldn't be too happy if everybody wore a uniform, would you? People need differentiation. Your examples are too personal to be applied more generally, I am afraid.

G. Of course, you are right. For if my ideas were to have a wider application, deeper social changes would be required. Particularly a change of the existing, consumption-oriented value system.

O. Who could introduce such changes? And how?

G. The same forces that would be able to resist the power which drives the whole mechanism of consumption.

O. What are these forces? From your books one can take an impression that the enlightened electorate could become such a force?

G. No doubt the introduction of any significant change is a very slow process, especially in the United States; primarily because so many people, perhaps the majority, live quite well within the existing system. Therefore I believe we should concentrate first on those areas about which the private corporations care less—on housing, health care, or public transportation.

O. You presented this idea twenty-five years ago in *The Affluent Society*. You proposed then many steps that could ease the tensions resulting from these and other social problems. Would you write such a book again today?

G. Winston Churchill once said, "I have often had to eat my words and on the whole I found them a wholesome diet."

I would certainly revise some of *The Affluent Society* if I was publishing it again, as I revised it in some subsequent editions. But not the basic idea. The basic idea of *The Affluent Society* is that there are values above and beyond increased production. A further idea is that one needs a balance between public consumption and private consumption. And a still further idea is that with affluence one leaves a certain part of the population in deep poverty, intolerable poverty, in fact. All of these ideas I would still put in a new edition, some of them with increased emphasis.

I developed in *The Affluent Society* what I call the theory of social balance. One must respect the relationship between public expenditure and private consumption. I would argue that New York City today is an indication of how serious it is to ignore the need for that balance. We currently are having a great discussion in the United States of our educational system. Again, an example of what we have ignored: the public-private balance. All of these things I would emphasize, and I would, of course, particularly emphasize the way in which the affluent society leaves behind the poor of the great cities.

O. And you would still have to face the problem of how to bring about a social balance, how to introduce required changes. In your book *The New Industrial State,* you recognize the intellectual community, which you call the educational and scientific estate, as a force that could act on behalf of social changes. In *Economics and the Public Purpose* such a force appears in the enlightened society, acting within the existing political system.

G. I find no contradiction here. I still believe that the potential force acting on behalf of change is, first of all, the intellectual community. Members of the university and scientific community are able to recognize the necessity for changes and undertake appropriate action both in a political and an educational sense. They have certainly a greater power than, say, the traditionally conservative American unions.

O. Do you think intellectuals have been critical and influential enough? That their actions were effective?

G. It was the academic and intellectual community that led us to withdraw U.S. forces from Vietnam and admit that the war had been a political mistake. And similarly, it is forcing the issue on arms control.

O. Don't you think that an equally significant reason for the withdrawal from Vietnam might have been the fact that the war ceased to be profitable for the U.S. power elite?

G. No, I do not accept the view that the U.S. establishment needed that war. Whenever the end of the war was mentioned, stock exchange prices soared, not dropped. I'd say that a greater part of the responsibility for the Vietnam War lay in error rather than in economic interest.

I think in general, that it is a mistake to ignore the role of error and ill-considered emotion in human affairs and through the entire human history.

O. Now I understand your idea of changes: to oppose stupidity with the wisdom of the intellectuals. But this time, too, history would be against you. The rule of philosophers has never succeeded yet . . .

G. You do exaggerate, don't you? Upon practical observation, I think that the major force that acts on behalf of a change in the system is the academic and larger intellectual community. Of course, I am aware of the difficulties in any significant social and political change. But that is realism, not resignation. I write treatises on economic matters partly because it is my duty as a scholar. But in my practical activities, I try to be a realist and achieve what is possible.

O. Since you mentioned practical activities, I'd like to ask you what kind of activity gives you the greatest satisfaction?

G. I take pleasure from many kinds of activity. All my life I've been known as a hard-working person. People have felt sorry for me—I work so hard. I've spent time on public affairs, making speeches, helping political candidates, writing books. Some have wondered why I've been working so hard.

The answer is simple. I was born and raised on a farm in Canada. There, we really worked hard. We got our bread, as it is said, by the sweat of our brows. All I've been doing ever since has seemed quite easy to me.

14. Nicolai Tchavtchavadze

Nikolai Zuravovich Tchavtchavadze, born in 1923, graduated from the Department of Philosophy of the University of Tbilisi in 1949. He has since worked at the Institute of Philosophy of the Academy of Sciences of the Soviet Republic of Georgia. Presently, he is the director of the Institute of Philosophy.

Dr. Tchavtchavadze's main topics of interest include aesthetics, the theory of values, the philosophy of culture, and the philosophy of man.

He is the author of many books, most notably On Some Peculiarities of the Reality Reflected in Arts *(1954),* Problems of Aesthetics *(1958),* On the Nature of Aesthetics *(1964), and* Philosophy and Culture *(1980).*

Nicolai Tchavtchavadze is a member of the Academy of Sciences of the Soviet Republic of Georgia.

Wiktor Osiatyński: A recent prevailing feeling is that modern philosophy is too detached from life, that it doesn't address the most important problems of society or the individual, and that sophisticated philosophical speculations are of no interest to anyone except a handful of professionals. What, in your opinion, is the actual role of philosophy in contemporary society?

Nikolai Tchavtchavadze: Let's begin with what it should be. I believe that philosophy ought to be a guidepost, both in the individual life and in the entire culture. It ought to be a spiritual and intellectual activity that would help to answer the questions of life, such as: What are we living for? What should we live for? What is the meaning of life?

O. Do you know the meaning of life?

T. Man, I think, lives to find some higher values.

O. What values?

T. Nobody, including myself, will answer your question. For someone it may be virtue; for someone else, justice; for still another person, truth or beauty. The point is that philosophy ought to look for the values which can make the life of man meaningful. By fulfilling this task, philosophy would serve as the basis for human activity, a guiding force in individual and social life.

O. How could philosophy play the guiding role if, as you contend, there is no universal meaning of life and no universal hierarchy of values?

T. Good question. Now, you may find my answer paradoxical, but I think that the essence of life is the quest for the essence of life. Philosophy knows no single, universal answer to a question about the meaning of life. Each man has to look for it by himself.

O. Do you mean we all should be philosophers?

T. Yes, although not in the professional sense of the term. Philosophy ought to encourage people to become philosophers; to develop a serious approach to life; to contemplate the priorities of their values and to look for values of the highest standing.

There is hardly anyone who hasn't asked himself, at least once, what he lives for, and for what values. And it is philosophy that should remind people of such questions and help them not to live unconsciously or instinctively. Philosophy should exhort people to remember that these most vital questions should not be evaded. This is my view of the role of philosophy in the contemporary world.

O. You told me what philosophy ought to be. Now, can you tell me what it is?

T. It is not always what it should be, for many reasons. Our philosophy was once used primarily to justify questionable politics or mediocre propaganda. It was often done by philosophers themselves, forgetting the higher, humanistic purpose of philosophy. Moreover, we don't always act and behave as philosophers should.

O. What does that mean: to act as philosophers should?

T. It means, first of all, to seek spiritual values rather than material ones. This is, I believe, of the utmost significance today. For I know that once material things have the most important value in someone's life, that person becomes as much of a thing as his own possessions.

O. You say spiritual values are more important than the material ones. That is easy for someone like you to say, because you do not suffer from poverty and you have developed, through education and tradition, interests in the nonmaterialistic realm of values. Do the people who have until very recently been poor, hungry, and uneducated share your views? Isn't their vision of a "better world" closer to the ability to accumulate material possessions that were once completely out of their reach? Don't they dream now of the estates and riches that might bring them affluence and power? And how can one achieve harmony between the two kinds of values—material and spiritual?

T. I find the principles of Marxist philosophy useful here. They state that nobody should suffer from poverty or hunger, and that all people should have the same opportunity to live by and for spiritual values. These principles also state that material possessions should be relatively easy to obtain and, therefore, will lose their priority.

O. Can we so fulfill our material needs that they will not be important? Today everybody wants a car, while once much less was enough to make people happy. Someday we may want our personal rocket to the moon. Can you really say that at a certain point there will emerge conditions satisfactory enough to put materials needs aside and develop spiritual values?

T. Each of us must ask, What do I need this rocket—or car, for that matter—for? It may not be indispensable. One may only want it to reach a higher social status, to be "better" than one's neighbor. If so, it is wrong. To answer this question, each of us must apply this ethical criteria.

O. But to use such criteria, one should have a clearly and precisely defined hierarchy of values. And that doesn't happen easily or frequently.

T. I think that a person, under any circumstances, can easily tell ethical actions from unethical ones. If I place myself, my own interests, above everything else, it is unethical. But if I acknowledge the existence of something else—say, other people or even some abstract value—that is more valuable than myself and my ego, then I behave ethically.

O. Do you think this attitude, placing other people or abstract values above oneself, is popular in contemporary society?

T. No.

O. Why?

T. Because it is more difficult to live with this attitude. One has to think more about both oneself and others and make difficult choices. Moreover, we all respond to the influence of a great variety of motives: instincts, habits, personal interests, advantages. It is hard, therefore, to determine what motives are decisive. The line between higher motives and egotism is often fluid or blurred. And everyone likes undisturbed sleep, so they explain and rationalize things to find justification for self-serving behavior—for example, one may tell himself that he did an unethical thing to make other people happy.

O. Then, shouldn't philosophy attempt to show people the real motives behind their actions? Or, at least, encourage them to think about these motives?

T. Certainly; philosophy should also examine the reasons people act in ways they shouldn't. One of these reasons, I believe, is the fact that we live in an age of science, that science has become today's main spiritual force.

O. How can science be morally harmful? We believe that the growth of science is a driving force of progress, don't we?

T. We understand progress very one-sidedly, primarily as a growth of material well-being. As I said, philosophy should offer us guidance in life. Therefore, certain fundamental questions must be answered. What is it man needs? What is the essence of man? Let us look at what today's science, both natural science and social theories, says about man. I'm afraid that, in all sciences, man is just one among many things in the universe; he may be more complex, but principally, man is considered just a thing like all others.

O. Do you mean that for science, man is just a subject for observation and exploration?

T. Not only that. I am talking about the consequences of this fact. Since science usually considers man a subject whose behavior may be fully explained by external reasons, man himself may also explain everything in terms of such reason; he may blame these reasons for whatever he does.

O. But the essence of science lies in the search for causal relations. So it is only natural that science approaches man as it does.

T. I am not against science as such. I am against its domination, against an idolatrous attitude toward science and the methods it applies. I think that, for the reasons I've just mentioned, science should be only a tool; it should be subordinated to philosophical reflection. The philosophical approach to man, in contradistinction to the purely scientific one, should be that each individual is to be seen as a unique person able to make a free choice. That's why man is responsible for his deeds.

O. So your point is that science, concentrating on the external motives of human activity, may absolve man from a sense of responsibility for his actions.

T. Exactly. I also mean that, for the same reason, science gives man a faulty image of himself. It excludes contradictions, doubts, feelings, and conscience. I may read an erudite psychological treatise telling me many interesting things, but I can't find a man in it. Then I read *The Brothers Karamazov* and find a very lively and complete man there. Art has found a better path to present man than science, including psychology and philosophy. To an artist, man is obviously not simply another arrangement of molecules.

O. I've read in an article by the director of the Cybernetics Institute in Tashkent about a universal machine that could play chess, checkers, and poker. "When it plays a game, it is driven not only by calculation, but also by emotions. We fed into it a program containing such feelings as greediness, prudence, ambition. What is a feeling? It is no more than a particular state, resulting from an action or information relayed to the brain. And we merely built a model of such states."

T. Now, you see, what science is like: full of haughtiness and condescension, degrading man. The ideas you quoted are not only incredible; they are false and dangerous, too. How can feelings, human feelings, be preprogrammed if man himself cannot always identify them clearly enough?

Of course, each man is conditioned—socially, psychologically, and genetically. But he is also an active and free subject. What we need is a philosophy that will see man as a complex unity of conditional behavior and free choice.

O. How can we find such a philosophical route to man?

T. We should consider man as a subject. As does the artist.

O. What, then, is philosophy—a science or art?

T. I hold the current opinion that philosophy is the self-consciousness of culture, an inner theory of culture, as it were. Philosophy comprises reflection on nature, man, society, history. But what's most important in philosophy is, in my opinion, that it serves as a landmark or a guidepost to help us find our way in life more easily.

O. Philosophy, you say—answering the questions on what man is, should, or could be—ought to play a guiding role in society. Let's assume that, as a philosopher, I have found—or I believe I have—the answers to these questions, that I have conjured up a vision of the world in which everybody might—again, in my opinion—be happy. Moreover, my vision doesn't contradict the findings of other sciences, so it is possible. But it happens, strangely enough, that people don't want to live according to my vision and don't want to pursue it. It was you, professor, who said that there was no universal hierarchy of values and each man can have his own vision of happiness. Can I impose my own vision on other people?

T. No, you cannot. People must accept it of their own free will.

O. Do you know such a hierarchy of values that could be universally accepted? Is it to be found at all?

T. I don't have a clear answer to your question. I am looking for it myself, as does each man individually. I find one of Marx's thoughts remarkably valuable—that there are, so to speak, two histories: a history of man's actions and a history of man's evolution, the latter being a process of continual pursuit of the most important values. I think we can distinguish the most fundamental criteria of this pursuit: one of them is that man cannot force another man to do anything. Dostoevski came up with an interesting idea; he was an outstanding writer, but he opposed socialism. He criticized Socialists because they wanted to define how people should be happy whether the people agreed or not. And each man wants to have freedom of choice between being good or bad.

O. Thus we come back to the problem of responsibility. If I am made to be good, then I am neither good nor bad. I am responsible for nothing. I am only a preprogrammed machine. I can be held responsible for my actions only if I am let free to make my choice between good and evil.

T. Right; however, having been given the freedom of choice, you should also be offered such opportunities and education that—with your free will to make a choice—you'd always choose the good.

O. Do you think the modern system of education enhances the freedom of choice?

T. No.

O. Why?

T. Because in today's schools, despite formal rhetoric, there is hardly any true education, just teaching—dealing in facts, data, practical skills. Moreover, art is considered insignificant in schools, although it is art that, by its very nature, drives man toward human values. I would like today's schools to teach not only what the world looks like and how to change it in order to get more things, but also how to experience and appreciate the universe.

But our era is the era of technology. We are changing, producing, constructing; we are in a hurry, although we hardly know why or for what.

O. But supposedly, people do really want to change, construct, and progress, and not ask the abstract question: What is it all for?

T. That is exactly why they are so unhappy. Somehow it is hard for me to believe that people want to be unhappy.

O. Why then do people almost everywhere want more material goods and affluence, even at the expense of other values? Do they all believe in illusion? Or is it just an easier way of life?

T. The point seems to be elsewhere. I think the problem is lack of satisfaction in the spiritual sphere. Religion has become somewhat obsolete, especially in the highly developed nations. It doesn't play its former, traditional role. Having nothing to replace religion, man finds it difficult to live. He feels unhappy because his spiritual needs remain unsatisfied. My idea is that it is philosophy that should now take over the role religion used to play.

O. What position do these spiritual and ethical values occupy in the hierarchy of values of contemporary man? Do you share the view that—as a result of social change, industrialization, the breakdown of the former structures, the emergence of new opportunities, growing affluence, and other factors—ethical and spiritual values are further diminished?

T. Rather not. Let us take an example. There was an economic boom in Georgia right after World War II and people grew rich. There were many ways to acquire wealth, including illegal and unethical ones. Some of my friends engaged in unethical activities. It is interesting, what they used to say: they sacrificed themselves, in an ethical sense, so their children could live an honest but opulent life.

O. Wasn't it the kind of rationalization you've already mentioned?

T. I don't think so. Those people were mostly reasoning as follows: I may be a speculator, a thief, or a scoundrel, but I do what I do so that my children won't be like me.

O. They clearly confused the ends and means. Do you find the ends more important than the means?

T. Absolutely not. The means are equally as important as the ends. What's important is not only the task of creating a better world for the future, but the way in which it is done is of equal significance because its future form—and future man, too—depends on the ways and means applied today. Future man is not going to fall down out of a clear blue sky. He will be as we create him, he will be like ourselves. If we do unethical things, even in the name of a higher purpose, future man will be unethical, too.

O. As new man takes shape, he will be, by all evidence, a "consumer" man. Will he also be ethical? Will he be sensitive to nonmaterial values, the ones you mentioned at the beginning of our conversation?

T. I hope he may be ethical and sensitive.

O. What can help him be like that?

T. How about giving him a good example?

O. Who?

T. Those who are ethical and sensitive. Perhaps the philosophers, and other enlightened and sensitive people.

O. But such people usually keep to themselves while the example is set on top, by the prominent people.

T. In the short term that may be true, but it is not so obvious. You see, in the entire history of humanity, there has always existed a relatively small group of people who adhered to spiritual and ethical values. Those people were rarely successful: they suffered a lot. But we owe to them the preservation of our spiritual values.

O. Did they show other people the way? Did they serve, so to speak, as the conscience of society?

T. Right. It was always so. And I hope their influence will be even stronger now.

O. Because you are an optimist?

T. No; it has to do with one of your questions. The one about the poor and hungry people and their natural needs. Well, from every indication, hunger and poverty will gradually disappear from our planet. Science and technology will help to save humanity from hunger and danger. New, better living conditions will be created so that man can turn his attention to other, higher values.

O. So it is science and technology, after all, that are to save the world and humanity?

T. Science and technology alone will not save us. However, they may be helpful if they are subordinate to the higher, more important values. As I said, science and technology are only the tools. The point is to use them to promote ethical values, such as virtue, the common good, freedom, and justice. And this is the most important task for all of us.

PART THREE

ON THE FUTURE OF SCIENCE

8

On History and the Future

Galbraith and Tchavtchavadze postulate a drastic change in values. Is such a change possible? What will our civilization look like in the future? These questions are addressed by Alvin Toffler and Lev Gumilov. Toffler discusses history and the future in general terms, while Gumilov presents his own, highly controversial theory of the historical process and outlines his vision of the probable past.

Alvin Toffler, whose name is commonly associated with change, comments on constants and continuity in human social organization. He admits that continuity and discontinuity both operate and, therefore, we need a balanced temporal view that will enable us to look both backward and forward and to relate what we find in the past and what we expect in the future to the present. Perceiving differences between history and future studies, Toffler claims these differences are not as dramatic as we usually assume. Both history and future studies are structures of inference, and as we have many visions of possible and probable futures, we may have many visions of a possible past. Toffler stresses that there are no universal values and that human nature is constantly changing. Presenting his own vision of the future Third Wave society, Toffler explains his reasons why this vision is both possible and probable.

Gumilov exemplifies Toffler's concept of many possible and probable pasts. His theory of ethnogenesis can be, in fact, perceived as a "past fiction" of a sort. The crucial concept of Gumilov's theory is an ethnos, meaning a group of people, usually of the same ethnic origins, who are bound together by the judgment of other people and by their own self-identity. For Gumilov an ethnos is the elementary social group, and all history is a cycle of sudden expansions and slow disappearances of ethnoses.

15. Alvin Toffler

Alvin Toffler was born in 1928. After graduating from New York University in 1949, he worked in various capacities as a blue-collar laborer. From 1952 on, he wrote articles for numerous journals, magazines, and periodicals, and from 1959 to 1961 he served as associate editor of Fortune *magazine. His 1964 work,* The Culture Consumers: A Study of Art and Affluence in America, *established Toffler as an independent social critic.*

His particular interest in future studies led to Future Shock *(1970), which sold more than ten million copies in some thirty languages. Equally successful were Toffler's subsequent books:* The Eco-Spasm Report *(1975),* The Third Wave *(1980), and* Previews & Premises *(1983) in which he elaborated a vision of a new, highly technological but not industrial, civilization.*

Alvin Toffler was a visiting professor at Cornell University, a member of the faculty at the New School for Social Research, and a visiting scholar at the Russell Sage Foundation. His books are required readings in universities from the United States and Japan to Brazil, Zaire, and Poland.

Toffler holds five honorary doctorates in science, letters, and law. He has addressed numerous parliamentary and governmental bodies and lectured before scores of scholarly institutions and major corporations all over the world. He is also a member of the International Institute for Strategic Studies.

Alvin Toffler's books have won many awards, including the Prix de Meilleur Livre Etranger in France and the McKinsey Foundation Book Award. In 1983, Toffler was named Author of the Year by the American Society of Journalists and Authors for having "significantly influenced our attitudes and concepts of ourselves as an American society."

Wiktor Osiatyński: You are associated with change. In *Future Shock* you dealt with the acceleration of change in our time. In *The Third Wave* you compare today's world to an ocean, on the surface of which three great waves of change collide: you use the First Wave as a metaphor for agrarian civilization; the Second Wave represents industrialism; and the Third Wave, the new society toward which all the changes you deal with lead. You stress the differences among these forms of social organization, rather than continuity. Do you perceive anything that is unchangeable? What are the constants in human history and society?

Alvin Toffler: I don't believe anything is constant in human social organization. There are only structures and processes of long duration and other structures and processes that endure briefly. But all social structures and all social processes have a life span.

Therefore, when we say something is permanent or continuous, we are usually not talking about something truly eternal or unchanging; we are really talking about relative durations—the relationship between the duration of one phenomena and another. This is the background against which I may ask myself what is "continuous" in human social organization and what is not.

French historian Fernand Braudel begins his great history of the Mediterranean region with geology, with the fact that there is a strip of desert that runs all the way from North Africa across to India and China. This is the geological setting and it changes very slowly. He speaks, in fact, of three different temporal scales or rates of change. One is geological time, another is social time, and the other is individual time. This analysis is extremely powerful and valuable, but it is subject to the same charge that could be made against my own use of the metaphor of three waves of historical change. By dividing time into three categories, he distinguishes three perspectives through which he observes history. And one could, of course, say that we should look at the history from other points of view and that there are intermediate durations. An infinite number of different periods or intervals or durations are distinguishable, and therefore there are many possible temporal perspectives.

Now, the same thing can be said of the waves of change. And it bears on the question of continuity. If you look at my statement about three waves of historical changes in society, it is clearly a grand oversimplification, because one can distinguish many more changes in history and divide it into many, much smaller pieces. If you divide it into very small pieces, you tend to emphasize continuity and incrementalism. If you divide it into a relatively few pieces, you emphasize discontinuity.

O. Not necessarily. A minimal change in a very small piece can be as important as a dramatic change in a big part.

T. That's true, of course, but incrementalism usually denies drama and discontinuity. However, the very question whether history is continuous or discontinuous in a philosophical sense is one of a category of questions that I put into a special file in my head, and that file says: wrong questions!

O. Do you mean that there is no such phenomenon as the opposition of continuity and discontinuity?

T. When I hear a question that has been repeated for ten thousand years and not solved, my hypothetical assumption is that there is something wrong with the way the question is framed.

O. Perhaps it is one of the constant features of the human condition that we have to ask questions which we cannot answer? We ask, for example, what was there before the beginning of the universe, and where does infinite space end, and what is outside that end?

T. Let me put it this way: I am not suggesting that, because we ask the same question again and again, the underlying phenomenon is insignificant. There may very well be an underlying reality that we don't understand and which needs to be further explored. But there are many different ways of attacking a piece of unknown territory. To divide questions into a dualistic form—for example, continuity versus discontinuity—can be very powerful for certain classes of questions, but useless and obscurantist for other kinds of questions. Rather than an either/or solution to this problem, I would say that continuity and discontinuity both operate, and that what we choose to call continuity and discontinuity is relative to our position and our definitions.

O. You mean that an answer to the question of continuity and discontinuity in history depends on our models. Why, then, have you been so consistently emphasizing, even dramatizing, the discontinuities in contemporary life?

T. Primarily because all traditional culture was stressing continuity. Had I grown up in a culture that placed its emphasis on discontinuity, I would probably have stressed continuity.

O. But you grew up in the United States, and it has a culture that, as compared to all other cultures, stresses discontinuity!

T. Perhaps as compared with other cultures. But even in this culture there is an enormous emphasis on continuity. Its presence is strong in our Judeo-Christian religions; it is strong in the emphasis we place on precedent in law; it is equally strong in the American assumption that the ideas of freedom and democracy are instinctive and eternal in man. While Marxist historians tend to divide the world into the periods of revolutions, followed by periods of quantitative change, followed once more by periods of qualitative change, Western, non-Marxist historians tend to work in precisely the opposite way, emphasizing the continuity of underlying social and cultural patterns.

So despite growing up in American society, I found myself in a culture that in my judgment still heavily emphasized continuity as against the discontinuities of social and historical experience. I set out to challenge that.

O. Because it's wrong?

T. Not because it's wrong, but because it's one-sided and limits our abilities to think.

As a result of this emphasis on continuity with the past, we had little in the way of futurism. When I began to write very little effort was being made by serious people to examine the possibilities or the probabilities of the future, except in the form of science fiction. And what little futurist analysis there was tended to rely on straight-line trend extrapolation, which was, after all, based on the assumption of continuity.

In many academic quarters, even today, futurism is regarded as a crystal ball, pseudodiscipline. So I took the opposite position.

My work starts from what I've called a revolutionary premise: the idea that today's changes cannot be understood as mere straight-line extensions of the forces that have driven industrial society until now. I see what is happening today as a kind of mutation or transformation. Of course, today's changes are rooted in the past and can be analyzed that way, but if we merely point out the continuities, we may miss or conceal the special character of our period.

When I wrote *Future Shock* my impulse to fight against the predominant "continuist ideology" was very strong. I wanted to clear space in culture for systematic thought about the future. I was less sympathetic to history and to the uses of history then, perhaps, than I would be today.

O. My impression is that, at least now, you are quite sympathetic to history. In fact, in my opinion, the first ten chapters of *The Third Wave* provide one of the best historical analyses of industrial society ever written. Moreover, you place your description of today's transition to a new society, and your vision of that new society, in a broad historical perspective. So, in my judgment, you are by no means anti-historical.

T. In my own development I have come to believe that we need a more balanced temporal view, that I should attack not merely nostalgia and past orientation, but also, in a more general sense, every form of temporal provincialism. I think that we, as individuals and as cultures, need temporal perspective, the ability to look forward and backward, and to relate what we find to the present. The failure to look both backward and forward and today's obsession with the present is a dangerous cultural trend.

O. I would even say that we can hardly think about the future without an interest in history, without knowing where we come from. I wonder, however, if we are able to think about the future in the same way as we deal with the past?

T. There is an obvious difference between history and future studies. Historians have worked very hard, especially in this century, to move beyond sheer speculation and to apply more empirical methods to historical studies. As a result, an enormous amount of historical evidence has begun to pile up. We have papers, we have books, we have archaeological findings, we have carbon datings, we have facts—both physical and cultural—from the past, which help us fill in some of the blanks.

From the future we have nothing. We have no bones. We have no books. We have no great writers whose work from the future comes down to us today. We have no memoirs from the future. Therefore, we work with an absence of what would be scientifically regarded as empirical data.

But is this difference between history and future studies as deep as it looks? I would point out that history is itself a structure of inference. That the central questions in history are not so much given by the data as by the models historians apply.

O. Do you mean that what I am looking for determines what I find in the past?

T. Obviously, and in large measure. However, we don't need to take this argument all the way. I don't mean to imply that all historians are so unconscious of what they do that they are unaware of their own biases. But it is impossible to strip history of cultural bias, of the bias of the present, of the bias of the individual. And, as a consequence, we always model the past in certain ways, whether we wish to or not. Braudel models it one way. Lewis Namier another way. Arnold Toynbee still another way.

These models are powerful tools. They determine the inferences that are made from the raw data. And I would argue that what we do with respect to the future also depends on our creating a structure of inferences. Every culture, every individual, in fact, constructs an architecture of assumptions about the future, and that heavily influences our convictions about what is likely to happen. We then select historical data and data about the present period and feed it through our models to create a set of coherent statements about tomorrow.

O. About what is likely to happen or, rather, about what should happen tomorrow?

T. Well, any structure of assumptions about the future can be divided into various forms. There are assumptions about the most probable future—what you believe is going to happen. That's what most people who call themselves forecasters work with. But anybody who thinks imaginatively recognizes that more futures are possible than are probable. We select the future from a wide array of options. (Here I fall back, and most people who have thought much about the future in recent years also fall back, on French economist Bertrand de Jouvenal's concept of the array of futures: multiple possible futures among which some are highly probable and others less probable.) But one can go beyond this. I would divide our architecture of assumptions about the future into those that are possible, a smaller number that are probable, and a still smaller number that are preferable.

O. Cannot this distinction apply to the past as well? If history is a structure of inferences, can't we have an array of possible pasts of which some were more probable and some less probable?

T. Precisely; in fact, we have many versions of the past, and we can make post-dictions—the reverse of pre-dictions. If certain historical data are accepted as correct, then our models should identify gaps in our record. Subsequent research may or may not locate the missing data.

Your question has to do with parallels between a historian and a futurist. It is true we cannot know the future. But I also believe that we cannot know the past. We can only make hypotheses supported by varying amounts of verifiable evidence. In the case of the future, we can only verify our accounts later, when the world they describe becomes history. Indeed, our assumptions about the future are themselves a part of our historical records. Fred Polak has written a classic work *The Image of the Future*, about the views of the future held by various cultures throughout history.

O. Understanding what you are saying about history and the future, I am still looking for some constants in human history. You said that all processes and all structures are transient, but these processes and structures are usually the means to satisfy our needs and values. Are basic needs and values as transient as technologies and organizations or, perhaps, are at least some of them constant?

T. First, as to being basic: the argument can be made that values themselves are the products or effects of technology and social institutions, rather than the causes. My own view is that they are neither causes nor effects, but that there is a continuing, complex feedback relationship between the two. Our values shape our technologies, which shape our values, and so on.

As to whether values are permanent or transient, that primarily depends on one's definition of values. If we apply a very general definition of values, at a very high level of abstraction, we see values as less transient, or even permanent. When we apply a more concrete definition of values, we may see them in a constant change. For example, in *Values and the Future,* Kurt Baier and Nicholas Rescher, two philosophers at the University of Pittsburgh, defined values in a way that made them highly sensitive to change.

O. But, in any case, don't you think values change more slowly than, say, technology? That there is much stronger resistance to change in the realm of values and ideas?

T. Surely, because human beings resist changing concepts. We know about what the psychologist Festinger called cognitive dissonance and how the mind rejects ideas that are dissonant with the existing cognitive structures in the mind. So you can say that people's values change more slowly. But often it merely involves a semantic shift. People change their behavior while insisting it is to implement unchanged values. The Soviets often behave in a quite un-Marxist manner, while insisting they do so to serve the cause of Marxism. If we want to know whether values are changing, we need to look at the behavior, not the ideological rationalizations for it. When we focus on behavior, we see a lot more value-change than if we just listen to the words.

We also know of extreme circumstances of crisis, of death, of torture, of trauma, which sometimes result in very rapid religious or ideological conversion—instantaneous changes in the conceptual structure of the individual. So I would argue that values, in both the behavioral and cognitive sense, can change very rapidly.

O. How about human needs? Perhaps there exist some needs that do not change throughout history?

T. Obviously there are certain enduring human requirements. We all must take in oxygen from the environment. We all need so many proteins, so many calories. In turn, these needs are expressed in certain routine behaviors. But even these biological prerequisites are fulfilled or expressed in a thousand different cultural ways.

The question that we are revolving around is more popularly put in terms of human nature. Does human nature change? I think human nature does change, and the very notion has different meanings from culture to culture and from period to period. I remember, during the Vietnam War, going to see a production of *The Trojan Women*. They were weeping for the sons they had lost in the Trojan war. The play implied that the mothers of the sons lost in Vietnam must be experiencing the same thing as the mothers of those ancient Greek sons.

O. Which was not true?

T. Which, in my opinion, was decidedly false. What is common to the so-called universal experience that comes down to us through such a play? It is probably true that within the bodies of those Greek mothers and within the bodies of the Vietnam victims' mothers similar chemical and biological responses associated with high emotion may have occurred. But everything else was different. All the cultural associations, the entire meaning of the experience, were different. So is it correct to impute an identity of experience? Can we separate human nature from the culture that surrounds it? Only by reducing it to biology—and not even at that level.

Another example comes to mind in relation to the tragedy of the people who were aboard the South Korean plane struck down by a Soviet missile. There were citizens of thirteen countries aboard the plane. All were killed. For the relatives of the victims, however, the meaning of this tragedy was not at all the same. One of the highest values in Eastern tradition and religion is the integrity of the body of a dead person. Therefore, for the Koreans who were deprived of the bodies of their beloved, the whole experience was traumatic to a point that we, here, in the West, can hardly understand.

Therefore, I would be very cautious in identifying similarities between different contemporary cultures, and still more so between cultures of the past and present.

Anthropology has brought a heightened recognition of the profound differences among cultures that coexist on the planet at the same time. We have yet to learn the importance of differences between cultures in different periods of time. We assume that human reactions remain the same across time, when, in fact, I believe they do not.

So answering the question about human nature, I think the idea that human nature is continuous and permanent is either a mistake or is based on so high a level of abstraction as to make it a meaningless statement.

O. You distinguished between possible, probable, and preferable futures. How does this distinction apply to your own work? In your last two books you elaborated on a vision of the future Third Wave society. In it, all our industrial—that is, Second Wave—institutions, structures, and concepts have become obsolete and undergo transformation. Moreover, Third Wave society holds out hope for more freedom, democracy, and opportunity for individual fulfillment than exist now or ever before.

Is this vision possible, probable, and preferable?

T. The society I've described in *The Third Wave* is possible. It doesn't violate known science and doesn't violate anything that we know about the complexities of human experience. Nor does it ever require people to be angels in order to create this kind of a society. It accepts complexity, it accepts diversity, it accepts crime, schism, and a whole range of other characteristics of all societies. So that the picture of the Third Wave presented is not an impossible or utopian society. It is clearly a possible future.

I would also argue en passant that, because the model on which it is based is, in fact, a powerful tool for analyzing and understanding social change, the image of the Third Wave is rather more complex than many other visions. It is not a utopia and it is not simple.

I also believe it is probable. Indeed, *The Third Wave* is not speculative fiction. It is based on considerable, documented research, and many of the ideas in it have already come true. We are moving rapidly in the direction outlined in it, and, right now, it is a probable future in many countries. Of course, its probability can change. It changes every day, from moment to moment.

The answer to the third question—is it preferable?—depends on who we are and from what position we are looking at the future. Is it preferable to powerful vested interests with a great stake in preserving the existing industrial institutions in their present form? No, it is not preferable. But, on the other hand, to many people, who are, in one way or another, harmed by the existing social system, who feel alienated, who cannot find enough satisfaction within the existing system, for all these, I believe, the Third Wave is preferable.

O. I have a feeling that many people who are quite well off in the existing Second Wave system would also welcome the Third Wave society as a preferable future.

T. I didn't mean to limit the Third Wave to only those who are alienated in an economic and social sense. There are many people who occupy positions of importance today who welcome Third Wave changes. There is a growing number of people—people working in biology, in computers, in genetics—who have a great vested interest in the spread of the Third Wave system.

If you take the people who are discontent with the Second Wave, or left out of the Second Wave society, and you add to them the growing number who have new opportunities to develop psychologically or increase their economic and political power in the Third Wave sector, you have a powerful coalition for attacking and, I think, successfully overthrowing, the Second Wave structures.

Add to this another key fact: the unsustainability of the Second Wave system. If we look at the fundamental limitations of the traditional industrial system, we see that it cannot continue to grow at the rate and in the direction it has been growing until now.

O. Is this so because of shrinking resources and a growing ecological imbalance?

T. The limitations on industrial civilization are partly a result of changes in the population and resources of our planet. Partly they are a result of a radically changed geopolitical situation in which the rest of the nonindustrial world is no longer content to be the petroleum pump and garden for the industrial world, but has a strong economic interest of its own, and, in many cases, sufficient military power to, at least, attract the attention of the great powers.

I think, however, that the traditional industrial system, what I have called Second Wave society, cannot continue primarily because of its own internal dynamics. It has within itself the seeds of self-destruction because the entire system of mass production and mass distribution, which is a dominant characteristic of Second Wave, industrial society, was based on a single economic assumption: that it is cheaper to mass produce goods than to produce customized goods. Mass production, which is almost the defining feature of industrial society, is rapidly becoming an outmoded form of production, as I first suggested in *Future Shock* and spelled out further in *The Third Wave*.

This has tremendous social, cultural, and political implications. It is part of the entire society's shift away from its traditional industrial base and the emergence of a more differentiated societal structure. We are moving from an industrial mass society, a Second Wave society, to a highly technological, de-massified Third Wave society.

O. Do you mean that technology itself has outgrown industrialism?

T. Most people unfortunately misunderstand this because they confuse industrialism with technology. The assumption is made that a technological society is an industrial society. In my work, I have always argued the necessity for a clear distinction to be made between an industrial society and a technological society. We can regard industrial society as, perhaps, the first technological society, but it is not the only technological society. We are now moving into a new kind of technological society, a society that is highly technological but not industrial. Its social, economic, cultural, and political characteristics are, if anything, anti-industrial. Its science and technology transcend industrialism.

O. Are you, then, a technological optimist? Many critics of industrial society would like to return to an allegedly idyllic preindustrial past. You don't share that nostalgia, do you?

T. Not at all. Moreover, there are many optimistic potentials in modern technology, which I point out. But I am also aware of its pessimistic potentials. One has to be blind not to be aware of nuclear risk or of the power certain types of technology might confer on abusive, undemocratic regimes.

Nevertheless, on balance, I would regard myself as a technological-optimist-with-reservations because, while I recognize all the dangers of 1984 writ large, I think that the basic trajectory of technology has shifted.

During the dominance of Second Wave civilization, because our technologies were primitive, we moved toward greater and greater homogeneity and regimentation. Our basic technologies encouraged the centralization and concentration of power. By contrast, many Third Wave technologies move in the opposite direction. They have the potential for dispersing and decentralizing power, rather than centralizing it.

I have never been one-sided, either an optimist or a pessimist. Everybody who has read me closely knows that I have a mixed and bittersweet attitude toward the new possibilities racing toward us. A careful reading would show that even in *The Third Wave*, which is ostensibly a more optimistic book than *Future Shock*, and in which the major melodies are optimistic, there are important minor melodies that are extremely pessimistic.

So I would answer your question by saying that I am optimistic about the things that most people are pessimistic about, and pessimistic about many things they haven't even begun to think about.

16. Lev Gumilov

Lev Nicolaevich Gumilov, born in 1912, is the son of the great Russian poetess, Anna Achmatova. He graduated from the Department of History of Leningrad University and went on to conduct research in the Ermitage Gallery. In 1961 he obtained his doctorate in history and started lecturing on ethnology at the Department of Geology of Leningrad University.

Though his early works point to his interest in the history of oriental natives, in recent years he has developed an interest in the general problems of the evolution of nations and ethnic groups. He created a unique, if somewhat controversial, theory of ethnogenesis as a cyclical process of the rise and fall of an energy supply in individual ethnic groups. Gumilov has written extensively on this subject. His book, The Science of Ethnos, *was rejected as too controversial by major Soviet publishing houses, but was finally published in Hungary in 1980.*

Wiktor Osiatyński: What is "ethnos," the central notion of your theory?

Lev Gumilov: Good question: this notion is often misinterpreted. In my theory, I define ethnos as a group of people having a unique dynamic structure and an equally dynamic stereotype of behavior. To put it simply, the ethnos may correspond to the notion of such natural ethnic groups as tribes or nations . . .

O. Races?

G. No; while racial differences have no significant effects on human activities, ethnic differences do. Moreover, most ethnic groups consist of people whose origins can be traced to various races or mixed breeds. Race is a purely biological concept.

O. What, then, determines the membership of an individual in a particular ethnic group?

G. First of all, acknowledgment of the fact—one's own and that of other people. For ethnos may be defined as an enduring group of people who consider themselves, and are considered by others, different from the other groups.

O. Can one arbitrarily join an ethnic group?

G. Absolutely not if the members of such groups refuse to admit you. In Siberia, I met an Orthodox nobleman who had a Polish father and a Russian mother; he claimed to be a Pole, but other Poles did not accept him. For them he was not a Pole.

O. Did you consider him Russian?

G. Yes, because he behaved like one. And membership in an ethnic group is practically determined, or rather sensed intuitively, in terms of behavioral sterotypes. A Pole will always behave somewhat differently than a Russian, a German, or a Czech.

O. Do these behavioral differences result from cultural dissimilarities?

G. No, they just have an ethnical character. Culture is a homogenizing process, ethnos differentiating. The point is, how a person adjusts as early as childhood, or rather is adjusted, to the world and adjusts the world to himself. This is what creates the differences between various ethnic groups.

O. Can you look at someone and tell what group he belongs to?

G. Not if this person is silent and does nothing. If he begins to speak, and respond to my actions, I can begin to guess.

O. Will you take the language of the person as the criterion?

G. No; people can speak foreign languages. Do you speak English?

O. Yes.

G. So what? It is obvious that you are not English.

O. Well, I meant the mother tongue, the language one used to explore the world and find one's ways in it.

G. It doesn't matter. The Tartars today speak Russian better than Tartarian. But they are still Tartars.

O. Anthropologically, you mean?

G. No; you wouldn't be able to trace any anthropological distinctions to them. Since the Tartars have maintained close relations with the Russians, they have mixed with each other to such a degree that the Tartarian "type" is hard to distinguish now.

O. Then how do we define them?

G. On the grounds of behavior or, sometimes, by the facial expression, which is not determined anthropologically but psychologically. So it also belongs to the behavorial sphere.

O. And this stereotype of the ethnic group doesn't change, does it?

G. Of course it does! It changes with the evolution of the group. Ethnic groups are subject to a continuous, cyclical change. In fact, there is nothing equal to the changeability of ethnic groups in the entire evolution of humanity. You realize that just 1,500 years ago, there were no Russians or Poles, Slovaks or Czcchs, only one ethnos of Slavs. If we go back, say, to the tenth century, we will find that in Europe there were many an ethnos that have long since perished.

They might have left only some relics. And if we go back even further, to three thousand years ago, wc will find none of the present ethnic groups. The ones that might have existed have ceased to exist and none of their descendants are to be found anywhere today. You see, in contradistinction to races or societies, ethnos is an unstable systemic entity, appearing and disappearing with time.

O. How does an ethnic group emerge?

G. We can speak reasonably only of the formation of new ethnic groups since the history of ancient groups, their formation and demise, remains unknown. Historically, ethnic groups might have formed in two different ways. Imagine a vast territory inhabited for centuries by various ethnic groups: then a sudden regrouping takes place.

It results—mostly on the borderlines between the distinctly different cultures—in new, nonhomogeneous though increasingly closely interrelated, mixed communities. At first, the separate members of such communities are hardly different from their ancestors, taking directly after them; but just a few generations later, the behavioral stereotype changes and, gradually, becomes distinctly different. These three generational stages mark the dynamic phases of the formation of the ethnic group. This variant of ethnogenesis is clearly visible in the examples of various extra-ethnic systems, including the Roman Germanic/Teutonic culture of the eighth to ninth century; the culture of the seventh century called Islam; and Eastern European, or more precisely, the Great Russian culture of the fourteenth century.

Sometimes a new ethnic group emerges as a result of separation from another group. A number of individuals may leave their traditional group and adopt the behavioral stereotype of a different group. The newcomers may disperse and "melt" in the new group. Elsewhere, ethnic groups, given favorable conditions, form an entirely new nation. The Americans, Mexicans, or Boers provide good examples.

The difference between the two ways of formation of a new ethnos is obvious and extends far beyond their genesis. In the former case, the newly formed groups remain within the sphere of influence of the traditional culture, adopting only some local peculiarities. While in the latter case there emerges a completely new quality. The institutions and customs of the groups from which new nations descend will perish or be preserved only in the form of relics or insignificant borrowings.

Such phenomena constitute, to a considerable extent, the history of the cyclical evolution of ethnic groups.

O. What causes the intital change, the original regrouping of a nation?

G. The processes occurring in history correspond, nearly literally, to the thermodynamic processes occurring in nature. The initial impulse to change comes from an increased charge of energy that the inhabitants of certain territories receive: the new energy forces them to change their former behavioral stereotype. Imagine the quiet and leisurely people who had formerly lived in the territory of, say, Arabia before Mohammed. They never waged wars, but only had occasional harmless neighborly quarrels. They were rather passive and not very creative. They rarely did anything remarkable. They all lived much like today's most decent and straightest citizens. Suddenly —I stress it: suddenly—there emerged a generation of people whom I call the passionates, from the Latin word *passio*. They seemed to be excessively energetic and felt compelled to quit the drowsy life and set out to pursue idealistic or even illusory goals unheard of before. Thus they begin a struggle to achieve ideals that require laying far-reaching plans. Why did they plan and act? After all, they got nothing but trouble. But they had to discharge the excessive energy: they had to act. In our example, the Arabs decided to conquer the world for Islam. In a way, they succeeded, for they managed to spread their religion from the Caucasus to Spain; later their influence declined. At first, they plundered the conquered territories, but later they lost both the loot and their own lives in wars. All in all, they gained very little and lost a lot. But it could hardly be otherwise, for it was a spontaneous, uncontrollable process. Only from the more distant perspective of ethnogenesis can you see that the process ran along a strictly determined curve, which rises rapidly at the beginning, at the peak fluctuating slightly, and descends until it reaches the starting point. By then, the ethnic configurations of the group have been completely changed by this very process.

O. What is the mechanism triggering the process?

G. As I said, it is an energy mechanism. Vladimir Vernadski, an outstanding scientist, has named this new kind of energy "geo-biochemical energy." Only living organisms have it; it is not mythological *vis vitalis*, but a strictly determined form of energy that can be measured by kilocalories and kilogramometers. This form of energy spurs the emergence of species and helps each spread over the planet as rapidly as possible. This energy can also be found in people. Uusually its amount is steady, but somctimes it suddenly flares up. Then a relatively small group of people, 5 to 10 percent of the population, begin to absorb this extra energy and discharge it in the form of labor. The simplest expression of this energy is usually territorial expansionism.

O. But Vernadski's geo-biochemical energy, if it does exist at all, has not been scientifically identified yet. Let us assume, however, that you are reasoning correctly. Does it mean that we have a specific impulse for territorial expansion?

G. Right; expansion is a historic pattern, although it doesn't have to take the form of conquest. For example, the Byzantine Empire did not wage wars of conquest; instead, it expanded culturally and religiously. Byzantine missionaries traveled as far west as Ireland and as far east as China. Russia's conversion to Christianity in 988 further contributed to the ethnocultural Byzantine influence. Certain cultures have discharged surplus energy in the form of an attempt to change their own behavioral stereotype, but this is a rarity.

O. What is the source, the origin, of the surplus energy?

G. These energetic impulses have certain features that enable us to determine their sources. Each of the impulses was a strictly territorial phenomenon; it sprang up in different but always considerably limited areas, never beyond the Northern Hemisphere. Even if the territory happened to be divided by a mountain range or a sea, it didn't interfere with the energy transmission.

O. Could such a "shot" of extra energy have occurred in several parts of the Northern Hemisphere at once?

G. Right; when, for instance, the Arabs, led by Mohammed, set out to conquer neighboring lands, there was a revolution in India. In Tibet the first monarchy was established; in China a new dynasty took over to continue the restoration of the country's power.

O. What's the conclusion?

G. The nature and the source of energy that spurred all these occurrences seem clear and determinable. Earth receives energy from three sources. The first is solar energy, which is relatively steady and regular, and provides the grounds for photosynthesis. This form of energy has nothing to do with the processes we are discussing, for the sun heats the whole planet while the oscillation of energy triggering the ethnogenetic processes has a local character. It never occurs in the equatorial region, where solar radiation is most intensive. The second kind of energy is radiation, which results from decay of radioactive elements on earth; this energy, of more or less equal amounts around the globe, has nothing to do with ethnogenetic processes either. However, the energy "jumps" occur sometimes in areas where radioactivity is less intensive. Moreover, from every indication, this kind of radiation reduces the vital energy and activity of life forms rather than enhancing the energetic discharge. Thus we come to the third source: cosmic radiation, the genesis and essence of which still await full explanation. We have discovered, however, that the phases of intensification of cosmic radiation coincided with the initial phases of the cyclical processes of ethnogenesis.

O. Do you mean that the passionates can utilize the energy they get from cosmic radiation?

G. Not quite. This kind of radiation brings about a multiplication of mutations in a population. And the passionates, who abound in the third generation following the phase of intensified cosmic radiation, are just mutants endowed with the capability to better absorb energy and, consequently, engage in greater activity.

O. It sounds somewhat like a fantasy, but let's go on. Do these processes have to result in expansionism, or may they also lead to a creative activity?

G. Either way. It is a natural process and nature does not distinguish between good and evil. In nature we deal with quantitative notions: less energy, less labor; more energy, more labor. In what direction the energy is pushed, we cannot tell.

O. What does it depend on?

G. On the inner character of the groups showered with the new energy.

O. On their culture?

G. You can say so. But culture, too, results from energetic stimuli —not the other way around.

O. Can you give a historic example of the process you describe?

G. Here you are. There was a sudden increase of cosmic radiation in the first century. It affected the lands from Sweden to Abyssinia and Palestine. At first, no extraordinary activity or "passion" could be observed in Sweden, while a rather vigorous social movement of the first Christians sprang up in Palestine. In the mid-second century, when a Christian community was already organized in the Middle East, the Goths migrated from the Skansen island into the Vistula River basin, and further southward. And thus a great migration began. Christian expansionism and the migration of nations were the two forms of discharge of the extra energy. In both cases, the victim was the Roman Empire, but in different ways. The Christians let themselves be killed by others, and the Germans, on the contrary, killed others. The Christians, eventually, were the conquerors, while the Germans, who invaded the Roman territory, were totally annihilated.

O. Did the original German ethnos really perish completely?

G. Nothing was left of the Germanic tribes that entered the territory of the Roman Empire—the Goths, Ostrogoths, Longobardi, Vandals, Burgundi. Even the Dacians, who suddenly grew active at the same time, were destroyed by the swords of the Roman legionists.

The Romanians claim today that they are descended from the ancient Dacians, but, in fact, their ancestors were the Roman deportees. Thus the effect of the energetic impulse was, after a century or two, the annihilation of some of the migrant nations and the consolidation of the Christian community, which at that time constituted already a specific ethnos. Its members had a strong sense of group identity, the distinction: "we" versus "them" and a specific behavioral stereotype. The original Christian ethnos survived until the fifteenth century, which is the duration of a full cycle of ethnogenesis: from the rise of an ethnos till its fall . . .

O. I don't quite understand what you mean by "a full cycle of ethnogenesis"? Can you measure its duration?

G. I've already explained that ethnogenesis has an energetic nature. Therefore it is amenable to the second law of thermodynamics, that is, the principle of entropy. Energy is gradually dissipated. The human mechanisms of this process is relatively simple. All passionates are overactive. They wage wars, they risk life. Small wonder that they perish much more rapidly than quiet, yielding people. In times of peace, too, the former become adventurous, so they hardly ever settle down to raise families. As a consequence, their number decreases and, little by little, they disappear from the population. Under normal circumstances, such a process takes 1,200 years. It can be accelerated though, if strong external forces are involved.

O. Is the disintegration of an ethnos caused by a decrease of cosmic radiation?

G. No, it depends only on the events of our earthly history. What happens in space is important at the beginning of the entire process: the process, once set off, then depends on historic fate.

O. So it means that an ethnos may perish for two reasons, one being negative natural selection, since the passionates take all risk and are destroyed, and the other being the domination of a stronger, more aggressive ethnos.

G. It comes to the same thing. The passionates fight with neighbors and get killed.

O. Is war an inevitable fate of mankind? A specific law of human nature?

G. It seems, at any rate, to be an unavoidable fact of an unorganized process of ethnogenesis. If we ever come to know the process in detail and learn to control it in an organized way, we may decide to send all passionates into space so that they would discharge their surplus energy and we could live on peacefully, not disturbed by troublemakers. Then all violence will disappear from our history . . .

O. Will the best human accomplishments also disappear?

G. Yes. A homeostasis will prevail: all will be calm, people will be quiet, accepting their chores obediently. Life will go on normally and safely.

O. Will it be worthwhile at all?

G. Well, it's a matter of taste. We may either make allowances for the dramatic energetic "jumps" or live in homeostasis. And if we are troubled by an excess of energy, we may decide to get rid of it. The passionates can be isolated or killed, and the rest of humanity will be left strictly alone.

O. Don't you think that the attitude of the silent majority to passionate troublemakers is never very friendly in any society?

G. Yes, but with the exception of the initial phase of the cycle, when they usually attract many followers. However, before all the passionates are annihilated, they manage to accomplish something. For instance, Joan d'Arc, before she was executed, saved France. And besides, even if all passionates disappeared, there is no way to prevent the next flare of cosmic radiation. Quite fortunately.

9

On Futurism and the Paradigm Shift

Toffler pointed out that there are many futures possible—out of which a smaller number are probable, and a still smaller are preferable. What future will we and our children face?

Will technological change transform society? Is human potential for progress unlimited? Will we manage to use and benefit from human potential? Why is a change in human beliefs crucial to the future?

These and many other questions are discussed by Igor Bestuzhev-Lada and Willis Harman. Bestuzhev-Lada deals with the general problems of prognostications, while Harman points to the changes in human beliefs and consciousness that we are undergoing today in Western civilization.

Bestuzhev-Lada begins with the history of future studies and with the abilities and limitations of scientific forecasting, explaining why most recent prognoses turned out to be false. In contrast with Toffler, Bestuzhev-Lada stresses the differences between history and future studies rather than the similarities. He presents Marxist theory of social development as an example of a general prognosis, and admits that an interpretation of this prognosis as a historical necessity is a mistake based on technological determinism.

For Bestuzhev-Lada, thinking about the future is an inexhaustible source of social imagination and of personal energy. However, he also believes that an individual needs both practicality and optimism to act on the future in any sort of useful way.

In fact, with this in mind, Bestuzhev-Lada forecasts a crucial change in the future society: a drastically changed character of work and of people's attitude toward work.

For Willis Harman the present changes have even more dramatic character. He claims that we are undergoing a thoroughly fundamental change in our beliefs about man, his perceptive abilities and potentials, his values, and his relationship to other people and to the environment. This change in beliefs is what Harman calls a new Copernican revolution. Harman points out that the problems we are unable to solve today are a direct result of materialistically biased industrial beliefs. The so-called industrial paradigm is extremely successful in answering the "How to" questions, but it is totally inadequate to answer "What for"—value-oriented questions. To bring back the lost sense of meaning to the individual, we have to address today the "What for" questions. The most promising way to do so is to open our consciousness.

Harman stresses that science itself is more and more aware of these problems, and that the opening up of the exploration of human consciousness within the context of scientific inquiry signals a shift in the basic premises underlying industrial society. This shift, in turn, is being enhanced by an emerging new science.

17. Igor Bestuzhev-Lada

Igor Vasilievich Bestuzhev-Lada was born in 1927, and graduated from the Department of History of the Institute of International Relations in Moscow in 1950. In his first job he researched the history of social sciences at the Institute of History of the Soviet Academy of Science. In 1967, he became head of the prognostic section, the first such center in the Soviet Union, at the Institute of the International Workers' Movement. Two years later, he took over an analogous section at the Institute of Sociological Research of the Soviet Academy of Sciences, and has since become its director.

His main topics of interest include history of futurology, forecasting the future, and popularization of futurology. These subjects are reviewed and analyzed in his books, which include If the World Disarms *(1961),* The Outline of the Future *(1965),* The Family: Yesterday, Today and Tomorrow *(1978), and* Social Indicators of the Quality of Life of the Soviet Society *(1980).*

Dr. Igor Bestuzhev-Lada was the chairman of the Futurology

Section of the Soviet Sociological Association and the chairman of the Future Research Committee of the International Sociological Society. He also contributed to the book The Futurists, *edited by Alvin Toffler and published in the United States in 1974.*

Wiktor Osiatyński: Is futurology a science?

Igor Bestuzhev-Lada: You know, the very word *futurology* is rather vague and ambiguous. The first to use it, in 1943, was Osip Flechtheim, a German scientist who lived and worked in the United States; he used this notion to describe a new, peculiar "philosophy of the future." Futurology was to be distinguished from the social theories about the past and present, which Karl Manheim had divided into "ideologies"—theories defending the existing social system—and "utopias"—theories challenging the existing system. Flechtheim's futurology was not to justify or criticize anything; its purpose was the scientific research of the future.

The notion of futurology became popular in the West in the early sixties, at a time when prognoses of every sort boomed. It was perceived as a specific science of the future, or history of the future, which was to deal with the prospects of development of all phenomena, primarily of the social ones. Such history of the future was to be different from other scientific disciplines dealing solely with the past or current study of tendencies and trends.

O. It all sounds strange; isn't the word *history* synonymous with the study of the past rather than the future?

B-L. Right. And that is why all attempts to establish a "history of the future," analogous to the "history of the past" ended in failure. The point is that the history of the past examines the events that have already taken place, and does it with specific scientific tools, different from the ones used to examine current or future events. However, lack of the proper scientific tools is not the problem here. In fact, prognosis is an inherent part of every scientific discipline dealing with reality; for if the description and explanation of an event or phenomenon lacks a prediction of the direction of its further development, it will be quite meaningless. Whatever we do in science today, we must refer it, or assign it, to the future; our duty is to determine how present events may develop in the future. Futurology, then, does not have its own topic.

O. Wouldn't futurology have an identity if we understood it as an integration of all kinds of prognoses made on the ground of each particular discipline? There will be no separate future of physics, demography, economics, and so on, for all spheres of life are interrelated and affect each other. Therefore, should an integration of the sciences with regard to the future not become a leading—and distinct—subject of scientific research?

B-L. Yes. For when we think of the future, we have to take into account all its aspects. It is what the interdisciplinary research contributes to. With the reservation that a more adequate name for such research concerning the social sciences seems to be "prognostics" rather than futurology.

O. The argument about the term set aside, what can prognostics tell us about the foreseeing of the future? Can you foresee everything scientifically?

B-L. As with everything concerning the future, prognostics, too, has its limits, both the limits of concrete spheres of human activity and the limits of temporal horizons. Thus you can hardly foresee future scientific or artistic developments, or, in general, the concrete forms of social consciousness. Such questions can be the subject of considerations, sometimes of literary fiction or science fiction, but no scientific tools are available to set forth any justified prognoses for the further development of those spheres. As it appears, we are able to foresee but twenty to thirty years ahead. Any further perspective is likely to breed phenomena that we don't—or can't—have any idea about now. We may agree in substance that any particular prognosis should be reduced to the actually existing socioeconomic formation.

O. If I have it correctly, the theory of communism did extend, however, beyond the limits of the formation existing at the moment of its formulation.

B-L. The theory of scientific communism was, by no means, a detailed prognosis in the sense we are talking about. It described the prospects of the development of advanced communism somewhat, but, first of all, it described the requirements for a transition toward communism. As such, it dealt primarily with the trends appearing within the actual existing order. As far as the next formation is concerned, the theory of scientific communism presented only a most general vision, going into no specific details. Classic Marxism described attempts at a particular forecasting of the distant future as derivatory efforts to impose a standard of conduct onto the future generations who may be able to solve their problems with means and tools quite unheard of yet. This is just why Karl Marx, Friedrich Engels, and Lenin derided attempts of "preprogramming" the particular form of family to develop under communism, or of how love would look among the Communists . . . Classic Marxism formulated general laws of development leading to communism and to the realization of the principal goals and values of the new formation. To give this vision a concrete form is the task of present and future generations.

O. But is the realization of this general vision to take place automatically, only because such are the laws of social development?

B-L. I think it is more complex. We will never reach communism if people just idly wait for it to come. But we'd never reach anything if certain objective potentials weren't implied in the principles of social development. In fact, the theory of scientific communism points to an ideal as well as to the practical ways, leading to the realization of that ideal. What is necessary to reach this end is scientific planning in all spheres of human activity, and control over the changes aimed at the realization of that ideal.

O. It is sometimes believed that this can be achieved merely by the change of the means of production.

B-L. We call such an approach technological determinism. It is obvious that technological changes result in some social changes. But technology is just a tool that can be used for a variety of purposes—such as to maximize profits and power, or to introduce social progress. It is not the tool itself but the social organization that decides how it will be used. If we speak today about the "techno-scientific revolution" and the perspectives it offers for future development, we don't mean merely the development of science and technology, but, primarily, we mean the integration of this development with the social organization and goals we've set forth to achieve.

O. Can prognostics influence the goals a society sets forth for itself?

B-L. This question has been heatedly disputed. But at least one thing is clear now: we cannot rely just on the instruments of prognostics—on extrapolation, models, computers; a computer is only a kind of transmitter. It outputs what's put in. All by itself, the computer never answers questions concerning purposes or goals. It can make it easier to find optimal ways toward the realization of the goals. But ultimately, the result always depends on the human vision of these goals. On the other hand, however, the prognoses themselves may influence the future and the social goals. For the prognoses affect social consciousness; they influence people's ideas of the future, thus influencing their views and activities.

O. What is your opinion on the significance of the thinking of the future done not by experts of prognostics or futurologists, but by an every-man?

B-L. I consider it a potent source of social imagination and a factor accelerating the creative activity of man. Future is mostly conceived as a simple continuation of the present. It's hard to imagine that the future may bring something qualitatively new and unknown. A culture, ready to prepare us to face such a new future, would have a significant social quality.

O. What "personal" advantages can a person get from giving serious thought to the future of his or her own society and all mankind?

B-L. Thinking of the future develops consciousness. Consciousness, in turn, like participation in culture or in social life, enriches life. If you look ahead to the future—not only your own, but others', the whole society—you get much greater motivation for your activity. And your awareness of the just goals that the society aims at makes you—even if you are under difficult personal conditions—an optimist. In fact, without hope and optimism life would be unbearable.

O. Most predictions made during the last few decades have hardly induced any optimism.

B-L. Right. Western futurologists often preach about the coming global catastrophe; about the threat of hunger, overpopulation, food crisis, economic crisis, urban decay, psychological crisis, and the danger of manipulation of the individual personality.

O. Don't you think that such pessimistic predictions may encourage actions to prevent the catastrophe? And optimistic visions could lull our alertness in the face of truly difficult problems.

B-L. I am far from appraising a hurray-optimism, especially when we face so many critical situations. Obstacles, problems, and threats, as well as the complexity of their potential solution, should be presented and discussed openly. People will thus gain the necessary perspective and sense of purpose to solve the problems. The optimistic, but realistic, approach increases the feeling of social responsibility of all people and leads to greater harmony between the individual and collective aspirations.

O. Who is to decide on the ultimate goals determining the direction of social development and individual activity? Does not the selection of such goals ultimately depend on the hierarchy of social values?

B-L. Of course it does. However, until lately, we have not always considered it important enough. The analysis of the hierarchy of values was not very broad, for the principal goals were imposed on us by the historic situation; we had to reconstruct and develop our economy and try to fulfill the most elementary needs of the people. It has been but very recently that we realized the necessity of identifying long-term social priorities based on a multiaspect analysis of values. And not only of material values, but also the values of education, participation in culture, or even such personal values as friendship and love.

O. Can you plan or foresee these values at all? It is easier with economic problems; certain production potential determines the amount of material goods to be manufactured. But can you plan or just outline such abstract values as goodness, morality, harmonious relations among people, the purpose of life?

B-L. It is much more difficult, but not impossible. The very first step should be a thorough analysis of the hierarchy of human values and needs, which will provide a basis for a definition of abstract goals and for the selection of concrete means to carry out these goals.

O. What changes of the hierarchy of values do you consider the most important for our future?

B-L. It is hard to make a choice since all values are so tightly interrelated. I believe, however, that what's going to bear the most crucial significance for the future is a change in the character of work and the different attitude people may take toward it.

O. Do you have in mind just the development of technology, or the very purpose of work itself? So far, despite the growing automation of work in the world, regardless of different conditions, work has been treated mostly instrumentally, as a means of carrying out other purposes, most often as a means to satisfy the worker's needs.

B-L. Long ago, classic Marxism stated that work would become something greater than just manufacture, that it would become an independent purpose of life and a source of satisfaction and fulfillment for people. Today, it appears more and more clear that automation may soon replace man, especially at hard or repetitive work, while man will be preparing software for new machines—so this work will have a creative character.

O. Will it happen automatically?

B-L. No. It is what we are aiming at. And it is our chance. To achieve it, we need an overall social progress in education, culture, generally—in the way we think.

O. Does the growing popularity of narrowly specialistic education contribute to such progress?

B-L. I believe in education that results in highly specialized skills complemented with broad horizons. An educated person should be socially oriented, caring for the well-being of other people. Everybody should consciously contribute to the universal social cause, which, in turn, would be a source of his or her personal satisfaction.

O. But if your vision is to come true, a dramatic change of the hierarchy of social values would be required, that is, the predominance of material values would have to be replaced by a greater interest in different, higher values. Do you believe it's possible at all? Isn't it easier to increase the material standard of living rather than look for a new, more subtle and impalpable purpose of life?

B-L. Right. However, the very nature of the hierarchy of human needs suggests a dose of optimism here. The elementary material needs placed on its top level have quite clear limits: you cannot consume more than three thousand calories a day; you cannot wear more than one outfit at a time; even the space of your dwelling place has its psychological limitations . . .

O. But you can eat more expensive food, endlessly change your clothes, houses, furniture.

B-L. Right. That is why it would be our greatest mistake to narrow our interest to an insatiable pursuit of such desires, which, most often, are only for prestige. Such desires should have a rational limit, while the satisfaction of the other, higher needs, should become a source of prestige and self-esteem. The higher purpose might include a need to share in the social life, to contribute to friendly relations with other people, to self-development in the sphere of knowledge, ethical and aesthetical values, or, last but not least, the creative need to express one's own personality. All these needs have no limits. That is why I think the potentials of progress are unlimited. One of our most important tasks now is to abandon the path leading us to the desire for an endless number of material things. What we should do instead—still keeping up the production of all goods that help to make our lives easier and better—is to embark upon a path that leads to the expression of our creative needs, peculiar to our human nature. When we achieve this, we will have the right to speak of a revolutionary leap in the history of humanity.

18. Willis Harman

Willis W. Harman was born in 1918. After obtaining his doctorate in electrical engineering in 1948, he taught at Florida State University. In 1952 he became a professor at Stanford University. His initial research and publications dealt primarily with microwave electronics and theory of communication.

Dr. Harman has also devoted some of his research to psychology. He has been a cofounder of the Society of Humanistic Psychology, and published several works on the subject: Old Wine in New Wineskins *(1967) and* The New Copernican Revolution *(1969).*

Willis Harman turned to social politics in 1966. He was appointed director of the Center for the Study of Social Policy at the Stanford Research Institute (presently, SRI International) in Menlo Park, California. The team of researchers headed by Dr. Harman has authored several reports on educational policy, use of natural resources, and contemporary social problems. The Changing Images of Man, *a report Dr. Harman supervised, published in 1974, is considered one of the most significant contributions to the studies on change in social consciousness in contemporary industrial societies. Similar problems are discussed in Willis Harman's book* An Incomplete Guide to the Future *(1979).*

In 1977, Dr. Harman became president of the Institute of Noetic Sciences in Sausalito, California. Under the auspices of the institute, he has published many papers and reports dealing with consciousness changes, with the role of science, with changes in value-systems, and with the future society.

In 1980, Dr. Harman, who continues to work for SRI International, was appointed to the Board of Regents of the University of California.

Wiktor Osiatyński: You have been saying for almost fifteen years now that our generation is witnessing a new Copernican revolution. What do you mean by that?

Willis Harman: A fundamental change in our beliefs about man, his perceptive abilities and potentials, his values, and his relationship to other people and to the environment. This shift in human beliefs is, in turn, triggering such changes in social institutions, politics, and everyday life that we can hardly imagine today.

O. Why, then, don't we see this revolution?

H. Because it is difficult to recognize revolution in beliefs if one is actually in process. One can imagine attempting to make the case, say, in the middle of the seventeenth century that from the ideas of Copernicus and Galileo would emerge a conceptual revolution that would eventually shake society to its very roots. We can hear the arguments that these new ideas about the planets might be of great interest to theologians and philosophers, but they could hardly be expected to make much impact on the practical world of everyday experience. And yet, as we all know, they did in time affect every institution in society.

O. Do you mean that these ideas were the source of all other changes? Don't you underestimate social and economic changes that put an end to the medieval order?

H. There is no single cause in history. But one can hardly overestimate the role of beliefs. From all I know about history there were beliefs—and often unconscious beliefs—that most fiercely resisted change. People around the world for hundreds of years had watched ships disappear over the horizon. People back in ancient Egypt knew that if you moved in the north-south direction, then the position of the stars and the sky seemed to shift. All sorts of evidence seemed to suggest that the earth was spherical and orbited around the sun. But until Copernicus and after, people perceived the earth as a flat object in the center of the universe. It was an emotional, not even consciously articulated "gut feeling" that influenced their perception and caused resistance to Copernicus's ideas.

Similarly, people who grew up in different tribes perceived the world differently. In some tribes the trees talk to each other, and in our tribe they don't. When people change the perception and image of man in which they believe, then relatively rapidly a major transformation takes place.

O. Do you think that we live now in a period of such transformation?

H. No doubt. The gut beliefs of people living in industrial societies have been changing in the last fifteen years. And there had not been a comparable change on the same level of profundity since the time of Copernicus.

O. I do see some changes, but I'm not convinced they are really as deep and revolutionary as you claim. What evidence do you have that we are currently going through, as you say, a historical metamorphosis?

H. There are two sorts of evidence. First, there are ever growing indications that the industrial paradigm is unsuited to an ecologically resilient global society and sustained global peace. And second, there are numerous indications that the core image of man around which this paradigm formed has already undergone marked change.

O. In both cases you use the phrase "the industrial paradigm." It is like a cliché; everybody talks and writes about "paradigm" and "paradigm shift." What do you mean by the industrial paradigm?

H. Generally speaking, a paradigm is a set of unquestioned assumptions about an individual, society, and universe; it comprises a system of values that, in turn, guides individual and social activity. To be more specific, the industrial paradigm is fundamentally a consequence of the secularization of values and the shift in the image of man at the end of the Middle Ages. At that time, the basis for the values that guided societal institutions, as well as individual lives, shifted away from the traditional religious foundations to a more utilitarian and pragmatic base. A new image of rational and manipulative man, shaping his own destiny in a world neutral to his dreams and constantly concerned with material progress, emerged and took over. The nature of this man has been perceived in reductionist terms of needs, instincts, learning, and inherited predispositions.

The industrial man believes that material progress is the road to the promised land; that the manipulative—economic and technical—rationality is the most effective mode of logic; that science is the most reliable form of knowledge; and that the highest good is the social and material well-being of the individual. These beliefs and values comprised in the industrial paradigm fueled the impetus of the industrial society toward geographical exploration and colonization; toward science, capitalism, and industry; and eventually toward science-based high technology and modern society.

O. What was wrong with the industrial paradigm as described by you? Didn't it lead to the increase in the material standard of living, to elimination of toil and plagues haunting mankind for thousands of years, to modern science and high technology, and, finally, to more democratic government than ever before?

H. It's true. The basic premises of the industrial paradigm did very well for us for a while. But as they became progressively more dominant, dismissing and shutting out from people's minds transcendental premises underlying human, spiritual values, something began to go wrong. I don't think it's necessary to recite the familiar litany of today's global dilemmas: economic crisis, unemployment and inflation, maldevelopment in much of the world, shortages of resources, environmental disintegration, idea of national security through total nuclear insecurity, and so on.

O. Do you think all these problems are related to the industrial paradigm? To what people believe in?

H. Definitely. I would even say that the most serious global problems appear to be the more or less direct result of the materialistically biased successes of the industrial paradigm. The same basic premises I mentioned have developed into pathogenic forms and create our problems. Our belief that it is the destiny of humanity to control nature leads to uncontrolled devastation of environment and to the extinction of those species that "don't have any use." The belief that social progress consists in continuous expansion of the gross output leads to the conclusion that commercially structured hedonistic pursuits, pollution and pollution-cleanup, and the arms race are "good for the economy." Our belief that economic rationality is a suitable guide for social decisions leads to the neglect of both the future impact of today's decisions and the noneconomic ideas. And so on. As a result, we have got a lot of things that are "good for the economy," but we really don't need them. In the human sense we could do better without an arms race, pollution, and pollution control, as well as without all the hedonistic behavior we are persuaded to display. On the other hand, there are all sorts of things that we need, but they don't fit the economy very well. Good education for everybody, clean air, basic research, safe streets in big cities—all of these and many other things are not considered productive—a drain on the economy. So, there is something fundamentally wrong with our thinking when the useless things are being done because it is good for the GNP and the needed things don't get done because they don't make a profit for somebody.

O. I think you've just mentioned the main cause of these problems. It seems to me that there are very tangible interests of very powerful people rather than industrial beliefs that result in distorted priorities and the crisis.

H. Even if that is so, the dominant social beliefs enable the powerful few to impose their own goals on society. Until people do not reject persuasion, until they do not change their beliefs—the crisis will keep growing.

O. Do you think people will change their beliefs?

H. I am convinced about it. It has to do with the common denominator of all problems we were talking about. I think the single most important crisis is essentially the crisis in meaning in the industrial society. We are incredibly successful at answering the "How to" questions. How to put a man on the moon? How to create genetically new species? How to extinguish other species? We can handle practically any "How to" question. But at the same time, we are increasingly confused about the question, "What for"—the value question. And there is a growing recognition that there is nobody who knows what is worth doing. We are going faster and faster, but we have lost track of the goal.

O. This crisis in meaning has a very broad social context. One can live with it relatively at ease. I can always say: I have no impact on social values; it's simply the way things are going and I will not be able to change it.

H. Not necessarily, because more and more people become sensitive to "What for" questions. And that has to do with the fact that there is also a crisis in meaning in individual lives. When you have a production-focused society, then meaning comes from having a job in the economy; in producing something, consuming, and so on. This changes when production problems have been totally solved. The U.S. is producing three times as much wheat as it can use. It is producing much more goods and services of all sorts than it can make use of. And the meaning of an increased production does not suffice anymore. When the individual cannot get a full meaning out of doing his work on the job, the crucial question arises: where is the meaning? And it is this crisis in meaning that has caused the people to turn around.

O. To turn where?

H. To question basic assumptions of the industrial paradigm. To question the idea of competing nation-states confronting each other on a small planet with devastating nuclear weapons. To question the idea of mass consumption society. To question even—as some people do—the whole idea of a full-employment society. Because the full employment and mass consumption go together. And where the production problems have been solved, you don't need everybody in production. Then, the question comes up: what do you do with marginal people? Since the number of the so-called marginal people will increase chronically, we must be asking the wrong question. In a way it is the most fundamental challenge to a modern industrial society. What is the value of people when you don't need them for production jobs? And how do you reorder the society to assure these people the sense of meaning?

Another, equally fundamental, question is: how does it happen that our science and whole knowledge system has nothing to say about values and goals?

None of these questions can be answered within the framework of the industrial paradigm, whatever form of industrial society it is—capitalist or Socialist. These ultimate questions have little to do with the economic system in the usual sense. They have to do with what values should prevail in the institutions of society. And there are economic and technical values at one end of the axis and ecological, feminist, humane, spiritual values at the other end.

O. Do you think the paradigm shift will go in the direction of "ecological, feminist, humane, and spiritual values"?

H. It has to if we are to solve our problems, and not perish. We have to embrace transcendental values that are ignored by the industrial paradigm. And we have to develop the value-oriented resources of our minds, which are ignored by science.

O. Namely? What values do you have in mind?

H. The new values have been perceived by an ever growing number of people during the past fifteen years. There has been a growing sense that the quality of relationships is important: quality of lives; being in touch with oneself, being in touch with others, relationship toward the earth—all these kinds of values that were neglected by the power of economic hiatus.

O. How can we arrive at these new values? It seems to me that we all have an access to these values but we don't see them.

H. I think we underestimate the power and capacities of what is unconscious in us.

O. You mean that these values are in the unconscious part of our minds? And we repress them?

H. I think that, at least, the ability to rediscover these values is there. When we speak of unconscious, we have to separate two aspects of it. One is the "rubbish heap"—here are all the things that would make me uncomfortable if they became conscious: my secret beliefs that I am inadequate; my secret beliefs that I must fear others, the environment, the universe. We suppress such thoughts but all these unconsciously held beliefs contribute to the way we perceive the world. We do downgrade ourselves, we do fear other people, and we are in conflict with ourselves and with others.

For conflict is very largely a matter of perception. If I perceive you—even unconsciously—as having certain characteristics that I know are characteristics of Polish spies, I may find that I am very much in conflict with you. When I change those perceptions and I realize that there is a person who at the deep level is the same and identical with me and, therefore, we couldn't be other than brothers, if we only tried, then I see you in a very different way.

O. And such potential is in the other part of the unconscious?

H. Yes. It is the creative, aesthetic, spiritual, and intuitive side of the unconscious. In American educator Abraham Maslow's words, it is the "godlike" side of us. But we repress it together with the rubbish-heap part of the unconscious. By resisting to uncover the ways in which we secretly feel ashamed, we resist revealing our conscious awareness of the "godlike" in ourselves.

O. Is that why you emphasize so strongly the need for consciousness research?

H. Precisely. I am convinced there is a part of our unconscious that is blocked by the industrial paradigm, by science, by the way we perceive things and ourselves. This part of consciousness is the most valuable, creative, and humane aspect of mind. It is also sensitive to values. Therefore, we have to uncover this part, because it is only the rediscovery of values that can bring back the sense of meaning to the individual.

O. Now I see this crisis, I see the negative role of the industrial paradigm, I see the need for changes and even the required directions of change. The only thing I don't see is Copernicus, who would shake all our industrial-paradigm-oriented beliefs.

H. I do see Copernicus, in a metaphorical sense. For fifteen years I have been observing the process of gradual weakening of the authority of industrial institutions and values. I have been observing the growing interest in human internal experiences. And recently, the scientists themselves are suddenly far more willing to talk about the reality of the nonphysical and the nonmeasurable.

In a landmark invited paper in the 1981 Annual Review of Neuroscience the Nobel laureate, Roger Sperry—whose research gave us the left-brain-right-brain watchword of pop psychology—called attention to the relatively neglected area of human subjective experience. Sperry asserts that: "Current concepts of the mind-brain relation involve a direct break with the long-established rationalist and behaviorist doctrine that has dominated neuroscience for many decades. Instead of renouncing or ignoring consciousness, the new interpretation gives full reocgnition to the primacy of inner conscious awareness as a causal reality."

Such a statement, that an essentially nonmeasurable inner conscious awareness is indeed a "causal reality," would have been rank heresy not too many years ago. Even today, few scientists of comparable stature would venture such an assertion. However, British physicist David Bohm finds need for a nonmeasurable "implicate order" behind the measurable world of physics. And biologist Rupert Sheldrake is creating a stir with his hypothesis that nonmeasurable "morphogenetic fields," cumulative over generations, are necessary to account for the complex instinctive behavior of animals. Thus it is the scientists themselves who are finding the materialism of an earlier science to be inadequate to the understanding of reality.

O. But all these are at best hypotheses. And as to Sheldrake's theory, an editorial in *Nature* termed it ". . . an exercise in pseudoscience" and "an infuriating tract . . . the best candidate for burning there has been in many years."

H. It is precisely what the Church did with Galileo's hypothesis, isn't it? Today, however, things look different. The equally respectable journal *New Scientist* had observed that such responses as those in *Nature* were to be expected since Sheldrake's theory involves "putting aside our assumptions on how the world works." And the same journal established a special prize for the best experimental design to test Sheldrake's hypothesis. But let's not debate over the details. What seems more important is that in more and more theories—in physics, biology, neurophysiology, and other "hard" sciences—the spiritual and intuitive realms turn out to be not in conflict with science, as was once assumed to be the case. No scientific findings disprove it; some findings in consciousness research seem to support it.

O. And this is what you call a new Copernican revolution?

H. Yes. I think that the opening up of the exploration of human consciousness within the context of publicly validated scientific inquiry, and the parallel between the research findings there and the observable change in cultural beliefs in recent years, signal a shift in the basic premises underlying industrial society. And it seems to me that this shift rivals in significance the transformation in the image of man that took place with the Copernican revolution. It is difficult to imagine now the changes that might accompany such a profound shift. I am convinced that these changes will be for better understanding of a sense of values and of ultimate goals.

O. What do you think, how widespread are these changes? How many people question the basic premises of the industrial paradigm and engage in a search for the new values?

H. We have only incomplete survey data, so it will be a guess. I think, however, that eight years ago when we first met it was under 5 percent of Americans. Now, I would guess, it is between 10 and 20 percent.

O. If that is so, it really looks like a rapid change in belief. But the paradigm shift is going to challenge not only belief but very tangible vested interests as well. Aren't you afraid of a dramatic conflict? More generally, are you an optimist as to the future of mankind?

H. I would separate the two things. One is: are you optimistic or pessimistic? The other is: where are you investing yourself? In what image of the future? These are totally separate questions. And, on the one hand, there is no question in my mind where I am investing myself. I am deliberately focusing on and perceiving all the signs of a future that really works for people, all around the globe. And I know it is possible. So I will hold that image in my mind, I'll speak that image, I'll see that image.

Now, optimism and pessimism are just a matter of what are the odds. It's a gambler's game. And I don't really care what the odds are. If the odds are 95 percent that we will blow up the world or we will end up the way Rome did, it doesn't matter, because I'll invest myself the same way, anyway.

10

On a New Science

What is the emerging new science that Willis Harman emphasizes? What are new scientific questions?

These questions are discussed by Edgar Mitchell and Victor Iniushin. A man who walked on the moon, Edgar Mitchell argues that it is consciousness research that will pave the way for the new science. Kazakh biophysicist Iniushin stresses, in turn, a need for a new geometry that is a prerequisite for understanding life. This new geometry, however, will also result in an enrichment of the scientific paradigm. Both intellectuals believe a new science will embrace human values that are neglected by science as it is practiced today.

Mitchell foresees a spritual phase of evolution, which will complement biological and intellectual phases of human development. According to Mitchell, contemporary science is helpless in the face of numerous natural phenomena. Psychic and consciousness research, by contrast, attempts to analyze these phenomena. If some of the assumptions of consciousness research turn out to be true, we will have to revise many assumptions taken for granted in science. It doesn't mean, however, that a new science will replace traditional science; instead, it will enrich scientific methods and enlarge their applicability.

Mitchell explains one of the versions of the new science—a concept of the morphogenetic field and morphic resonance postulated by British biologist Rupert Sheldrake. For Mitchell, Sheldrake's hypothesis explains most of the mysterious phenomena.

Contrary to the scientific assumption that the universe is random, Mitchell holds that an order and a purpose, as well as a universal value system, are written into the universe. Therefore, the approaching revolution in science will pave the way for the recognition of fundamental moral values.

Iniushin analyzes the prospects for an integration of physicochemical sciences with biology. Such an integration seems extremely difficult to him, since life and inanimate matter are two qualitatively different forms of space. If this is the case, the precondition of an integration of biology with physics is a development of a completely new geometry. As a step toward this geometry Iniushin introduces the concept of a biological field that results from the interaction between living organisms.

In Iniushin's concept, life is a unique form of space in which physical and chemical processes occur. The living form of space is different from inanimate space. Moreover, inanimate space by no means can by itself become a living one, which means that, contrary to the opinions established in science, life could not have emerged on earth.

Iniushin explains, in the perspective of his theories, many psychic phenomena. He discusses in detail such problems as acupuncture, Kirlian photography, and telepathy, finding them all explicable from a bioenergetic perspective. However, to understand them completely we have to enlarge the scientific paradigm. Even more desperately we need to create a new worldview that would recognize the preservation of every living form as the main purpose of all human activity, including science.

19. Edgar Mitchell

Edgar D. Mitchell, born in 1930, graduated from Carnegie Institute of Technology in 1952. Shortly thereafter, he joined the U.S. Navy. In 1964 he obtained a doctorate in aeronautics and astronautics at the Massachusetts Institute of Technology and two years later was admitted to the NASA Astronauts Corps. In 1971, as a lunar module pilot, Dr. Edgar Mitchell was the sixth man to put his foot on the moon.

*While in transit to the moon and on his way back to earth, Dr. Mitchell attempted to send messages to earth by means of telepathy (*Journal of Parapsychology, *July 1971). Afterward, he decided to engage more fully in studies of human consciousness, a challenge that he had wanted to undertake for several years. In 1972 he left NASA to found the Institute of Noetic Sciences (from* nous—*mind, in*

Greek) in California. The institute was to support research and to collect information on those potentials of the human mind, which were of little interest to contemporary science. Among its many projects exploring the nature of human consciousness, the institute cosponsored (with Stanford Research Institute) the well-known experiments with Uri Geller in 1974 and opened five chairs for outstanding scholars who would like to engage in studies of the changing concepts of reality and their impact on the twentieth century. Dr. Mitchell edited Psychic Exploration—A Challenge for Science *(1974); the book is considered the most comprehensive study on psychic phenomena. It is a compilation of modern studies by eminent individuals into this mysterious realm of human functioning.*

After helping establish psychic research as a valid and promising field of inquiry, Dr. Mitchell focused on the studies of consciousness in its various forms. He presented a broad outline of these studies in the paper "Consciousness: The Ultimate Enigma" (1972).

Dr. Mitchell is now working on conceptual and mathematical models that could help provide synthesis of our physical and metaphysical notions of reality.

Wiktor Osiatyński: You are considered one of very few people of the new era—the era of space flights, highly developed technologies. What is your personal image of this era?

Edgar Mitchell: I may be a man of the new era but not exactly in the sense you have in mind. For me, it's not only an era of people walking on the moon for the first time. Rather, it's a new phase of human development and evolution. Throughout history mankind has been subject to biological evolution; now we have entered the current era of intellectual evolution in which we are creating the environment in which we live. I'd like to believe this era will be of short duration and we might soon enter a stage of the spiritual evolution of man in which our intellectual development merges with and becomes influenced by a renewed spiritual sense.

O. You mean, spirit will replace intellect?

M. No, one will complement the other. Spirit will enhance our rational, scientific knowledge; thus it will help us to use our knowledge in a better way. The two spheres of human experience, rational and spiritual, which are artificially separated, will be put together. Now we recognize some of our experiences as scientifically valid; we reject others because we have no scientific explanation for them. But science in its true sense is an attempt to understand the universe. Therefore, ignorance of certain facets of the universe and certain phenomena, only because we find it difficult to apply traditional scientific tools and methods to them, is sheer nonsense. Our goal is to comprehend the world and man's role in it. When we find tools of science helpful, we use them. But when they seem to be useless toward understanding human experience, we should try to find new tools or improve the old, so they might be more effective.

Often, however, we reject the experience rather than look for new tools of understanding. Sometimes, we must reexamine the most basic assumptions of science, which we have taken for granted without question. Such a reexamination and change of assumptions can result in a paradigm shift. Many observations in recent years seem to suggest that some of the premises and methods accepted in science are not as useful as they might be. It may be worthwhile to re-verify them now. I personally have become convinced that knowledge of the existence of human subjective facilities or "inner knowing" should be sufficient for theoreticians, at least, to understand the need for a paradigm shift.

O. Do you suggest that the scientific tools we use are not good enough for us to understand the universe precisely and fully?

M. Yes, exactly. I think that not only the tools but also some methodological assumptions of science are inadequate. Let us take as an example the total objectivity of an observer. With the acceptance of Werner Heisenberg's principle of uncertainty we have admitted that the very fact of conducting an observation affects the observed process. Now, however, it is time to find out whether the very fact that a scientist thinks of undertaking an observation doesn't affect its further course and its results.

O. Do you mean that there is nothing like an "aimless" observation and the preordained aim or goal or purpose influences the nature of the observation?

M. Right. We first create a hypothesis and then we start looking for experimental data to confirm it. The process itself affects our perception. It is the hypothesis, or more generally, the paradigm—a set of accepted principles and axioms—that determines what we know and what we don't. The paradigm causes us to see what we expect to see. If an observation fits our paradigm, our accepted way of perception, then we accept it much more easily than in a case where it doesn't. If it doesn't, it causes an emotional stress. In such a case, it's easier to say that the observation doesn't exist or is in error than to change the paradigm to fit the observation. This is one of the main problems of our modern science. We are throwing away vast amounts of human observation and experience because they don't fit within existing "official" knowledge.

O. Too many facts do not fit the dominant paradigm?

M. Yes; I think that in the development of a new science there is a phase when you accumulate facts. At first, you find facts that are beyond your worldview. You either ignore them or put them aside. In the long run you have so many of them that they can't be ignored any longer. At this moment an honest scientist will think that something must be wrong. "I must discard too many observations; it's time to face them and determine whether or not a new paradigm, a new set of assumptions, could be created on the basis of these facts."

That's the way it is now with consciousness research. The phenomena with which it deals have existed for a long time. Philosophers for centuries have proclaimed that consciousness is at the base of reality. But evidence of such existence has been ignored or put aside. And now we say, "Let us put together all the facts we ignored and try to create a new model." It can be expected that new concepts will emerge, covering the nature of the relationship between man and the universe. These relationships go beyond the classic scientific paradigm, but they include both the ignored facts and most of those phenomena that are accepted by traditional science. Therefore, our research should lead to a relatively smooth transition from one set of assumptions to another.

The history of science has already known similar processes. The relativity theory has not canceled the concepts of Sir Isaac Newton. Albert Einstein, simply, has built a more comprehensive model, covering Newton's laws as well. The situation now is quite similar to that one. When we understand the phenomena of human consciousness, we'll be able to build a new paradigm. It will not have to contradict the theory of relativity or quantum mechanics. It will extend the present sphere of our research.

O. What kind of a new theory do you have in mind?

M. No complete theory exists yet. There are growing doubts as to the existing paradigm and numerous hypotheses of how the physical and spiritual universe may function. I think the most promising new tool is the hypothesis of formative causation and the concept of morphogenetic fields postulated recently by British biologist Rupert Sheldrake.

O. From what I know, Sheldrake supposes that systems are organized in the way they are because similar systems were organized that way in the past, and, more specifically, that the characteristic forms and behavior of physical, chemical, and biological systems in the present moment are determined by morphogenetic fields acting across space and time. Is there any proof that these invisible fields, without mass or energy, exist?

M. Sheldrake's hypothesis has not been proven yet, but there is substantial scientific evidence that he may be right. This concept may explain, for example, the well-known findings by Harvard psychologist William McDougal, that given the same learning task, subsequent generations of rats were learning more quickly than the generations preceding them. McDougal made his experiments in the 1920s; since then his findings were confirmed in other laboratories. These results are, however, completely inexplicable in terms of conventional science. And now, Sheldrake's hypothesis offers a possible explanation: the first generation of rats established a morphogenetic field for the specific behavior being learned. That field then guided the behavior of subsequent generations, making it easier for them to learn the task, through a process that Sheldrake calls morphic resonance.

Generally speaking, Sheldrake's hypothesis says that if something happens once in a certain way, it will be easier for it to happen the same way a second time because of the influence of an established morphogenetic field.

O. Would this hypothesis put in a new perspective the problems of consciousness and spirituality you deal with?

M. Of course, when we develop physical and mathematical models for Sheldrake's field concept, we may discover a missing bridge between the physical and the metaphysical, for this theory provides us with a basis for an information model of the universe. Physical theories and physical cosmologies up to this point have simply talked about the material nature of the universe. Now, Sheldrake's concept gives us an informational property for matter that science has heretofore ignored. And if that informational property is there, it provides a basis for much of our thinking, particularly in the realm that we have called spiritual experience. What we call spiritual may be thought of as experiencing information about what we are.

O. Now I see the possible consequences of Sheldrake's theory. Is there a way to prove it?

M. As I've said, it hasn't been proved yet. And let's be careful about the word *prove.* To prove is to reach agreement on a way of perceiving reality.

But in principle Sheldrake's hypotheses, in contrast to many other new concepts about consciousness, is testable in a traditional way. In the spring of 1983 at the Institute of Noetic Sciences a number of specialists in a variety of fields were discussing with Sheldrake experiments that might verify his theory. An interesting observation is that in the case of many experimental designs, the only alternative explanation to the existence of morphogenetic fields would be the existence of telepathy combined with psychokinesis. To achieve positive results from such an experiment would create quite a dilemma for traditionalists.

O. Do you mean that the morphogenetic field and morphic resonance could help explain psychic phenomena?

M. I like to think of psychic phenomena as simply a manifestation of human awareness, like intuition, creativity, and so on. It seems quite clear, if the morphogenetic field can transfer information across space and time, that's precisely what most of psi functioning is about. However, what seems to me even more important is that this theory explains why only relatively few people have fully developed, easily accessible psychic capability.

O. Because most of us use rational channels of communication?

M. Precisely. We are trained to use our mind/brain in a particular way. That way enhances our deductive processes and suppresses our intuitive processes. I think that there is potential for deepening our subjective facilities to enhance our knowledge. Development of these capabilities, however, is an evolutionary process. Knowledge seems to accumulate both from our deductive and intuitive processes. Presently, when a relatively small number of people explicitly use that capability, no strong morphogenetic field has been established. We all have little flashes of insight into ESP and other psychic faculties, but it has not evolved yet to the point where we can more effectively use it. Using Sheldrake's model, it seems to me that as we learn to know our potentials better, the ability to use psychic understanding will become stronger.

O. Do you have in mind the process of establishing the morphogenetic field for the psychic phenomena by getting more and more ordinary people involved in using and developing these capabilities? But don't you think that there is much less popular interest in parapsychology today than, say, eight years ago when we first talked?

M. I don't think that the popular interest in parapsychology has decreased. It's simply not as sensational anymore. Further, more important than psychic is the broader question of what are *all* of our deeper subjective faculties.

On the one hand, many people take psychic events for granted because it is a natural part of their functioning. On the other hand, it is less newsworthy because there is nothing really new in it. Many people would like to better understand psychic faculties, to even have training methods by which one could develop these capabilities. But there are few new developments because the official paradigm proponents refuse to analyze psychic phenomena. However, to continue to compartmentalize psychic as distinct from the totality of human subjective experience is an old paradigm, a reductionist way of looking at things.

O. Do you believe that official science will recognize and explain psi phenomena?

M. Yes, I do. I have lost, however, all expectations that we are going to see this happen quickly. The reason for this is that traditional scientists are pretty well stuck in the old-paradigm thinking. And the psychic experience has to come from the exploration of the subjective, which forces one into a personal paradigm shift. In order to understand the subjective, one has to experience it. If you are mired in old-paradigm thinking it is very difficult to experience the new paradigm or to experience a different reality.

Part of the problem is that an intellectual exercise in understanding the subjective is not sufficient. It is to cause theoreticians to experience the inner world so that they can know what they are talking about. That's why I believe in the necessity of evolutionary pressure to bring this about.

O. By convincing the scientists that psychic phenomena exist?

M. No, rather by the slow process of establishing a morphogenetic field for this knowledge. We cannot persuade anyone to investigate the validity of inner experience or to believe in it if he or she doesn't want to. And as long as they resist investigating it, you are wasting your time trying to convince them about it. Most of the people currently existing in the scientific establishment are not likely to abandon the traditional paradigm in order to explore the new one, because it requires personally investing in the subjective, which is something they have previously rejected.

O. Are you, then, more skeptical about the prospects of a paradigm shift than you were eight years ago?

M. No; I think we are starting to go through a major transition right now. My skeptical remarks were addressed precisely to your question about the prospects for the integration of the psychic domain in a new paradigm. I don't think anymore that it will happen soon.

O. Where, then, do you see the evidence of a paradigm shift?

M. Well, perhaps there is more hope to it than fact. But I seem to be seeing in society a sort of change that foreruns the paradigm shift. John Naisbitt, for example, in his book *Megatrends* is documenting some very pragmatic and easily discernible parts of the paradigm shift: on one hand, such things as decentralization and the trend to smaller systems; on the other, changes in the system of values, more sense of personal responsibility.

O. Do you, then, foresee the paradigm shift without the psychic part of it?

M. You keep dwelling on the psychic even though I continue to emphasize that it is not a productive way to think about subjective experience. Of course, I hope that psychic phenomena, sooner or later, will find their way to science and will enrich our concept of human potentials, but I am not happy with the notion of psychic development as a product of our effort. I prefer to think of all spheres of subjective understanding and inner development of which the psychic is only a tiny part. And it is not of primary importance what facet will challenge the dominant scientific paradigm and force the change in our perspective. What is important is the result of this change.

O. What do you perceive as the most significant and the most desired result of the paradigm shift?

M. I believe it will be a drastic change in our attitude toward values, or, more precisely, what it is that is ultimately worth doing. The old paradigm is firmly entrenched in the existing morphogenetic field with its own concept of values or, more precisely, ignoring the question of values. Scientists assume that science itself and the material world are independent of any intrinsic value, so science doesn't have to be concerned with the question. This lack of interest in moral values is the main aspect of the crisis of our time. In order to change it, we have to address once again the old philosophical question of how we arrive at values.

O. You once said that a value system is inscribed in the universe. Do you still believe that?

M. Yes, but I would now modify it by saying that this value system really comes out of the wisdom of the ages. It is the information about what permits optimum survival and in the case of humans what produces ultimate satisfaction. The information is in the morphogenetic field that has been building up since the beginning of the universe.

O. Along with evolution?

M. Along with the material aspect of evolution, which we now understand reasonably well. But what we do not understand is the effect of a constant interaction between the material and the informational aspects of evolution. As the species evolved, not only were there genetic manifestations evolving but the informational characteristics underlying that material aspect were evolving, too. And values are a part of this informational field of evolution.

O. And you think that a "new science" should find this value system in the universe?

M. I don't want to be misunderstood. The search for the value system is not reserved to scientists. Their task is to explore the universe. But if the value system is an inherent part of the universe, then science, even in the most traditional sense, should not ignore it any longer. To put it more basically, if the universe has an informational mechanism for propagating knowledge of its successes to future generations, that is of scientific importance.

O. And then would we have an ethical image of the universe and man?

M. We have an ethical image even now. A science ignorant of value considerations creates an ethic, too. A dangerous one, for that matter. So let's say, we could have a new ethical image of the world. One in which the value system would play a much more significant part along with our rationally discovered knowledge. One in which the respect for knowledge of moral values will play a primary role in human life and activity. It must be so if we want to survive.

20. Victor Iniushin

Victor Mikhailovich Iniushin, who was born in 1941, graduated from the Kazakh University in Alma Ata in 1963 and took an assistant's job in biophysics at the same university. In 1972 he obtained a doctorate at the University of Lvov and, three years later, became a professor at the University of Alma Ata, where he holds the biophysics chair.

The main subject of the research and writings of Dr. Iniushin includes the problems of bioenergetics of the organism and the theory of the biological field. He published more than a hundred dissertations and papers, and a book, Biostimulation and Bio-Plasma *(1975).*

As chairman of the Committee on Bioenergetics at the Kazakh Scientific-Technological Society, Dr. Iniushin has coordinated the research in bioenergetics conducted by more than thirty scientific institutes all over the U.S.S.R.

His latest research, focusing on the influence of laser radiation on living organisms, resulted in a 30 percent increase of crops and an increase of the vitamin and sugar content of fruits. In his experiments he also uses laser radiation to influence the genetic code. His theoretical work concentrates on the means of finding a better understanding of the complex energetic processes occurring in living organisms. Victor Iniushin's conceptions of bioplasma and biological field, while still in the hypothetical phase, is considered controversial by the majority of scientists.

Dr. Iniushin is a member of the Academy of Sciences of the Kazakh S.S.R.

Wiktor Osiatyński: The advantages gained from your bioenergetic experiments and, in particular, the use of lasers for biological purposes, are well known. It is not known, however, what the theoretical consequence of biophysical research is. Will it be of any use in determining the very substance of living matter, of the properties that make it distinct from the inanimate world? Will it perhaps help to establish the relationship between the subjects of physics and biology, to integrate these sciences? If so, then on what level?

Victor Iniushin: Our research has not yet gone beyond the preliminary stage; it pertains, in general, to the questions you've just formulated. Concentrating on the study of life at the level of elementary biophysical reactions and analyzing the energetic processes of living organisms, we have managed to collect data enabling us to say more about the difference between animate and inanimate matter. It appears that the difference goes far deeper and is of quite a different nature, than it had been popularly believed.

O. What is it?

I. There are two fundamentally different forms of space, I contend, and this is why a condition of the integration of physicochemical sciences with biology seems to require the formulation of an entirely new geometry: the geometry of the living organism—taking into account this other form of space that we have only begun to explore, the one we've sensed only intuitively.

O. Can you describe the difference between the two forms of space and your conception of the new geometry in more detail?

I. In brief and put simply, the geometry of physico-chemical space is Euclidean, three-dimensional. When approaching the speed of light, time is reduced to the dimensions of space, and we must switch to four-dimensional geometry so we can grasp the essence of physicochemical processes. If we, however, enter the realm of biological processes, we face a geometry of more than just four dimensions. Some of the greatest scientists, including Vladimir Vernadski, have long hypothesized that biological space was multidimensional. It also is heterogenic. It exists in more than three or four correlatives; therefore we are not to speak of the homogeneity of space, not even in two symmetrical points.

O. In biological space, I guess, everything is in motion, in a continuous change?

I. Right; from the point of view of our traditional thinking it is, so to speak, a quasi-space, a quasi-state that changes depending on the situation of each point in this space. The situation of the point depends on many coordinates. It means, in practice, that no point unrelated to a great number of other points and independent from their properties, is to be found there. Suppose there are a million points in a space. We want to select just one from the million. But this one depends on the situations and properties of all the others.

O. While the situations and properties of those other points are in a continual change?

I. Exactly; in fact, this seems to be the next quality of biological space.

O. Does this mean that we cannot isolate the point, seize its essence, and describe it? If so, it reminds me of a problem of quantum physics where it is also impossible to determine in what point an elementary molecule is situated at a given moment.

I. You mean the uncertainty principle, don't you? I'm afraid these cannot be compared. The uncertainty principle describes the random character of phenomena occurring on the molecular level, while in biological space, we have the contrary phenomenon: a determined nature of life processes that are influenced by a great number of factors.

O. Let's return to the different forms of space. Do you mean that each point is defined by the great number of other points?

I. Yes, and the problem is to create a geometry that makes it possible to grasp and describe the peculiarities of the whole space and each of its points. It is very difficult because of our cognitive habits.

O. Isn't it as if, through the entire history of human knowledge, we have worn eyeglasses with a special kind of lens, providing us with a three-dimensional vision? And in order to integrate physics with biology, we will have to switch to another kind of lens, because the ones we've used so far have proved inadequate?

I. Right; such integrative attempts have often been undertaken. Whenever a discovery was made in physics or chemistry, scientists attempted to apply it to biology. When the mechanistic approach dominated in physics, biologists, too, tried to interpret life as a kind of a mechanism. When reductionism took over, it led to an approach reducing the processes of life to the elementary physico-chemical processes. All these attempts have led to a dead end. It appears that it is not enough to possess superb tools of physical cognition and the most sensitive instruments. What is necessary, instead, is a revolutionary shift of world outlook. But it is extremely difficult to adopt one, for it is opposed by those who have long been accustomed to their, as you put it, three-dimensional eyeglasses, which provide bas-relief vision.

O. I understand that to have the lens changed, we need a new geometry. Are you doing anything to formulate its principles?

I. First, we have to outline the methods of exploration of that space and its characteristics. For instance, we need to find out how the space itself changes within the biological field. When a plant is sprouting, although it is not yet structurally mature, the surrounding space is also changing. When a forest begins to grow, very close interrelations constituting a specific biological field, as I call it, develop among the crowns of the trees. What we are studying now is how the biological field affects the optical properties of the living organism. We have discovered, in fact, that we are exploring a fluid space with a kind of flow. This space can be explored and its map can be made—a map like a mosaic, changing with the flow of time while life in this space lasts. The map of this mosaic space changes continually because the space is in a continual "flow." We've only begun our research; a route must be projected first; mathematical models and detailed research will follow.

O. Let me ask you once again: how would you, on the basis of your conception, distinguish what's animate from what's inanimate?

I. I think the most vital difference lies in the quality of existence —in other words, in the way of interpretation of the physical and chemical processes within a peculiar spatial matrix. What is alive is a synthesis of elements and processes of the animate world, interrelated with each other in a great number of dimensions. In brief, life is one of the two modes of existence of space, one in which integrated physical and chemical processes occur. In this sense, it is opposite from inanimate space.

O. Is it possible that the surrounding space may, somehow, change the matrix, make the synthesis, and get animated?

I. Do you have in mind the artificial creation of life? It's absurd! It would contradict the principles of thermodynamics. As there is the thermodynamic principle of conservation of energy, there also is a law, according to which the inanimate form of space cannot automatically change into a biological space. There is, simply, a thermodynamic situation in biological space that rules out such a transformation.

O. But if inanimate space cannot automatically become animate, how did life on earth begin?

I. It could have hardly happened on earth. Moreover, I am not sure that the question about the origins of life makes much sense at all. We no longer ask how did matter begin; we assume that matter is eternal and infinite.

O. But from every scientific indication, earth is more than four billion years old, and life appeared much later in the earth's history. Some scientists claim that life emerged from an inevitable chemical evolution; others say that the evolution was ignited by a kind of flare.

And you say that the proto-forms of life could have existed from the very beginning of earth. Can it be that we are just not able to find any traces of those primordial forms?

I. I think that many arguments speak for the cosmic origins of life. For me, personally, the most convincing is the ancient theory of panspermia that says there are, in space, the "germs" of life: some of them might have made their way to earth and found favorable conditions in the form of—and this is acknowledged by science as actually existing here three billion years ago—the so-called primordial soup. What was it? It was an energetic substratum, a huge mass of energetic and chemical material providing optimal conditions for further development of those germs and for the entire evolution of life.

O. It means that life may not be limited to earth.

I. Right; the anthropocentric view of the exceptional nature of life on earth is more appropriate for knowledge from the time of Ptolemy rather than for our time.

O. The hypothesis of the extraterrestrial origins of life has been ruled out for some time now as implausible, or, at least, too mystical. To an outsider, your own theory sounds mysterious, too. In connection with this, I have a question about the subject of your research. People often believe that biophysics will help to explain mysterious and puzzling phenomena, such as telepathy, acupuncture, or Kirlian photography. On the other hand, however, many scientists accept no such phenomena and charge those who study them with idealism, mysticism, or a kind of occultism. What, in your opinion, should be the approach of science to those mysterious phenomena that, so far, have not been explained?

I. I'll tell you why we cannot explain those phenomena: because our theoretical approach is wrong and obsolete. Reductionism applied to biological phenomena means that we study them analytically, dividing them into parts, as it were, but losing the vision of the whole. Why, for instance, is the theory of the biological field so poorly described and why are so few scientists interested in it? Because in recent decades, the major tendency in biology has been slanted toward chemistry. All the processes were reduced to chemical molecules and to their interactions. The structures above the molecular level were of no interest to anyone. Moreover, the scores of unknown areas and parascientific phenomena clearly seem to scare the scientists.

O. Why?

I. Because to explain strange phenomena, completely new theoretical concepts would have to be formed. And scientists don't like to do that. Besides, it is far more difficult than to follow the beaten path, even though it may lead to a dead end. In effect, experiments dealing with those phenomena are conducted only by enthusiasts in my country or yours or elsewhere. They are often very successful scientists, but they carry on their research all by themselves. They get no financial support. This is why their research doesn't reach a high standard.

O. Do you think it should become the recognized subject of an "official science"?

I. Positively; more and more of today's scientists share this opinion. Psychologists have even proposed studying telepathy, telekinesis, and other psi phenomena on the most advanced scientific levels.

O. Thus acknowledging the real occurrence of such phenomena?

I. Yes; there is no doubt today that they are real. The majority of Soviet scientists admit it. But many official science representatives are dead set against the exploration of these phenomena. I think it is because they would have to give up many traditional beliefs and theories, and it's so difficult.

French physiologist Claude Bernard once said that if a single fact challenged a theory, this fact was to be acknowledged, and the theory rejected. We have more and more such facts nowadays. It means it's high time we start working on new theoretical frameworks to accommodate these facts.

O. Are you working in this direction? Are you trying to find a biophysical explanation of the phenomena still considered mysterious?

I. Yes, we hope that the way for new theoretical principles may be paved by the geometry of biological space. We also conduct experiments in an attempt to explain some of the mysterious phenomena. Our research on acupuncture has proven most successful. Chinese folk medicine localized over six hundred points of the human body. A needle inserted in one or more of these points will cure a patient of his affliction, whether it is physiological or emotional. Our biophysical study of the subject has clearly proved that these very points, unlike all others, emit a specific, unique radiation. This has given rise to the idea of laser biostimulation.

First, we select particular points—different ones in each case—

from among these traditionally known in the Chinese acupuncture technique. Then, we insert into these points minute portions of energy, thus "animating" impaired tissues, or healing wounds, or curing certain diseases. We may use radiation instead of drugs to treat patients in the future. Acupuncture is not mysterious any longer; in other domains there is also significant albeit slow progress.

For instance, research conducted in Novosybirsk on a specific communication between isolated cells by means of optic radiation, microwaves, or long electromagnetic waves may someday result in an explanation of such phenomena as, say, telepathy. We have also studied Kirlian photography and now it poses no mystery either.

In general, all seemingly mysterious phenomena become understandable if we acknowledge that there is a specific biological field in each organism, which can emit and receive signals.

O. And should we decode these signals of the animate nature, incomprehensible and unrelated to each other as they seem?

I. Yes, and to achieve this, we need to start with the innermost part of the organism. Modern science, and, generally, contemporary people, concentrate on the outside world, taking no account of what happens inside an individual.

O. What philosophical consequences can result from the research you've already done and that yet to be done?

I. I think this research demonstrates the unity of the universe: the unity of the macrocosm and microcosm. I believe this research may confirm an old Eastern idea of harmony between man and the universe. Man is the microcosm: what surrounds him and precedes him is the macrocosm. We have to find a harmony between the two spheres. So far, it has never been achieved, but in the future it will be a necessity.

O. Harmony, you say, has remained unreachable; how about the philosophy of the East: has it also failed in this respect?

I. Yes, it has. Eastern culture has followed an inner way; it has concentrated on the microcosm of man, ignoring the outside world. The latter was, in turn, what Western culture concentrated on. It has developed the technology, the methods of domination over nature, while neglecting the inner world. Now we are reaching a point where nature and life and technological progress are increasingly in conflict with each other. We must choose now: either further technological progress, or nature and the development of man as a living organism. Hence the need for a new world outlook.

O. Is it not possible to accept technological progress within a new world outlook?

I. I think it's our major task. Emphasis ought to be removed from the conquest and domination over nature and put instead on the effort to multiply the bioenergetic potential of all life on earth. I mentioned the thermodynamic impossibility of creating life artificially. I think there is a remarkable thing to the law of thermodynamics: it demands the protection of all of nature.

Therefore, the major task of humanity should not be the destruction of man's natural environment in his insatiable greed to satisfy his desires; rather, it should be the development of humanity's potentials, perceived as an integration of human beings, their natural environment, and the whole ecosystem.

O. It would really require a dramatic change of the world's outlook, of human needs, attitudes, and values.

I. That's true. However, such a philosophical shift would be of tremendous significance to the development of a full-fledged society of men capable of changing not only the planet but also, in the future, the entire surrounding universe. For mankind shall face the necessity to change the universe, so that it could extend its "household" beyond earth.

O. Do you believe that if the research you told me about results in a shift of the world's outlook, it will point to mankind the right direction to pursue?

I. I hope so. For man should not build his hopes upon the destruction of life, but rather on the continual development of his own biological potential. It will be possible, if he comes to know the entirety of living nature and enhances its biological potential, too. Then, and only then, will one of the most important functions implied in life itself—the protection of humanity and the protection of all life—be accomplished. If this is done, biology will unite with the humanities to serve man and his survival. Isn't this the very purpose of all sciences, including biology, and of art and of the entire human culture?

II

On Science in Perspective

What is science? How did it emerge? When did it happen? And, why did it happen? What was "before" science?

What was the essence of the Cartesian breakthrough that led to modern science? What were the basic tenets of the Cartesian worldview? Why was this method so successful? What are its limitations? What is the new scientific worldview? How will it influence our lives? Does science deal with truth?

These are the questions addressed by Sergei Semenov and Fritjof Capra, who put into historical perspective the problems discussed throughout the entire book. Semenov presents the way of life and surprising technological capacities of the people who lived in a prescientific epoch, while Capra analyzes the short history of science from the Cartesian revolution to the second turning point, which is taking place today.

Semenov presents the basic principles of the development of technology that, according to him, have been the same in prehistoric and modern times. In contrast with Toffler's emphasis on change and turning points, Semenov stresses the gradual process of the accumulation of human skills and experiences. He points out the perfection of Neolithic man in his fields of manufacture and explains the mechanism of the emergence of new technologies and skills. They all evolved together with the evolution of human needs and intellectual capacities.

Capra seems to agree with the concept of an intellectual evolution. He rejects, however, Semenov's incrementalism, emphasizing the turning points in the intellectual history of womankind. The first turning point took place in Europe during the Renaissance and gave birth to modern science. For Capra, the essence of science is the empirical nature of knowledge and the process of model-making, which permits the putting of empirical observations into a coherent order. The scientific method was extremely successful in explaining most natural phenomena; no wonder the scientific worldview took over human minds. Today, however, this vision of science becomes more and more obsolete. A new vision emerges, which rejects the reductionism and mechanicism of the post-Cartesian science, and stresses interconnectedness and interdependence of all phenomena. The emerging new worldview acknowledges the fundamentally dynamic nature of the universe, which is alive. Together with the new worldview, a new, holistic and ecological consciousness emerges.

One of the most important aspects of these developments is, for Capra, a growing awareness of the scientists themselves that they do not deal with truth. What they are aiming at is, at best, an approximate description of reality. Capra uses a metaphor of a map and a territory: being based on the observations and being internally consistent, a map still isn't a territory. Similarly, science is not truth. The confusion of a map and a territory was the reason for Galileo's condemnation by the Church. The same confusion underlies the cult of science that characterizes a modern society. This cult, however, will wither away in a new worldview that will perceive science as one of many capabilities, existing in a broader framework of human potentials and subordinate to ecological ethics.

21. Sergei Semenov

Sergei Aristovich Semenov, born in 1898, graduated from the Institute of Pedagogy in Leningrad in 1927; interested in a career as a writer and explorer, he joined several expeditions to Eastern Siberia. He wrote numerous reports, essays, and short stories about these trips. In 1931, Sergei Semenov took a research job at the Institute of Archaeology of the Soviet Academy of Sciences in Leningrad, where he has been working ever since.

Dr. Semenov has written and lectured extensively on experimental archaeology and traceology, the latter being one of his major topics of interest. His findings and ideas have been presented in his many books, the most noteworthy of which are: Primitive Technology *(1957),* Development of Technology in the Stone Age *(1968), and* The Origins of Agriculture *(1974).* Prehistoric Technology: An

Experimental Study of the Oldest Tools and Artifacts from Traces of Manufacture and Wear *was published in the United States in 1964.*

Dr. Semenov's ideas have been analyzed in numerous books, scientific papers, and articles all over the world, and the laboratory directed by him attracts scientists from many countries. In 1977 a special international congress in Vancouver, Canada, was discussing the traceological method developed by Sergei Semenov.

In 1974, Dr. Semenov was awarded a State Prize for his achievements in the field of prehistoric archaeology.

Wiktor Osiatyński: What is really new in your method of research called traceology? How is it related to traditional archaeology or to historic research in general?

Sergei Semenov: In the broadest sense, traceology is a study of tools and artifacts from traces of manufacture and wear that we find in archaeological excavations. It is much like a detective's job, to put it figuratively. A detective, on the basis of available remains—fingerprints, footprints, single hairs, or other clues, some practically invisible—traces, or reconstructs, the probable situation. He may take photographs, use a variety of other devices, or even undertake certain experiments—all in order to find out what happened in the time he was not there. We, too, study all features of the prehistoric tools very carefully: we examine traces left on them either by the makers or the users; our findings help us learn more about the people who handled the tools or even reconstruct a picture of prehistoric societies. This method of research enables us also to study the development of tools used by man, the process of his technological advance from Australopithecus all the way to feudalism.

O. But isn't it the very sphere of research of the history of modern science and technology that deals with somewhat less distant epochs? In what way can archaeology add to our knowledge if it goes so far into ancient technologies that are no longer used?

S. The history of science and technology covers but a small section of a very long process; it deals with the science of modern times and the technology originating with the Industrial Revolution. However, if you ask historians about the patterns of scientific and technological development, they will hardly know what to say. Engrossed in a multitude of specializations and tools, they have no perspective from which to comprehend the whole. The historical process began not two centuries ago but hundreds of thousands of years ago. If you want to learn about the laws guiding this historical process, you have to begin where once everything took root. You have to find the "ends of the threads." These ends are to be found in prehistoric culture, in the most ancient times.

O. Haven't the threads been broken many times since then? Do you think the same principles that have ruled technological and economic development from the Paleolithic to the Neolithic to the Ancient Age have continued through the Industrial Revolution to modern times? Hasn't each particular epoch given rise to new principles of development?

S. Although it is hard to believe, the most basic pattern of technological process in the development of the tools man uses does not change; it's independent of an epoch. Let us think about the characteristics of contemporary scientific and technological development: precision, automation, differentiation, and specialization of tools; acceleration of their operation; transformation of matter and energy from one form to another. However, it hardly occurs to anybody that the same characteristics of development appeared as early as the Stone Age; it may seem incredible, but that is the way it was.

O. It seems incredible indeed, especially if we are accustomed to the stereotypes of primitive culture.

S. True, the astonishment results from our own bias. We have heard too much of great turning points, of sudden upheavals altering human life, and we may also be preoccupied too much with the future, totally ignoring the past. What I, personally, consider the most important feature of our development is a gradual, continuous accumulation of human knowledge and skills. Progress in the way people work has not consisted only in the replacement of old tools and technologies with new ones; this progress also has been a gradual development of working skills and accumulated experiences. The accumulation protected and preserved old skills and methods that were modernized in time but never totally rejected. As new tools have emerged, people did not forget what could be done with a piece of an ordinary rock. At the archaeological sites displaying excavations from, say, 25,000 years ago, we often find tools that had been in common use a hundred or several hundred thousand years before; these tools were still useful, as we sometimes find old tools and skills useful today—an old-fashioned stone hatchet, an oil lamp or a torch, a drafthorse, or even our own skill of climbing a tree.

O. Don't we forget such simple skills every so often?

S. Yes, we do, I'm afraid. Hence our growing dependence on technology. We are so anxious to go forward as fast as possible that we'd rather get rid of an encumbering past. But nothing must be renounced from the human heritage. Everything still has value, even if just educational. While human development is an achievement of new things, it also requires a preservation of old things. Man's existence depends on what he remembers from the past. All his activities are based on what he has done earlier. If I forgot everything I knew, I would accomplish nothing, even if my senses and my mind still worked correctly. I'd end up in a mental institution. The same applies to the society as a whole. I also think that all our historical experience bears a tremendous contemporary consequence.

O. How do you see an idea of progress in a broader historical perspective? Tell me, professor, what is progress: a number of fundamental turning points in the history of mankind; an accelerated march of humanity along the same road; or a continuous process of perfection of technological devices, a process of constant improvement of the tools' efficiency and the standard of living?

S. Progress is a relative concept, for it depends on the criteria used for its evaluation. Labor efficiency has certainly increased as have our security and standard of living. But it would be highly questionable to use the idea of technological efficiency as a criterion of progress. All evidence suggests that primitive man achieved technological perfection in all areas of his activity. We have found several hundred stone disks, used as knives, in a four- to five-thousand-year-old vault in Yakutsia. The jewelers to whom we showed the stone blades said that such geometrical prisms must have been cut with a machine of great precision. We know from detailed analysis that the Neolithic man knew how to strike the stone with a piece of horn; to make a hundred blades an hour, each requiring a single arm movement. We cannot do it today, can we? We make things out of rock that the Neolithic man wouldn't, but we are not able to outdo him in the technical perfection of his fields of manufacture. For in all he did, he reached top mastery and perfection. Nothing more could be forced out of rock.

O. Does that mean that as long as man could develop the potential offered by stone, bones, and horns, he proceeded in this direction? When he reached the end and he still had some unsatisfied, or new, needs he turned to another material?

S. Right; man reached a dead end and he could not go any further. Then a pattern of development we call rationalization came about: man had to switch to another pathway, free of the imperfections and inefficiencies of the former.

O. So he discovered metal ores?

S. It was a very long and slow process. I imagine that many people were skeptical about using metal at first. Stone was a ready-made material, which just had to be given a desired shape, while metal had to be processed: melted, cast, forged. All the same, metal finally prevailed, because it proved more malleable and economical than stone. A Neolithic man needed fifteen minutes to chop through a 25-cm-diameter log with a stone hatchet; he did it three times faster with a copper ax. Although copper was softer than stone, it could be made sharper. A copper ax was, in fact, heavier and did not break as easily. Hence it quickly replaced the stone hatchet.

Moreover, a similar process of transition from one tool to another took place during an epoch we could observe. When Indian hunters in North America first encountered guns, they felt contemptuous toward the firearm. Such preparations as loading the gunpowder and setting the bullet took an unbearably long time, time in which an Indian huntsman could shoot many arrows from his bow. Nevertheless, firearms soon replaced bows because the force of an arrow or spear could not compare with that of a bullet. The more effective weapon prevailed.

O. Does that mean that the development of tools has been a response to human needs? That those technologies and tools that better serve man's needs have taken over?

S. Right, or quite new needs have emerged that couldn't be satisfied with the traditional tools, and then new ones had to be invented. That which was more effective and more useful always prevailed. What is the advantage of metal? Primarily, it is plastic. All kinds of tools can be made of it: dull or sharp; soft or hard. Almost any property can be given to metal. That is why our entire technology is based on metal.

O. Does that mean that the transition from stone to metal at the end of the Stone Age was of critical importance for future technological development, even to modern times? How did man come to use metal, or generally, how did he discover all his new inventions? By chance? Or did he know that he had exhausted the possibilities of any further development of stone and bone and therefore he had to discover something different? How did man arrive at the idea that metal had so many useful properties?

S. Ever since people have manufactured earthenware and pottery, they have known that properties of a material can be changed by temperature. Minerals were just another earth stuff.

O. And before, how did man first arrive at the idea to link fire and clay, to actually fire earthenware?

S. I think it was a gradual and slow process. Earthenware was in wide use in the Neolithic Age, but as early as the Paleolithic Age 25,000 years earlier, inhabitants of today's Czechoslovakia had fired clay statuettes. People living in other regions at that time utilized bones or stone for this purpose. In fact, in the same area, no other ceramic artifacts from a later period were found. It's as if the people tried a new method and then gave it up, as if they'd learned a skill but did not consider it really useful or significant enough to continue. It was developed only later, when the use of earthenware, and especially ceramic vessels, became widespread.

Aborigines in Australia did not make earthenware; they made wooden utensils instead. Pottery was quite useless for nomadic tribes; it broke so easily. And besides, they had nothing to store. When man settled down and started to store excessive produce, he had to have vessels to hold and preserve it. Agriculture, or even hunting or fishing—any economy that was dependent on storing food supplies, as well as the settled life-style itself—contributed to a growing demand for pottery. And further development of ceramic technologies has extended the utilization of pottery.

O. Do you mean that the evolution of tools is the result of the evolution of human needs?

S. I believe these are parallel processes. Needs might have come first sometimes, or at other times, technological processes might have created new needs; the demand for pottery resulted from the rise of agrarian culture; but agriculture was not a new need. It was a more efficient means of satisfying man's need for food.

O. In looking for the origins of today's technology, we trace a backward sequence of development: from metallurgy to ceramics, and from ceramics to agriculture. How have the milestones of human civilization been laid? Could it be that a chance mutation of wheat once yielded a bigger crop but then "required" man to cultivate and tend it, forcing him to settle down in one place?

S. You are right in substance, but there is one more thing. Before the agricultural civilization, man might have harvested wild crops. In a week, an average family, furnished with stone sickles, could have gathered enough grain for the whole year. Hence, wherever wild wheat grew, agricultural settlements have developed in time, because people who happened to inhabit the area did not have to lead a nomadic life; they could, or rather had to, settle down, for it was more difficult to wander dragging all their food supplies along. It would be quite senseless. So they built huts; their life became safer. Out of necessity, they placed natural manure and unknowingly fertilized the soil surrounding their houses—at first with no purpose, just out of the necessity—with natural manure and waste, and couldn't have ignored the fact that wheat ears in the direct vicinity of their dwellings were bigger and more lush than elsewhere. Thus they've gained a piece of important information: that fertilization fosters crops. However, at the time, they still had no hoe, or colter, or plow—these came later; they cut the grain, burned the stalks, and harvested even bigger and richer crops the next season. Thus the first agricultural system developed, which was found literally all over the planet: in China, America, west and east Asia . . .

O. May this similarity or, in general, all similarities in farming, tools, and culture suggest intercultural contacts or only the similar trends of development?

S. Contacts between the European and American agricultural civilizations don't seem very likely at all. The Japanese and perhaps the Chinese probably lived in isolation. People had scattered all over the globe long before agriculture emerged. While the tools used in various regions were slightly different, the overall methods of farming and their evolution followed the same pattern. I simply believe that the human intellect has developed in the same way although the particular circumstances might have differed from place to place. Everywhere people invented and developed working tools; without work and tools intellectual development would not have been possible at all.

O. No intellect would develop without tools? Or no tools would be invented without intellect?

S. We cannot know what the actual order of events was for we never saw a tribe of, say, Homo neanderthalensis. We cannot make any comparative study of the relationship between their intellectual development and the tools they used. I think, however, that it must have been a particular kind of feedback. Intellectual development made it possible to develop tools, and improvement of tools, in turn, accelerated the intellectual development of man. In fact, a similar interdependence can be seen in the development of a child or any individual. One's intellect enables one to work, but the stimulation of work is what makes possible one's further intellectual development. The evolution of humankind must have been based on the same principle. Intellect, language, and tools have developed simultaneously and interdependently in all cultures.

O. How much has man changed from his Neolithic or Paleolithic childhood?

S. Not as much as is popularly conceived. Paleolithic man already had a brain like ours. He also had language, enabling him to communicate and convey his skills and knowledge from one generation to the next. And he had the tools he needed. Only his actual living conditions were different; his surroundings were different, and his culture was not like ours. We read books, as he must have "read" nature. He understood signs that are quite unintelligible to us. He coped, in his own way, with adversities, enemies, diseases. And he endured, or, rather, he constantly developed; in fact, if he hadn't, there would be no "us." Even then, he followed the very pathway we are following now.

O. Are the stages of man's evolution distinct enough to justify the term "primitive man," which is often applied both to our prehistoric ancestors and to the islanders living far away from our civilization?

S. I don't think so. Certainly nothing justifies this term as used in a popular, pejorative sense that results from our condescending attitude toward other civilizations. We are proud and we boast of our achievements, so we say of others that they are primitive. But it is not true, and not only because there would be no "us" without them. If we look at the requirements their environment imposed upon them, we see that those people were as much adapted to them as we are to ours. The fact of their very survival is the best proof of this adaptation. They have a unique, magnificent art. They have built structures we might fail to erect even now. If they had the opportunities we have, they'd probably create cultural values no worse than ours. Moreover, it's astonishing how quickly the so-called primitive people living in remote regions adapt to modern technological devices. Even in our culture the majority of people lived a very old-fashioned life a few generations ago. Flexibility and adaptability are the most common qualities of man.

O. Do you mean that man reached maturity, or "adulthood," a long time ago?

S. Historically, the childhood of man lasted very long, but not much can be known about it. We hardly have any documents. Documents and traces provide the necessary data on the stages of human evolution. To know more about evolution, we must compare the artifacts of man—that is, his tools—from various periods. When he actually started making tools, he was already an adult. Humanity may now have entered an age of seniority, only very little wiser than it was thousands of years ago, when man first came of age.

More than half a century ago, when I was twenty-seven years old, I went to a far away region of Siberia to study the life of Nenets, or as they were sometimes called, the Samoyeds. The Nenets bred reindeer and their life hadn't changed much over the millennia. Most surprising of all were not only their practical skills, but the simplicity, straightforwardness, and extraordinary honesty of these tribesmen. They couldn't read or understand much of our culture, but they were fully mature human beings in every other way. They might even have reached a higher level of morality than ourselves.

O. Having this in mind, wouldn't it be more correct if we talked of the historical development of tools rather than of the progress of humanity?

S. But I think there is human progress, too. You can see it in culture, arts, science, and in the human consciousness. There are men of genius, individuals who give new direction and open new horizons for thought and action that make progress possible. However, in a more general way, we are not very much different from our forefathers or from the people today who live a life not as technologically advanced as ours. We have books, television, many sophisticated devices, but they don't need them. They have their own culture, customs, their own life. They enjoy it. When they visit us, they hardly ever appreciate our noise, pollution, haste—their life is so clean and calm . . .

O. And when we visit them?

S. When we don't come across hunger or poverty, we are enchanted. I think that this difference in responses says a lot.

22. Fritjof Capra

Fritjof Capra was born in 1939 in Vienna. After obtaining a doctorate in physics at the University of Vienna in 1966, he did research in high-energy physics in several European and American universities and laboratories. From 1966 to 1968 he was at the University of Paris, from 1968 to 1970 at the University of California, Santa Cruz. In 1970 he spent a semester at the Stanford Linear Accelerator, and from 1970 to 1974 he did research at the Imperial College of the University of London. Since 1975, Fritjof Capra has been a guest researcher at Lawrence Berkeley Laboratory at the University of California, Berkeley. He also teaches a course on physics for nonphysicists at Berkeley.

In addition to his high-energy physics research, Fritjof Capra is interested in the history of science, the philosophy of science, and the relationships between science and social problems and social movements. The Tao of Physics *(1975), the book in which Capra elaborated on the parallels between the basic tenets of today's physics and traditional Eastern philosophies, was a great success. In* The Turning Point *(1982), Capra describes today's social and moral crisis as primarily a crisis of perception, and explains the new ecological worldview that is replacing the Cartesian mechanistic paradigm.*

His latest book is Green Politics, *which concerns the activist political movement in West Germany.*

Wiktor Osiatyński: We live in a time when, for many people, science is the best, if not the only, road to the truth. For some, science is the only acceptable form of human cognition. How do you see science among other human cognitive capacities?

Fritjof Capra: This question already contains many problems. I could make the opposite statement that we live in a time when scientists know that there is no truth in science and that they do not deal with the truth. Scientists deal with approximate descriptions of reality.

In fact, I would distinguish between a good scientist and a bad scientist along these lines. A good scientist knows that whatever he or she says is an approximate description of reality.

O. What, then, is science? What is the scientific approach?

C. I accept any approach to knowledge as scientific that satisfies two criteria. The first criterion is the empirical nature: all knowledge has to be based on systematic observation. The second criterion is the process of model making: that in order to interpret observation we build theoretical models, which are internally consistent. But we know that these models are limited and approximate. Knowledge that is based on observations and organized on a basis of a consistent model is science.

O. How about mathematics and quantification? Aren't they necessary for science?

C. It is extremely useful to use mathematics in science, because there is a basic consistency built into mathematical language, but I don't think mathematics is necessary for science. In many sciences we are not able to use mathematics, and they are still scientific because they are internally consistent.

Similarly, quantification is very useful but not necessary for science. Our conventional framework of science would accept only those aspects of reality within its domain that can be measured and quantified. But you cannot quantify values or experience. Therefore, disciplines like economics and psychology, which deal with values and experience, would not be considered sciences. I think, however, that they are sciences because they are based on the systematic observation of reality and use consistent models.

O. So everything that is based on observation and is consistent is science. But it isn't truth. Am I right?

C. Yes; I often use the metaphor of the map and the territory. The map is internally consistent, but it describes the territory only approximately. And this is the whole confusion. I think Galileo was condemned by the Church because the Church confused the map and the territory. Galileo proposed a model of the universe whereas the Church was dealing with the truth. And it was the confusion between the truth and the scientific model that got Galileo into trouble.

So I think that science does not deal with the truth. For me the empirical nature of the knowledge and the process of model making are two criteria of science. And they both emerged in Europe during the Renaissance. But I want to make it clear that I am talking now about European, Western science, not, say, Chinese science.

O. European science emerged during the Renaissance? Why so late?

C. I think that it is connected with a level of abstraction. Perhaps humanity as a whole reached a certain level of abstraction at a certain age, and it was then that science came into being.

O. Do you mean that science had to emerge at a certain point in the development of humanity?

C. No, I don't think science is necessary. But the emergence of science has to do with an essential aspect of life. Human curiosity, ingenuity, and creativity are aspects of life. From the modern point of view, the phenomenon of self-transcendence is an essential phenomenon of life. Living organisms, whether they are a single cell or an animal or a human being or a society, have a tendency to transcend themselves, to go beyond their limitations. So when a certain level of abstraction is reached, human ingenuity and creativity will, among others things, take a scientific path. I don't think science is necessary to survive, but it is one manifestation of the general property of self-transcendence that is essential to life.

O. And you say this point was reached during the Renaissance. Wasn't science a result of social and technological changes? Growing cities, the power of the bourgeoisie, the disintegration of the feudal order, approaching industrialization—weren't all these processes creating more and more room for science? Isn't science, in fact, an industrial phenomenon?

C. I don't think so. Of course, from the perspective of close relationships among the realms of ideas, science, technology, and industrialism, we could debate what came first. We would see that René Descartes worked out his scientific model at a time that was still quite similar to the time of the Middle Ages. The change that occurred with the Industrial Revolution—the invention of the steam engine and the mechanization of production—was much later. Descartes and Sir Isaac Newton were living very much in the material culture of the Middle Ages. They used the same clothes, lived in the same houses, rode in the same carriages as people had thousands of years before them.

The Cartesian revolution was more of a philosophical, conceptual revolution; it was connected with the emergence of the individual rather than with industrialism, which followed relatively shortly afterward. As of then, of course, they both influenced each other.

O. Do you agree that industrialism accepted science and used it as an instrument of its own development?

C. Yes, and something important was added to Cartesian science.

Neither Descartes nor Galileo nor Newton nor any of their contemporaries had an evolutionary view. The concept of evolutionary change was not a part of their worldview.

O. Weren't they dealing with change?

C. Of course, they were dealing with change in the motion of objects and so on, but evolutionary change was not a part of their worldview. Their world was a machine, but it didn't evolve. In the nineteenth century the thought of evolution was suddenly everywhere. It was in geology, in arts, in astrophysics, in biology, and in every other discipline. It was accompanied by the Industrial Revolution, which showed a very radical change. Within a single lifetime, people began to perceive radical changes on the face of the earth.

O. And they needed the evolutionary theory to explain these changes as something that is in the natural order of things. But you say that the real breakthrough was before that, during the time of Descartes and Newton. Could you explain the meaning of this breakthrough? What was the essence of the Cartesian-Newtonian worldview?

C. First, it was the analytic method of reasoning. Descartes developed the method that says: when you have a complicated phenomenon to describe, the way to do it is to take it into pieces and describe the parts and then you put them together again. And the properties of the whole, and in particular the dynamics of the whole, will be determined by the properties of the parts. The properties of the parts are not to be explained unless you again take parts into pieces, into smaller parts. At the very end of this road are inexplicable, fundamental constituents, particles, and principles.

So the idea of the Cartesian paradigm is that the parts are primary and the whole is secondary—that the dynamics of the whole is derived from the properties of the parts.

This is very closely related to the mechanistic approach, to the conviction that the world is a machine. As you know, the time of Descartes was the baroque era, when people were building automatic ballerinas, animals, and other automata, when mechanics became a really fascinating study. Descartes was fascinated by these toys and actually built some himself. So the image of the machine was a model, and the prototype of the machine in the seventeenth century was the clockwork. And in clockwork it is true that the dynamics of the whole is determined by the properties of the parts. This is how a clock works.

O. But even the clockwork has an organization of the parts that is something different from the parts themselves.

C. This is precisely where Descartes had to turn to God. Descartes could say he didn't need the authority of the Church in order to say that this is true and this is false. But he was certainly a very religious person. He postulated the strict division between mind and matter. But, in fact, what he postulated was a triangle: mind-matter-God. And God was the creator of both mind and matter. God organized the world; he was the clockmaster. Later on, God was left out of the picture and people found it impossible to reconcile this division of mind and matter. When people forgot about the clockmaker and wanted to carry through the mechanistic paradigm, the only way they could do it was to accept chance as an explanatory principle of the universe.

To come back to Descartes, the third aspect of his worldview was the separation of mind and matter. A machine is not alive, doesn't have mind, hence the rigorous separation between mind and matter is necessary.

O. So we have three aspects: the separation of mind and matter, the vision of the universe as a machine, and the reductionist method. Is this all that constitutes Cartesian science?

C. These are the basic tenets. Of course, we also have the linear relation of cause and effect and other principles of science. But they all are connected with the model of a machine. Then comes Newton, who marks the completion of the Cartesian paradigm. Newton actually constructed the mathematical model for the Cartesian vision. And with Newton, we have the properties of space and time, and so on.

O. How did it happen that this vision of the universe became the predominant worldview? Why did it shape all disciplines—from physics to economics and psychology? How did it become a new religion?

C. First of all, both Descartes and Newton—as well as Copernicus, Galileo, and other figures of that era—were geniuses. They were creative, revolutionary minds. They dared to state, as I mentioned, "I don't need the Church, I don't need Aristotle, I can figure out for myself how the world works, and I postulate the world as a machine." So this vision was very daring.

And also the mechanistic model of the universe was extremely successful. It was first applied to the solar system and to various astronomical phenomena, to comets and to tides—and it worked very well as an explanatory model. It was also applied to the motion of bodies here on earth. It was then applied to the motion of gases, where the hypothesis that gases are made of little particles helped to define the relationships among pressure and volume and so on. Then it was also applied successfully to thermodynamics. It just worked everywhere. In biology, at the beginning, it didn't work so well, but when chemistry and electromagnetism were developed the concept of the body as a machine was again very successful.

O. Didn't the concept of an organism evolve in the last two centuries?

C. Of course it did. But what is interesting is the fact that the body in every phase in the development of biology was thought of basically as a machine. At the time of Descartes, the body was a mechanical machine. Then it became a chemical machine, and subsequently it became an electro-physico-chemical machine. The latest step is the computer. Now the brain is a computer. But it's a straight continuation of the Cartesian metaphor of the body as a machine.

O. What you are saying explains why people only relatively recently realized what, in fact, the heart is doing within an organism. In the premechanistic worldview people simply didn't ask questions about functions. The functional approach comes with the machine.

C. That is true. And I should say right away that the Cartesian model now seems limited in many ways, but it is still very useful. Living organisms are not machines, but they do develop machinelike functions and processes. The human heart works like a machine, but it is still not a machine; it is a living organism.

O. Do you know what a living organism is if it is not a machine?

C. It has to do with the broader problem of the whole mechanistic concept. If you assume that the world is a machine, the question appears: how do you get life into a machine? And you cannot find a scientific answer to this question within the mechanistic model. People—for example, French biologist Jacques Monod—try to do it, but it is unsuccessful whenever you start with the assumption of a lifeless universe. If, however, you start with the idea that the universe is alive, you have no problem introducing machinelike operations. And then, humans emerge with their creativity, which enables them to build machines. When you start the other way around, from the world as a machine, you need a creator—or, for that matter, chance

—who blows the soul into a human being. And it is also a kind of model. It is not a scientific model, but it is a model.

O. You said that the universe is alive. What do you mean by that?

C. Life is associated with a certain form of organization. Matter is organized. There is no nonorganized matter.

O. But not all kinds of organization are associated with life.

C. That's true. We can make a distinction between living and non-living matter. However, this distinction is pragmatic, and the question of scale is relevant here.

If you take a rock, we say this is nonliving matter. The organization of the molecules, of its atoms, of its structure, is that of nonliving matter. If we take the organization of the planet Earth, we say it is alive.

O. How about the rocks that that living planet contains?

C. That's the question. To the extent that those rocks are parts of the entire larger living system, they participate in the organization of that living system and, as such, are alive. But to the extent that you can separate it from the system, you can say that, in that framework, as a distinct physical entity, the rock is not alive. In itself, internally, it does not have an organization that would qualify it as living matter.

O. What kind of organization do we associate with life?

C. The type of organization that we associate with life is known as self-organization. Living organisms are self-organizing systems, which means that their structure and their pattern of organization is not determined by the environment, but by the system itself. Of course, there are interactions with the environment that influence the system, but they do not determine it. A living organism has a tendency "not to surrender," so to speak, to the environment, but to maintain itself in a stable state. On the other hand, as I mentioned earlier, there is also the opposite phenomenon of self-transcendence. Every living organism has a tendency to transcend its limitations, to reach outward in a creative step, to create new structures and new forms of organization. I should mention that this theory of self-organization, worked out by Nobel prize winner Ilya Prigogine and his colleagues, is only about ten years old.

O. If all life is characterized by the tendency to transcend itself, what, then, are significant differences between various forms of life? Do they transcend themselves in different ways?

C. The detailed patterns, of course, are different. But there are general principles of organization that are common to all life forms.

O. Are they transmitted in DNA?

C. Now, you are mixing the two approaches. This is a very important question of yours, because you are still talking about the elements of a system. You are talking about what it consists of, about the molecular structures.

O. No, I am not talking about the parts of the system. I am talking about the plan it is based on.

C. But the plan it is based on is not in the DNA. It is not located anywhere, it is distributed. DNA is an integral part of it, but it is not its basis. This is the error of molecular biology known as genetic determinism—to assume that the genetic part is the basis of everything else. There is much more to self-organization than DNA.

O. Does this mean that the very question about a basis is irrelevant?

C. Right, and there are also cases of self-organization without DNA.

O. How would you distinguish in this perspective a human being from other living organisms?

C. There is an enormous difference in complexity.

O. How about the symbolic world, language, and mind?

C. Here I can refer to the work of Gregory Bateson, an English cultural anthropologist, who postulated that mind be seen as the dynamics of self-organization. So mind is a set of processes that represent the dynamics of self-organization.

O. But that is precisely what you have said life is.

C. I asked Bateson the same question. His criteria for mind sound like criteria for life. And he said, "Yes, you are right. Mind is the essence of being alive."

O. We are close to the concept of the mind of a blade of grass.

C. Why not? The confusion is that you don't distinguish clearly between mind and consciousness, self-awareness. And this is where we have symbolic language, rational thinking, and all of that.

Today's science does not have a way of explaining what the nature of consciousness is. Because consciousness is first and foremost an experience and, as I said before, as long as science only measures and quantifies, it cannot deal with experience.

O. And we also will not solve this problem in the framework of a traditional physical and chemical approach, will we?

C. No, the new system's view of mind already goes beyond the traditional mechanistic-reductionist view. The new view of consciousness will go even further than that; it will be two steps removed from the Cartesian paradigm and today's molecular biology.

O. We were not so long ago at the point of saying that the Cartesian approach was extremely successful. Now you are saying that it is outdated, at least as applied to life. When did the first problems with the Cartesian-Newtonian paradigm appear?

C. I would say that in our culture the 1950s were perhaps the culmination of the Cartesian paradigm. The fifties saw one of the greatest triumphs of the mechanistic paradigm, and, I think, the last great triumph, that of molecular biology. Technology had its heyday; this was the time when the first Sputnik was launched. It was an age of undoubted technological optimism.

In the sixties came the decline. The movements of the sixties to a large degree marked the beginning of the end of the Cartesian paradigm; there was an intuitive feeling of its limitations. In the seventies there was a much more conscious perception of these limitations.

O. But these were not the first doubts?

C. Of course not. In the sixties and seventies these doubts were expressed in the society at large. But in physics it happened much earlier, in the twenties. It was then that the physicists were thrown into a crisis of perception. They tried to use the basic concepts of the Cartesian paradigm to describe atomic and subatomic phenomena, and it simply didn't work. So they were forced to question the very basic concepts of this paradigm.

German physicist Werner Heisenberg went to India and had a long discussion with Rabindranath Tagore, the Indian poet. Heisenberg told me that he found great consolation in the fact that there was a culture based on the very concepts that were so problematic for the physicists, the concepts of impermanence, relativity, and interconnectedness. The things that emerged in quantum mechanics were the very basic concepts of Hinduism and Buddhism.

Niels Bohr had a similar experience in China and found Chinese philosophy extremely compatible with his own ideas. Erwin Schrödinger, an Austrian theoretical physicist, read the *Upanishads* and wrote about them. Robert Oppenheimer, an American physicist and director of the Manhattan Project, later on studied Sanskrit in order to read the Bhagavad Gita in the original. Wolfgang Pauli, a German theoretical physicist, was sort of a mystic right from the very beginning.

So many of the leading physicists of that time were extremely attracted by Eastern thought, and the reasons they were attracted were the same as in the case of the hippies in the sixties. First of all, they were confused. So they just looked around for whatever help they could get in building the new conceptual framework. The breakdown of the mechanistic worldview was accompanied by people looking around to cultures from other parts of the world to find the similarities between those cultures and the new worldview.

O. Did they find it? What is the modern scientific worldview? How does it differ from the Cartesian assumptions? How popular is this new worldview?

C. When I am talking about the modern scientific worldview, I am now talking about the minority view, about the view of the people on the leading edge of science—Ilya Prigogine, David Bohm, and other people like them. I will call this modern view the ecological worldview.

There are two themes that go through the ecological worldview. The first theme is the fundamental interconnectedness and interdependence of all phenomena. And with that theme comes the reversal of the relationship between the part and the whole. I said that in the Cartesian worldview the dynamics of the whole is derived from the properties of the parts. Now, it is just the opposite. The properties of the parts are derived from the dynamics of the whole. The dynamics of the whole is primary, the parts are secondary. Heisenberg entitled his autobiography *The Part and the Whole*. I think that is very significant because this was the key issue in the development of quantum physics.

O. Does it mean that the parts cannot influence the whole? That they are meaningless?

C. Ultimately, I think, we will have to give up the distinction between primary and secondary; we will have to say that they are complementary and both are necessary. But until now so much emphasis was put on the parts that we turn around.

The second basic theme is the fundamentally dynamic nature of the universe, of reality. Structure is seen not as fundamental, but as a manifestation of an underlying process. And again, ultimately there will complementarity—structure and process will be seen as complementary.

Both these themes—interconnectedness and dynamics—are being played but again and again in scientific theories and also in Eastern philosophies.

O. What do you mean by scientific theories? Physics only?

C. Not only physics. There is Ilya Prigogine, who does some work in chemistry and biology. There is physicist David Bohm, and they don't know each other. And then, there is Karl Pribram and many others. There are all these people working in various areas, and then, moreover, there are various social movements: the ecology movement, the feminist movement, the peace movement, the so-called holistic health movement, and the human potential movement. All these movements go in the same direction without, at the beginning, knowing of each other. So there is really a very broad evolution of consciousness.

O. Is there any clear direction of this evolution?

C. Yes, there is. A new ecological worldview is now emerging that, in its scientific formulation, is given by the system's theory. This worldview is enhanced by the three great transformations that are taking place today. One is the shift from patriarchy to postpatriarchal society—in other words, the rise of feminist awareness. This is a very profound transformation, because it transforms our value system and the way we see ourselves. The second shift is the decline of the fossil fuel age. And the third shift is the paradigm shift that we are talking about. As a scientist I am mostly interested in the paradigm shift, but the other ones are as important.

O. What will the new scientific paradigm look like?

C. First of all, the new paradigm is not just a scientific paradigm. It is also embedded in a larger ecological consciousness. Second, the science that we are doing today will have to be expanded in order to serve the new paradigm. In particular, it will have to expand in the directions of values; it will have to include values. This means that we will have to move away from the requirements of quantification. Scientific models that cannot be quantified will also have to be accepted as valid models.

O. As I understand it, the new paradigm does not render science obsolete. Science will still exist, but in a broader framework.

C. Yes, I would say that the scientific formulations of the paradigm will be embedded in a broader ecological awareness. To be ecologically aware you need not be a scientist.

O. You can, but you don't have to?

C. It is easier when you are not a scientist. Scientific, rational thinking is very linear and ecosystems are highly nonlinear. Therefore, the intuitive mind finds it easier to deal with the nonlinearity of ecosystems. But at the same time, it is also very exciting to approach it, as I do, from the point of view of a scientist.

O. But as you said, most of the scientists are reluctant toward the paradigm shift.

C. That is true. But the previous paradigm shift faced the same problems. There were Descartes, Galileo, and others who were fighting the establishment. The establishment was extremely powerful. Both Galileo's *Dialogues* and Descartes's *Discourse* were published in Holland. They could not publish them in Italy or France because the establishment, meaning the Church, was too powerful.

Today, it is very similar. If you want to do research on the systems' view of mind, you can do it, they will not persecute you, but you won't get a grant. The technique has changed, but the domination of the establishment is exactly the same.

O. But Galileo and Descartes eventually prevailed.

C. Yes, and the new paradigm will prevail, too. I think today's struggle somehow mirrors the struggle at the end of the Middle Ages. Galileo and Descartes were very revolutionary persons. Their revolution was to oppose the dogma of their time. It was the dogma of the Church and of Aristotle, who was supported by the Church.

It is a fascinating observation that the very theory they developed has now become the dogma. And what people like myself are now fighting is again the establishment, which today is no longer the Church but the corporate world, the industrial world, the academic world—all these entrenchments of the mechanistic-reductionist worldview that has become as much a dogma as the Aristotelian worldview at the time of Descartes.

INDEX

Accidental discoveries, 8, 36–37
Achmatova, Anna, 143
Acupuncture, 183, 184–85
  biophysical explanation of, 184–85
Adaptation (in evolution), 44–46
  change in mechanisms of, 45–46
  complexity and, 45–46
  criteria for, 45
  dinosaurs and, 44–45
  environmental conditions and, 44–45
  ideally adapted species, 45
  principles of, 44–45
  vertebrates and, 46
Affluence, 54–55, 117–18
  overpopulation and, 54–55
  theory of social balance and, 117–18
Affluent Society, The (Galbraith), 117
Anatomy of Power, The (Galbraith), 113
Anesthesia, 8
Angiography, 33–35
  brain, 34–35
  coronary, 33–34
Anichkov, Sergei, 77–84
  biographical sketch of, 78
Animal experiments, 78
  application to humans, 78
Animate and inanimate matter, 180, 182
  biophysical research and, 180, 182
Anochin, Pyotr A., 62
Archaeology, 189–96
  intercultural contact, 194
  man's development since Paleolithic Era, 195
  pre-agricultural civilization, 194
  "primitive man," 195
  progress and, 190, 191
  stone-to-metal transition, 193
  technological perfection and, 191
  tools, development of, 190, 192–93
  traceology and, 189–90
Aristotle, 9, 201
Ark II (Ehrlich and Pirages), 54, 55
Art, 15–16, 155
  ethical role of, 16
  future developments in, 155
  intuition and, 15–16
  purpose of, 16
Artificial hearts, 89
Atom, composition of, 32

Bacon, Francis, 9
Baier, Kurt, 138
Bateson, Gregory, 204
Bernal, John Desmond, 9
Bernard, Claude, 46, 78, 184
Bestuzhev-Lada, Igor, 152–60
  biographical sketch of, 153–54
Bhagavad Gita, 205
Big Bang theory, 27–29
  "existence" before, 27–28
  infinity and, 28
  time and, 28–29
Biochemical processes, 41–42
  fundamental principles of, 41–42
Biological space, 180–86
  acupuncture and, 184–85
  animate and inanimate matter and, 182
  artificial creation of life and, 182
  beginning of life on earth and, 182–83
  Eastern philosophy and, 185
  human potential, development of, 186
  panspermia theory and, 182
  parascientific phenomena and, 183–85
  philosophical consequences of research in, 185–86
  thermodynamics and, 182
  uncertainty principle and, 181
  unity in universe and, 185
Biophysical research, 179–80
  animate and inanimate matter, 180
  biological space. *See* Biological space
  new geometry and, 180
  two forms of space and, 180

INDEX

Bohm, David, 72, 167, 206, 207
Bohr, Niels, 37, 38–39, 72, 205
Brain studies, 34–35, 61–76
  angiography and, 34–35
  cognition process and, 71
  consciousness and, 62–64
  cultural similarity and, 76
  decision making, 64
  ecological model of perception, 71
  emotions and, 64–68
  "holographic reality" and, 72–73
  holographic theory of, 69–76
  introduction, 61–62
  localized representation, principle of, 69
  memory and, 63
  motivation and, 63
  research, 75
  sensory apparatus and, 73
  spiritual experience and, 73–74
  stress, 64–68
  as tabula rasa, 71
Braudel, Fernand, 133, 137
Brothers Karamazov, The (Dostoevski), 123
Bureaucratic dynamic, 114

Cancer, 81–82
  central nervous system and, 81–82
  "healers" and, 82
  stress and, 82
Capra, Fritjof, 187–88, 197–208
  biographical sketch of, 197
Cartesian science, 199–202
  as limited but useful view, 202
  living organisms and, 202
  mind and matter, separation of, 200–01
  molecular biology and, 205
  reductionist method, 200–01
  universe as machine, 200–01
  world view, development into, 201–02
Central nervous system, 47, 81–84
  cancer and, 81
  emotions and, 83–84
  genotype and, 81
  influence upon organism, 81–82
Charmonium, 32
Chemistry, 5–6, 100
  dramatic changes in, 5–6
  scientific progress and, 100
Chomsky, Noam, 93–101
  biographical sketch of, 94–95
Churchill, Winston, 117
Clark, Dr. Barney, 89
Cognition, 19, 71, 95, 96–97, 105
  "feeling" and, 97
  holographic brain theory and, 71, 72–73
  infiniteness of, 19
  linguistics and, 95, 105
  nonlinguistic forms of thinking, 96–97
  as rational and linear, 97
Cognitive dissonance, 138
Communication, 97–98, 105–06
  animal vs. human, 105–06
  language and, 97–98
Communism, 155–56
  futurology and, 155–56
  law of social development and, 156
  technological determinism and, 156
Comparative linguistics, 103–04
  understanding man and reality through, 103–04
Consciousness, 62–64, 157, 166–67, 173, 204–05, 207
  Cartesian science and, 204–05
  ecological worldview and, 207
  evaluation of activity and result, 63
  facts ignored by science and, 173
  futurology and, 157
  growing interest in field of, 166–67
  introduction, 61–62
  memory and, 63
  morphogenetic fields and, 174–75
  motivation and, 63
  new paradigm and, 173
  new science and, 173
  research in, need for, 166
  scientists' interest in, 166–67
  working definition of, 62–63
Consumer values, 114–17
  affluence and, 117–18
  American values, exportation of, 114–15
  consumption-for-prestige attitude, 114–15
  cultural revolution of 1960s and, 116
  enlightened society and, 118
  intellectual community and, 117–18
  Japan and, 115–16
  shopping and, 116
  social change and, 116–17
Copernicus, Nicolaus, 161, 166, 201
  See also New Copernican revolution
Coronary angiography, 33–34
  synchrotion radiation and, 34

INDEX

Corporations, 112–14
bureaucratic dynamic in, 114
compensatory power of, 113
condign power of, 113
conditioned power of, 113
neoclassical economics and, 113
political power of, 112–13
public perception of, changes in, 113–14
social problems and, 113–14
Cosmic radiation, 148
Crick, Francis, 13
Crystal Ball, 32, 36
Curie, Marie, 35
Curiosity, 9–11, 35–36
scientists and, 9–11, 35–36
motivation and, 10
Cyclosporine, 89, 91

Death, 86, 90–91
legal-medical recognition of, 86
uncertainty about, heart patients and, 90–91
Descartes, René, 199–202, 208
See Cartesian science
Decision making, 64
emotional reactions and, 64
Density of universe, 28–29
Dialectic theory of knowledge, 19
Dialogues (Galileo), 208
Diary of a Madman (Gogol), 28
Dinosaurs, 44–45
Discourse (Descartes), 208
Dostoevski, Fyodor, 124
Double-helix structure of DNA, 13
DNA, 13

Ecological worldview, 206–08
consciousness and, 207
dynamic nature of universe, 206–07
feminist awareness, 207
interconnectedness of all phenomena, 206
new paradigm and, 207
in scientific theories, 207
See also New science
Economics, 109–19
affluence and, 117–18
consumer values and, 114–17
corporations and, 112–14
enlightened society, changes by, 118
group interests of economists, 112
inflation, 111–12
intellectual community and, 117–18
interest rates and, 111
introduction, 109–10
misuse of the science of, 112
money supply, control of, 111
negative consequences of growth, 110–11
neoclassical, 112–13
Reaganomics, 111
social balance, theory of, 117–18
status quo, protection of, 112
Economics and the Public Purpose (Galbraith), 112, 118
Education, 124–25, 159
human values and, 124–25
narrowly specialized, 159
Ehrlich, Paul, 40, 50–57
biographical sketch of, 50
Einstein, Albert, 16, 35, 37–38, 72, 173
Electricity, discovery of, 19
Electrons, 17, 28, 33
observability of, 33
orbit, 28
properties of, 17
Emotions, 64–68, 83–84, 123
central nervous system and, 83–84
conflict situations, 64–65
control of, 66, 67, 76, 84
decision making and, 64
evaluation of actions and, 64
"inquisitive response" and, 64
motivation and, 75–76
negative feelings, elimination of, 67–68
philosophy and, 123
prolonged responses, dangers of, 66
science and, 123
suppression of, 66
See also Stress
End of Affluence, The (Ehrlich), 55
Ends vs. means, 124–25
Energy crisis, 24, 53, 56
expansionism and, 24
overpopulation and, 53
waste of energy and, 56
Engels, Friedrich, 156
Enzymes, molecular structure of, 9
Ethics, 6, 121–22, 125–26
future man and, 125–26
philosophy and, 121–22
scientific basis for, 6
See also Value systems

INDEX

Ethnic groups, 143–49
  behavior and, 145
  cosmic radiation and, 148
  culture and, 143
  evolution of, 145
  extra-ethnic systems and, 146
  formation of, 145
  geo-biochemical energy and, 147–48
  language and, 143–44
  new groups, emergence of, 146
  stereotype, changes in, 146
  territorial expansionism and, 147
Ethnogenesis, theory of, 143–51
  disintegration of ethnos, 150
  ethnic groups. *See* Ethnic groups
  "ethnos" defined, 143–44
  full cycle of, 150
  historic example of, 149–50
  race, 144
  war, inevitability of, 150
Evolution, 40–57
  adaptation. *See* Adaptation (in evolution)
  anthropoids, first appearance of, 48
  ape into man, 47
  biochemical mechanism vs. physiological changes, 46
  biochemical processes, principles of, 41–42
  central nervous system and, 47
  complexity of organism and, 45–46
  dinosaurs and, 44–45
  diversified forms at beginning of life, 41
  environment, independence from, 46
  first appearance of life, 41–42
  "freedom of life," increase in, 46
  human evolution, 47–50
  ideally adapted species, 45
  introduction, 40–41
  language and, 47–48
  mutations, 44
  order in, 50
  overpopulation and, 51, 52–56
  photosynthesis and, 41
  prevailing life-mass, 43
  "progress" and, 50–51
  purpose in, 49–50
  race and, 48
  replacement of some life forms by others, 43–44
  saturation of life, 43
  selection and, 48
  spontaneity in, 49–50
  tools, use of, 48
  vertebrates, 46
Expansionism, 24–26, 30–31
  as destiny of mankind, 24–25
  fears about, 25, 30
  solar energy and, 25
  space colonies and, 24
Experiment, 9, 13
  intuition and, 13
  theory and, 9
Experimental medicine, 77–92
  animal experiments, 78
  central nervous system and, 81–84
  folk medicine and, 82–83
  heart transplants. *See* Heart transplant operations
  herbs and, 83
  humans, experiments on, 78, 79–80
  hypotheses and, 83
  introduction, 77
  main purpose of, 80
  primim non nocere principle, 80
  risk and, 79
  working at molecular level in, 80
Experimental method, 78–79, 80
Extinction (Ehrlich), 51
Extra-sensory perception, 18
  See also Parapsychology
Extraterrestrial intervention, 23
Euclid, 13

Feinberg, Evgenii, 3, 11–20
  biographical sketch of, 11–12
Feminism, 207
Festinger, Leon, 138
Flechtheim, Osip, 154
Fleming, Sir Alexander, 36
Folk medicine, 82–83
Freedom of choice, 124
Frequency domain, 75
Future Shock (Toffler), 132, 135, 142, 143
Futurism, 131–51
  assumptions about future, 137
  change as extension of present, 135
  consciousness and, 157
  continuity in history and, 135
  ethnogenesis theory. *See* Ethnogenesis, theory of
  historical perspectives and, 135–36, 137–38

industrial society and, 141–43
introduction, 131–32
multiple possible futures, 137
probable futures, 137
technological society and, 142
temporal perspective, need for, 136
Third Wave society and, 140–41
today's changes and, 135
work and, 158–59
See also Futurology; New Copernican revolution
Futurology, 154–60
artistic developments and, 155
communism and, 155–56
consciousness and, 157
creative needs and, 158, 159
education and, 159
goals influenced by, 156–57
as "history" of future, 154
ideologies and, 154
the individual and, 157
interdisciplinary research and, 155
laws of social development and, 156
limits of, 155
Marxism and, 155–56
material needs and, 159
optimism and, 157
origin of term, 154
pessimistic predictions, 157
"prognosis" in science generally, 154
scientific developments, 155
social imagination and, 157
social values and, 158–59
technological determinism and, 156
"utopias" and, 154
work and, 158–59
See also Futurism; New Copernican revolution

Galanter, Eugene, 68
Galbraith, John Kenneth, 109–19
biographical sketch of, 110
Galileo, 161, 167, 188, 198, 201, 208
Geller, Uri, 171
Geo-biochemical energy, 147–48
Geometry, 13
intuition and, 13
See also New geometry
Gibson, Jane, 71
Ginseng root, 83
Goethe, Johann Wolfgang, 104
Gogol, Nikolai Vasilievich, 28
Gumilov, Lev, 131–32, 143–51
biographical sketch of, 143

Halle, Morris, 94
Harman, Willis, 152–53, 160–68
biographical sketch of, 160
Healers, 82
central nervous system and, 82
Heart transplant operations, 85–92
animal hearts, use of, 89
artificial hearts and, 89
blood group type and, 85
death of donors, 86
decision making by patient, 90
donors for, 86
family permission and, 87, 88
hope and, 91–92
immunological problems, 89–90
increase in, 85
initial controversy over, 92
keeping donor heart alive, 86–87
medical centers performing, 88
poetic and cultural significance of the heart, 92
postoperative survival time, 88–89
selecting patients for, 85–86
"selling bodies" for, 87
tissue diversity, research in, 89
uncertainty about death and, 90–91
Heisenberg, Werner, 16, 37, 72, 172, 205, 206
See also Uncertainty principle
Herbs in medicine, 83
Herder, Johann Gottfried von, 102
Herman, Edward, 95
History, 131–51, 189–96
American culture and, 134–35
assumptions about, 137
constants in, 133, 138
continuity and, 133–34
cultural differences at various periods in, 140
discontinuity and, 133–34
ethnogenesis theory. *See* Ethnogenesis, theory of
future studies, 136, 137–38
futurism and, 131–51
geological time, 133
human nature and, 139
human needs, permanency of, 139
individual time, 133
models for, 136–37

History (*cont.*)
post-dictions, 137
prehistoric culture and, 189–96
relative duration of processes in, 133
social structures in, duration of, 133
social time, 133
as structure of inference, 136–37
temporal perspective, need for, 136
three states of change in, 133
unanswerable questions and, 134
value systems, changes in, 138
See also Archaeology
Hofmannstahl, Hugo von, 107
Hofstadter, Robert, 21, 31–39
biographical sketch of, 31
Holograms, 70
Holographic theory of brain function, 69–76
anatomic localization vs., 69–70
confirmation by experiments, 71–72
defined, 69
frequency domain and, 75
hologram defined, 70
"holographic reality" and, 72–73
memory distribution pattern, 69–70
neurophysiology and, 74–75
parapsychology and, 74
principle of localized representation and, 69
psychology and, 75–76
research and, 75
sensory apparatus and, 73
spiritual experience and, 73–74
See also Brain studies
Hope, 91–92
How to Be a Survivor (Ehrlich), 55
Human nature, 95–96, 139
changes in, 139
cultural influences and, 139
genetic predisposition and, 96
language and, 95–96
as neglected field of study, 101
Humboldt, Wilhelm von, 101, 107
Hughes, Dr. E. B., 33
Hypothesis, 9, 36–37, 83
experimental medicine and, 83
impetus for, 36–37
theory and experiment, 9

Ideals, 10–11
science and, 10–11
Image of the Future, The (Polak), 138
Imagination, 7–8
as scientists' attribute, 7–8
Inanimate matter. *See* Animate and inanimate matter
Indeterminacy principle, 16–17
Industrial paradigm, 162–68
consciousness and, 166–67
defined, 162
economic rationality and, 163
global problems resulting from, 163
"godlike" aspect of self and, 166
gross output and, 163
human needs and, 163
limitations of, 162–63
"marginal people" and, 164
meaning, crisis in, 164
nature, control of, 163
powerful elite and, 163–64
questioning of basic assumptions in, 164–65
scientists and materialism, 166–67
spiritual and intuitive realms and, 167
successes of, 162–63
transcendental values and, 164
unconscious values, rediscovery of, 165–66
values, changes in, 164–66
"what for" questions, 164
See also Industrial society
Industrial society, 141–43, 162–68
limitations of, 141
mass production and, 143
nonindustrial countries and, 141
self-destructive capability of, 141–42
See also Industrial paradigm
Infinity, 28
Big Bang and, 28
Inflation, 111–12
Iniushin, Victor, 169–70, 179–86
biographical sketch of, 179
Instrumental approach to man, 107
Intellectual community, 117–18
social balance and, 117–18
Vietnam War and, 118
Intuition, 12–16
art as authority behind, 15–16
conjecture and, 12–13
decision making and, 14
as direct recognition of truth, 13
experiment and, 13
need for authority to enforce, 14

INDEX

James, William, 76
Japan, 115–16
  consumer values and, 115–16
Joan d'Arc, 151
Jouvenal, Bertrand de, 137

Kant, Immanuel, 28
Kirlian photography, 183, 185

Landau, Lev, 17
Language(s), 47–48, 93–108, 143–44
  agrarian culture and, 106
  animal communication and, 105–06
  biological differentiation and, 104
  communication and, 97–98
  comparative linguistics and, 103–04
  as compensation for biological inadequacy, 102
  differences among, 99–100, 102
  environmental harmony and, 107
  ethnic groups and, 143–44
  genetic predisposition for, 96
  human nature and, 95–96
  industrial culture and, 106
  instrumental approach to man and, 107–08
  introduction, 93–94
  as nation-formation factor, 104–05
  nature and culture, 102
  noncommunication functions of, 107–08
  nonlinguistic forms of thinking, 96–97
  as nonrational, 97
  perception of world and, 106
  phonetics and, 105
  primates and, 47–48
  social existence and, 102
  social functions of, 97–98
  as spiritual sphere of nation, 107
  tower of Babel and, 104
  uniformity of human societies and, 99–100
  universal grammar and, 98–99, 105
  See also Linguistics
Languages of the Brain (Pribram), 75
Laser biostimulation, 184–85
  acupuncture and, 184–85
Lashley, Karl S., 68, 69
Left-brain—right-brain dichotomy, 167
Lenin, V. I., 156
Linguistics, 93–108
  achievements in field of, 98
  cognition and, 95
  comparative, 103–04
  introduction, 93–94
  phonetics and, 105
  psychology and, 98–99
  tower of Babel and, 104
  uniformity of societies and, 99–100
  universal grammar and, 98–99, 105
  See also Language(s)
Lobachevsky, Nikolai, 13

Macrocosm and microcosm, 21–39
  accidental discoveries, 36–37
  ancient civilizations, 25
  Big Bang theory, 27–28
  catastrophe and mankind, 30–31
  communication with other civilizations, 23
  coronary angiography, 33–34
  curiosity, 35–36
  expansionism, 24–26, 30–31
  extraterrestrial intervention, 23
  future developments, 28–30
  hypothesis, 36–37
  introduction, 21
  outer space, life in, 23–27
  quark hypothesis, 32–33
  randomness, 37–38
  research, 35
  solar system, conquering of, 30
  space cities, 24
  space research, 26–27
  the sun, 29–30
  wave model and particle model, 38
Manheim, Karl, 154
Mars, 26, 27
Marx, Karl, 124, 156
Marxism, 121, 155–56, 158
  futurology and, 155–56
Maslow, Abraham, 166
Mass production, 143
McDougal, William, 174
Medicine. *See* Experimental medicine; Heart transplant operations
Megatrends (Naisbitt), 177
Memory, 63, 69–70, 71
  consciousness and, 63
  holographic theory and, 69–71
  pattern of distribution in brain, 69–70
  retrieval mechanisms of, 71
  storage of, 70
Microcosm. *See* Macrocosm and microcosm

Miller, George A., 68
Mitchell, Edgar, 169–78
  biographical sketch of, 170–71
Mohammed, 148
Molecular biology, 205
  Cartesian science and, 205
Monod, Jacques, 202
Morality. *See* Ethics; Value systems
Morphogenetic fields, 167, 174–75
  consciousness and, 174–75
  McDougal learning experiments and, 174
  psychic phenomena and, 175
  verification of theory, 175
Motivation, 63, 75–76, 123
  consciousness and, 63
  emotions and, 75–76
  philosophy and, 122

Naisbitt, John, 177
Namier, Lewis, 137
Nature, 167
Nenets, 196
Nervous system. *See* Central nervous system
Neurosis, 65
Neurotropic drugs, 81
New Copernican revolution, 160–68
  defined, 160–61
  current metamorphosis, evidence for, 162
  impact today, 161
  industrial paradigm and, 162–68
  optimism about, 168
  perception of world changes in, 161
  self, investment of, 168
New geometry, 180–83
  exploration of, 181–82
  purpose of, 181
New Industrial State, The (Galbraith), 114, 117
New paradigm, 173–74, 177–78
  formative causation, hypothesis of, 173
  morphogenetic fields and, 174
  new science and, 173–74
  shift from old paradigm, 177–78
  values and, changes in, 177–78
New science, 169–86
  biological space, 180–86
  biophysical research and, 179–80
  consciousness research and, 173
  intellectual evolution and, 171
  introduction, 169–70
  morphogenetic fields and, 174–75
  new paradigm and, 173–74, 177–78
  parapsychological phenomena and, 183–85
  reexamination of assumptions, 172
  scientific method, inadequacy of, 172–73
  spiritual evolution and, 171
  tools of science, inadequacy of, 172
  uncertainty principle and, 172
  value system and, changes in, 177–78
  See also Ecological worldview; Science in general; Science in perspective
New Scientist, 167
Newton, Sir Isaac, 173, 199, 201
Nuclear energy, 53
  overpopulation and, 53

Oparin, A. I., 41
Oppenheimer, Robert, 205
Outer space, civilization in, 23–27
  communication, 23
  evolution of, 23, 25–26
  space cities, 24
  See also Space research
Overpopulation, 51, 52–56
  affluence and, 54–55
  distribution of resources and, 53–54
  food scarcity and, 52
  governments and, 56
  hidden power structures, 55–56
  individual independence and, 55–56
  nuclear energy and, 53
  social consciousness and, 54–55
  waste of energy and, 56

Panspermia, 182
Parapsychology, 17–19, 74, 175–76, 183–85
  biophysical explanation of, 184
  extra-sensory perception, 18
  holographic brain theory and, 74
  infiniteness of cognition, 17–18
  morphogenetic fields and, 175
  popular interest in, 176
  telekinesis, 18
  telepathy, 17–18, 183, 185
  traditional science and, 176, 184
Part and the Whole, The (Heisenberg), 206
Pauli, Wolfgang, 205

INDEX

Pauling, Linus, 3–11, 19
  biographical sketch of, 4–5
Pavlov, Ivan Petrovich, 64
Philosophy, 119–27
  defined, 123
  education and, 124–26
  egotism vs. higher motives, 121–22
  ends vs. means, 124–25
  ethics and, 121–22
  feelings and, 123
  freedom of choice and, 124
  individual's quest and, 120
  introduction, 109–10
  Marxism, 121, 124
  motivation and, 122
  poverty and, 121
  religion and, 125
  role in contemporary society, 119–20
  science and, 122–23, 126–27
  spiritual values and, 120–21, 125–26
  universal answers, 120
Phonetics, 105–06
  signal and symbol, 105–06
Photosynthesis, 41
Physics, 12, 16–17, 35, 100
  hidden order of world and, 16–17, 19
  medical uses of research in, 35
  physical image of world and, 12
  scientific progress and, 100
  uncertainty principle and, 16–17
Plankton, 43
Polak, Fred, 138
Pollution, 24
  expansionism and, 24
Polypeptide chains, 7
Population. *See* Overpopulation
Population Bomb, The (Ehrlich), 52, 53, 55
Poverty, 121
Prehistoric culture. *See* Archaeology
Pribram, Karl, 61–62, 68–76, 207
  biographical sketch of, 68–69
Prigogine, Ilya, 75, 203, 206, 207
Primim non nocere principle, 80
Prognosis, 154
Progress, 50–51, 100, 190, 191
  evolution and, 50–51
  formation of sciences and, 100
Proteins, spatial structure of, 8
Psi. *See* Parapsychology
Psychology, 75–76, 98–99
  holographic brain theory and, 75–76
  linguistics and, 98–99
  visual space and, 99
Ptolemy, 183

Quantum mechanisms, 5, 17
Quark hypothesis, 32–33

Race, 49, 144
  anatomical differences, 49
  ethnogenesis theory and, 144
  potential for development and, 49
Radiation, 148
Ramishvili, Guram, 93–94, 101–08
  biographical sketch of, 101–02
Randhana, M. S., 110
Randomness, 37–38
  causality and, 38
  Einstein and, 37–38
Rational philosophy in science, 5–6
Reaganomics, 111
Reductionism, 6
Religion, 14–15, 125
  as authority for science, 14–15
Rescher, Nicholas, 138
Romeo and Juliet (Shakespeare), 15
Rubenstein, Dr. E., 33
Rutherford, Ernest, 35

Sagan, Carl, 22
Samoyeds, 196
Science in general, 3–20, 100–01, 122–23, 154
  absolute truth, 19–20
  accidental discoveries, 8
  art as authority in, 15–16
  cognition, influences of, 19
  curiosity and, 9–11
  defining, 197–98
  dialectic theory of knowledge, 19
  dramatic discoveries in, 5–6, 19
  experiment and theory, 9
  faulty image of man by, 123
  feelings and, 123
  fundamental problems and progress, 6–7
  "good life" and, 10–11
  idolatrous attitude toward, 122–23
  imagination and, 7–8
  introduction, 3
  intuition and, 12–16
  man's responsibility and, 123

Science in general (*cont.*)
parapsychological phenomena and, 17–19
patterns underlying, 7
philosophy and, 122–23
physics and, 12
predicting developments of, 8–9
prognosis and, 154
rational philosophy and, 5–6
religion as authority for, 14–15
sociopolitical order and, 10–11
as subordinate to higher values, 126–27
theoretical approach, 12
ultimate knowledge and, 7
uncertainty principle and, 16–17
See also New science; Science in perspective
Science in perspective, 187–208
archaeology and, 189–96
Cartesian science, 199–202
defining science, 197–98
Eastern philosophy and, 205–06
empirical nature of science, 198
evolutionary view, 200
historical experience, importance of, 191
industrial phenomenon, science as, 199
introduction, 187–88
map-and-territory metaphor, 198
mathematics and, 198
models, 198
progress defined, 190, 191
quantification, 198
self-organization, 203
self-transcendence, 199, 203–04
traceology and, 189–90
truth and, 198
See also New science; Science in general
Scientific method, 172–73
new science and, 172–73
observation, errors in, 172
Scientists, 7–8, 9–11, 35–36
as creators of universe, 36
curiosity and, 9–11, 35–36
ideals and, 10–11
imagination and, 7–8
Schrödinger, Erwin, 205
Second Wave society. *See* Industrial society
Selection in evolution, 48
Self-organization, 203
Self-transcendence, 199, 203–04
Semenov, Sergei, 187–96
biographical sketch of, 188–89
Shakespeare, William, 15
Sheldrake, Rupert, 167, 169, 174–75
See also Morphogenetic fields
Shklovskii, Iosif, 21–31, 40
biographical sketch of, 21–22
Shumway, Norman, 77–78, 84–92
biographical sketch of, 84
Social balance, theory of, 117–18
Social change, 113–14, 116–18
affluence and, 117
consumer values and, 116–17
corporations and, 113–14
intellectual community and, 117–18
See also Value systems
Solar energy, 25, 53, 148
expansionism and, 25
Solar system, conquering of, 30
Space colonies, 24
Space research, 26–27
benefits of, 26–27
philosophical effects of, 27
Sperry, Roger, 166–67
Spiritual experience, 73–74, 120–21, 125
holographic brain theory and, 73–74
needs and, 125
philosophy and, 120–21
See also Parapsychology; Value systems
Stanford Linear Accelerator, 36
Stravinsky, Igor, 16
Stress, 64–68, 82
cancer and, 82
negative emotions, usefulness of, 67–68
physical exercise and, 66
Sudakov, Konstantin, 61–68
biographical sketch of, 61–62
Sulphur minerals, structure of, 10
Sun, 29–30
future of, 29–30
white dwarf and, 30
Synchrotron radiation, 34

Tagore, Rabindranath, 205
Tatarinov, Leonid, 40, 41–50
biographical sketch of, 41
Tchavtchavadze, Nicolai, 109–10, 119–27
biographical sketch of, 119
Techno-scientific revolution, 156
Technological society, 142, 156
futurology and, 156
industrial society compared to, 142
Telekinesis, 18
Telepathy, 17–18, 183, 185

Temporal perspective, 136
Territorial expansionism, 147
Theory, 9, 12
  experiment and, 9
  theoretical approach to science, 12
  See also Hypothesis
Thinking. *See* Cognition
Third Wave, The (Toffler), 132, 135, 140, 142, 143
Third Wave society, 132–34, 140–41
  continuity and, 133–34
  decentralization of power, 143
  as preferable future, 141
Time, 27–29
  Big Bang and, 27–29
  infinity and, 28
Toffler, Alvin, 131–43, 154, 187
  biographical sketch of, 132
Tools, 48, 189, 192–93, 194–95
  evolution and, 48
  intellect and, 194–95
  prehistoric; traceology and, 189
  as response to human needs, 192–93
Tower of Babel, 104
Toynbee, Arnold, 137
Traceology, 189–90
  defined, 189
  history and, 189–90
Trojan Women, The (Euripides), 139
Truth, 19–20, 35
  absolute, in science, 19–20
  in physics, 35

Ultimate knowledge, 7
Uncertainty principle, 16–17, 37–38, 172, 181
  biological space and, 181
Universal grammar, 98–99, 105
  defined, 98
  phonetics and, 105
  understanding human nature and, 98–99
Upanishads, 205

Values and the Future (Baier and Rescher), 138
Value systems, 109–27, 138–39, 164–66, 177–78
  behavioral changes and, 138–39
  cognitive dissonance and, 138
  industrial paradigm and, 164–66
  as inscribed in universe, 178
  introduction, 109–10
  new paradigm and, 177–78
  permanent and transient, 138
  technology and, 138
  transcendental, 165
  unconscious values, rediscovery of, 165–66
  See also Consumer values; Corporations; Economics; Philosophy
Vernadski, Vladimir, 147, 180
Vietnam War, 118, 139
  changing values and, 139
  intellectual community and, 118
Visual space, 99

War, inevitability of, 150
Watson, James, 13
Wave model, 38
White, Virginia, 88
Work, 119, 158–59
  creative character of, 158–59
  futurology and, 158–59

Xenon (anesthetic molecules), 8